AMERICAN FIX

INSIDE THE
OPIOID ADDICTION CRISIS—
AND HOW TO END IT

AMERICAN **FIX**

RYAN HAMPTON
WITH CLAIRE RUDY FOSTER

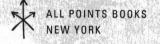

ALL POINTS BOOKS
NEW YORK

Although this is a work of nonfiction, the names and identifying characteristics of certain individuals have been changed to protect their privacy, and the dialogue in this work has been reconstructed to the best of the interviewer's recollection.

www.allpointsbooks.com

Designed by Jonathan Bennett

Library of Congress Cataloging-in-Publication Data

Names: Hampton, Ryan, author.
Title: American fix : inside the opioid addiction crisis - and how to end it / Ryan Hampton.
Description: First edition. | New York : All Points Books, 2018. | Includes bibliographical references and index.
Identifiers: LCCN 2018025770| ISBN 9781250196262 (hardcover : alk. paper) | ISBN 9781250196279 (ebook)
Subjects: LCSH: Opioid abuse—United States—History. | Drug abuse—United States—History. | Drug abuse—Political aspects—United States—History.
Classification: LCC RC568.O45 H35 2018 | DDC 362.29/30973—dc23
LC record available at https://lccn.loc.gov/2018025770

ISBN 978-1-250-19626-2 (hardcover)
ISBN 978-1-250-19627-9 (ebook)

Our books may be purchased in bulk for promotional, educational, or business use. Please contact your local bookseller or the Macmillan Corporate and Premium Sales Department at 1-800-221-7945, extension 5442, or by email at MacmillanSpecialMarkets@macmillan.com.

First Edition: August 2018

10 9 8 7 6 5 4 3 2 1

For Mom, Lorraine, and Katy—**you never gave up on me.** And to everyone else on this journey—thank you for showing me the way.

CONTENTS

AMERICAN **FIX**

INTRODUCTION

WHAT'S THE TRUE SCOPE OF THE OPIOID CRISIS? WHEN I try to describe it to someone who hasn't experienced it themselves, I find myself falling back on the terms we use to encompass genocide, natural disasters, and global war. It's a tsunami of loss.

It's so big that words fail to describe it.

Imagine that, every three weeks, 9/11 happens again. That's how many people are dying due to opioids in this country.[1] Or, imagine that a full jetliner crashes every three days: every man, woman, and child on board is erased. Dead. Gone. That's what the opioid crisis is doing. But it's not just in one city: It's everywhere, killing people from every walk of life. And we're not hearing those planes hit the ground. Most people go about their lives without thinking twice about these catastrophic losses. They are unaware of the tragedy happening all around them.

In 2017 alone, according to the *New York Times*, "about as many Americans are expected to die this year of drug overdoses as died in the Vietnam, Iraq, and Afghanistan wars combined." That's an increase from 2016, when 59,000 lives were lost to drug-related causes. Drug overdoses are now the leading cause of death for Americans under the age of fifty.[2] It's a massive crisis, gaining momentum every day.

If we do not take action now, predictors show that another 500,000 people could die of opioid-related causes within the next decade.[3] Half a million people. That's a sharp increase, even from the record death tolls we experience today. Easy access to synthetic opioids, a new generation of extremely potent prescription painkillers, and the prevalence of fentanyl all contribute to the daily body count. Ultra-strong painkillers have become the norm in our country, and we take them at obscenely high rates. In 2016, 236 million prescriptions were written for opioids in the United States. That's about one for every American adult.

As America's dependency on prescription painkillers has increased, our overdose rates have grown as well. That's not a coincidence. The pharmaceutical companies that dump millions of dollars into our advocacy programs, launder money through local and national nonprofits, and buy elected officials in every branch of government have created a national drug crisis. Our dependency on those pain pills was supposed to garner higher profits. And it did—but it also spiraled into a massive public health crisis, spurred by irresponsible prescribers, ignorant lawmakers, and ineffective treatment centers.

The American drug epidemic has further exposed the deep inequity of race, class, and gender in our country. *Who* gets help for their substance use problems, *when*, and *how* are all reliant on how white and well-off they are. Although addiction is a universal problem in America, we don't have universal care to combat it. We're on the *Titanic*, and there are no seats in the lifeboats for the people in steerage. Soon we'll all be underwater. That's why we haven't stopped the crisis in its tracks: The people who have the most power to make noise, call for help, and effect change get *just enough* help to maintain the status quo. The system is set up to privilege them, but that help doesn't trickle down. The rest of us are too poor, sick, and ashamed to take on the deeply flawed system that criminalizes addiction, pushes Big Pharma's agenda, and doesn't educate people about harm reduction or recovery options.

We cannot stop a crisis that we do not understand. *American Fix* will help you understand what the opioid crisis is, why it is happening, who it affects, and how we can stop it. We must find a solution; this is our Black Plague. It's our AIDS crisis. It is real, and we are sinking fast. If we are going to survive, we can't wait.

It's easier to explain and express what's happening inside the opioid epidemic through personal stories. After all, we're not statistics. We're people.

I walked into treatment for the last time on Thanksgiving Eve, 2014. It wasn't exactly a Kodak moment. I was terrified, exhausted, and sick of myself. My addiction had ruined every aspect of my life. I wasn't proud of who I had become. As I filled out the intake form, I swore I'd never speak about this moment or the years leading up to it ever again. I wanted to get help, get my life back together, and just move forward. I didn't ever want to think about what I'd been through, much less write a book about it.

But as I began to heal from my addiction and lost some of the people closest to me to overdoses, I became more willing to share my experience. I learned that my story was a jumping-off point. It created connection and community. So

I started reaching out. Yet every time I spoke up, many people told me to keep my mouth shut. They said I had nothing to offer. They lectured me to wait until I was "ready." But when would that day come? Ultimately, it wasn't up to them. It was up to me. I stopped waiting for permission to tell my story. And when I began speaking up, it opened the door for many others to do the same.

However, my recovery didn't begin and end with *me*. If anything, it opened my eyes to the extreme difficulties my peers were experiencing. Recently, I found out that Mikey, one of my best friends who'd been sober for three years, had relapsed on heroin. He was kicked out of his sober living and was couch surfing. That hit me hard, right in the gut. Mikey was my first roommate in sober living. We were in rehab together multiple times, both trying *for years* to reach the other side of our addiction. Mikey'd just had a kid. Things were going really well for him. But then his relationship soured, and he picked up something to cope with his emotional pain. Without insurance, his options for treatment were incredibly limited.

Although I talk to literally hundreds of people every day about *their* friends, kids, and family members, and speak to groups about recovery and advocate for policy reform, I was totally unprepared to deal with Mikey's relapse. I was dumbfounded. I panicked. I found Mikey and put him in touch with his mom, and only then did he feel comfortable asking for help.

He was homeless. At the bottom again. But his voice was so ashamed and scared. I could tell what it had taken for him to actually admit he needed help.

If Mikey hadn't made that call—if his mom hadn't talked to him first—if his family hadn't had the cash to cover part of his treatment—if he hadn't qualified for a scholarship at the rehab—if I hadn't been able to jump into my car and pick him up—what would have happened? What happens to people who don't have an immediate safety net in place?

We know what happens. They don't make it.

I have lost many friends to the disease of addiction, and each time, it's like another part of my heart is ripped out of my chest. It hurts. But there are certain friends, like Mikey, whose death would *permanently alter* me. My ability to love, to be close to others, would change forever. I didn't want to feel that pain. But because I feel it, and because I know so many moms and dads in America are feeling it right now about their own children, I need to share this story.

I can't be silent, knowing what I know about the opioid crisis. I can't sit still. It's just not who I am; the mentality of standing by while hundreds of lives are lost every day is an injustice to the dead and the families who mourn them. This book is for them—for the people who didn't make it—and for those of us who did. This book is for our parents, friends, families, and the vast network of people who are working for justice in recovery.

I set out to write this book with the intention of bringing you into my world. It's closer to yours than you think. It's a multibillion-dollar industry built on seedy rehabs, struggling families, jails and prisons, emergency rooms, community centers, syringe exchanges, methadone clinics, pill mills, and pharmacies. It is a place with a lot of pain in it—but a lot of hope too. This book will introduce you to the world of addiction and recovery and explain what it's like to live there.

This book is not about me. It's about *you*. It's about the people you love, the friends you've known. It's about your neighbors and the people who work in your office. It's about your kids, your parents. It's about the secret America that is all around you, whether you realize it or not.

Throughout this journey, I questioned myself every day. Why haven't we been listening to recovery? Why are the same old stories being told about addiction? Most of them are dead wrong. Now we have a new way to talk about this illness and the crisis that feeds off our silence. Some of the solutions to it have been staring us in the face, without our acknowledging them.

The opioid crisis is at your doorstep. It may not have impacted you yet, but it is just a matter of time before addiction touches your life. One in three Americans is affected by this crisis. If you do not have substance use disorder, you can be certain that at least one person you know *does*. That person may be suffering in silence, unable to ask for help—as I did, for more than a decade. They may have chosen to live in the dark, isolated from their friends and family.

This book is for the person who does not have a voice.

Please keep an open mind. Put aside your assumptions. Forget your prejudices and preconceived notions. You don't need those old ideas. Everything you think you know about this public health crisis is wrong. Believe me: I've lived it. Let me show you what I've learned.

1. IT STARTED WITH A PILL
A Single Irresponsible Prescription Initiated the Perfect Storm of My Addiction

IN 2005, I WAS LIVING IN FLORIDA, directly in the path of Hurricane Katrina. As the storm closed in, the blue sky faded to yellowish gray. My town's streets were empty. News stations played nonstop warnings about staying inside, stocking up on water, and preparing for the high winds and heavy rains that the hurricane would bring. Normal people complied. But not *my* people. We were out in the storm. Because the thing is, drug addiction doesn't take a day off. It doesn't matter what the weather is like. As the local news played yet another dramatic clip of palm trees being buffeted almost sideways, I was carefully counting my pain pills and wondering how long the storm would last.

The number of pills I had wasn't enough. It was never enough.

A day before Katrina hit, I got a last-minute appointment at a pain clinic. The place was crammed with people, standing room only. I was rushed through a ten-minute "checkup" and given a prescription for the medication I desperately needed. Then it was on to the pharmacy. However, I was out of luck. Most businesses had shut down due to the hurricane. I tried my usual pharmacy and called a dozen more, but no one answered. Then the storm came, and the whole city lost power. Two days later, when the rain and wind had eased up, I was strung out, shaking, and desperate. The people I knew who would sell me extra pills or trade prescriptions with me told me about a new pharmacy that had opened right before Katrina hit the Florida coast.

Clutching my scrip in my sweaty hand, I drove as fast as I could to this new place. Fort Lauderdale was still a ghost town. Fallen branches, debris, and even parts of houses littered the abandoned roads. I saw downed power lines and trees that had been crushed by the storm. Yet my addiction gripped me so strongly that I didn't give a single thought to my own safety. I made it to the new pharmacy and pulled into the already full parking lot. Sure enough, this was the place—and I wasn't the only person who'd heard about it.

Inside, the power was still out. Fluorescent bulbs powered by a plug-in generator lit the pharmacy with a ghostly, flickering glow. The waiting area was crowded with people moaning, complaining, sighing, fighting, and just *waiting* for their number to be called. This place charged almost double what I paid at my usual pharmacy. I didn't care. Nobody here cared. We just wanted our drugs.

Without power, there was no way to operate a cash register or any kind of computer. A huge, heavily muscled bodyguard stood next to the pharmacist's counter, arms crossed over his chest, glowering at anyone who moved. He wore a pistol in a shoulder holster. I had no doubt that he knew how

AMERICAN **FIX**

to use it. I slid into a chair. The pharmacist called someone's name, and I watched them hurry to the counter, eager to collect their pills. The pharmacist took a wad of hundred-dollar bills from the person, put them into a lockbox, and noted the purchase in a long, thin ledger. *Next.* Another bottle of pills. *Next.*

By the time it was my turn, I'd dissolved into a puddle of anxious sweat. *Hampton.* I couldn't get to the register fast enough. I was so desperate that I wasn't even trying to be cool, even under the intimidating stare of the armed guard or the strangers watching me. I had the cash, and I practically threw it at the person who held my pills.

"Thanks," I croaked, wishing I'd brought a bottle of water with me. I could have taken a handful of those pills on the spot. There was still no electricity and no running water, but there were drugs. I dry-swallowed two on my way back to my car. As I turned the key in the ignition, I felt them stick to my throat. I swallowed hard again, willing my hands to stop shaking. I'd be fine now. In just one more minute, everything would be fine.

The pills were small, round, and white, with an "M" marked on one side. Four milligrams of hydromorphone, in a smooth coating. Dilaudid. They came in a prescription bottle with my name on it. The pills were supposed to take my pain away. I tried them for the first time in 2003 after I'd hurt my ankle, and it just wasn't healing. I laughed about my klutziness with my doctor at the urgent care center, who nodded and smiled and handed me a piece of paper with the prescription written on it.

"We'll order you an MRI," she said. "Come back if your pain gets worse."

I took the first pill and my pain, the dull throb that followed me everywhere I went, went away. Four hours later, it came back. So I took another pill. And another one. I never got that MRI, because my ankle didn't hurt anymore. What I did get, after my first bottle of pills ran out, was another prescription.

At the time, there was almost no information available about prescription pill addiction. I didn't know what questions to ask, or even that I should be asking questions. Alcoholism was a taboo subject, and I'd never heard of substance use disorder. I was given the prescription in a doctor's office, a place we are all taught to trust. My "dealer" was a source we are taught to believe has our best interests at heart. There was no discussion of the addictive risks of opioids. After a few jokes and a handshake, I made my exit with a full prescription of extremely powerful opioids that blasted me into the stratosphere.

What I didn't know was that just that week the doctor had probably seen a sales rep from a pharmaceutical company who had assured her of the minimal addictive risk of opioids. Opioids were by no means a new drug, but the information that this new army of sales reps were presenting to physicians was. In 2003, a massive, organized effort on the part of the manufacturers of opioid pain medications had already been in motion for ten years.[1] Primary care and urgent care physicians everywhere were being given fraudulent information packaged as scientific studies that misrepresented and minimized the addictive risks of these drugs. It had made them the biggest-selling and most commonly prescribed drugs in America. Later in the book, we will examine the specific steps that led to what I believe is nothing less than medically sanctioned mass murder.

By seeking care for my ankle, I stumbled into a massive and

AMERICAN **FIX**

dangerous sea change under way in conventional medicine. Physicians were being taught to treat pain more aggressively, while pharmaceutical companies were consciously and deliberately presenting false research on the dangers of opioid painkillers. It was the white-coat equivalent of walking past a gunfight in a bad neighborhood. I heard the gunshots but didn't realize I was in danger. I was in harm's way. I didn't know it, and neither did my doctor.

Times were different in 2003. We were more focused on the war in Iraq than the drug war in America. As a kid, the only messages I got about drug and alcohol use had come from my school's D.A.R.E. program. In school, I saw videos of people driving drunk or racing through the streets, going crazy on crack or PCP. *Just say no* was a slogan and rallying cry popularized by First Lady Nancy Reagan, who talked like a sweet little grandma on an evening sitcom. Addiction could be avoided with simple good judgment, and all you had to do was "say no." America's grandma reassured you, with a pat on the head, that you wouldn't get hooked, as long as you avoided illicit substances, shady characters, and "the wrong crowd."[2] That's the message I got. And I said no, truly believing that I was on the straight and narrow. I followed the advice of all those smiling parental archetypes who seemed to cheer me on every time I made the "right choice." It was fine. Until those pain pills came along.

Up until then, I'd been a weekend warrior. The occasional joint, a few drinks with friends. There was a small margin of socially acceptable drug and alcohol use in young adulthood. I knew about hangovers; like most young adults in their twenties, I'd learned through experience where alcohol fit in my life and the broader culture. I had definitely enjoyed my college years and the period of socially acceptable excessive drinking that came with them. I wasn't a serious drinker, and I knew I'd mature out of my partying years, like most of my friends. What I didn't know was that nine out of ten people can use alcohol safely throughout their lives and not switch into an addictive pathology. However, the 10 percent who do become addicted only exhibit symptoms when their disease has progressed far beyond its early stages. Our understanding of the disease of alcoholism is further complicated by the fact that the medical diagnosis of what constitutes "problem drinking" is constantly in flux. The most recent revision was made in 2016 by the US Centers for Disease Control and Prevention.[3] Yet rarely has the medical definition of "problem drinking" been in sync with the societal definition, which is far more narrow. The myth of "functional alcoholism" has always undermined the true scale of this deadly problem and allowed people to avoid confronting the truth that alcoholism may have existed in their families or in their own lives.

I also didn't know about pills or their dangers. I used pills casually for two years. The pills weren't a big deal, in my mind, because they didn't come from a street dealer. The packaging made all the difference; it gave the hydromorphone an air of legitimacy. It looked like medicine. For me, though, it was poison.

I bounced in and out of urgent care clinics, collecting a new prescription every time. My ankle had long since healed, but I'd tell the doctors that it hurt, and they'd reach for the prescription pad.

"Let's take care of that," they always said.

Having doctors provide the prescription meant I had a cosignature, the same way a parent cosigns for your first apartment. When someone who's smarter than you tells you that what you're doing is legitimate, it's reassuring. I took comfort in it. I didn't think to say no to a substance that could be prescribed by a doctor. That changed two years later, in 2005, when I found Dr. Leah.

Dr. Leah had been an OB-GYN in Fort Lauderdale, Florida, but was now in the pain prescription business full time. "Pain management," she called it. At the time, pharmaceutical companies were paying enormous amounts of money to help doctors set up pain clinics instead of their regular practices. These clinics advertised in the back pages of local papers—I found Dr. Leah's clinic among the many ads in the *Miami New Times*. I was looking for a refill on my prescription, and I had plenty of places to choose from.

IN PAIN? WE CAN HELP! said one ad. Another one said: DON'T BE SHAMED FOR YOUR PAIN MEDICATION. WE PRESCRIBE OXY! I chose a clinic nearby, and the next day, I met Dr. Leah.

She was tall, like a model, with long blond hair. She was poised and confident, in her late thirties. When I went to her clinic, I sat in the waiting room for about twenty minutes. Then a nurse took me into the back and did a "physical."

"My ankle is swollen," I told her.

She nodded, took my temperature, and had me step onto a scale. That was it. Within fifteen minutes, I had *two* new prescriptions for pills. Dr. Leah gave me 120 OxyContin (80 mg) and 60 oxycodone (30 mg) and told me to come back next month.

"What if I need to stop taking them?" I asked her. It was a huge number of pills, and even I knew that the dosage was unusually high.

"You won't have any problems," she told me. "We'll just taper you off at ten to twenty percent of your dosage per day

IT STARTED WITH A PILL   13

until you're completely off the medication. We can do that at the clinic or you can control your dosage at home."

She handed me the prescription. "We'll see you in a month."

I lasted three weeks.

At first, I felt fantastic. A euphoric rush happened when those pills dissolved in my stomach. Opioids flick certain circuit breakers in the brain and flood you with feel-good chemicals like dopamine. For certain people, this is an elusive sensation. I didn't realize how much anxiety and depression I had until the medicine did its work and cleared away my mental fog. I felt so clear. So strong. It was the best feeling in the world, and I would do anything to hold onto it.

I was full of energy, my mood was positive, and I was even more productive at work than usual. I left the prescription pill bottle on my desk, where anyone could see it. This wasn't classic impairment, like a drunk stumbling along the sidewalk. It was simply the best boost I'd ever felt. I was totally functional (or so it seemed). If any of my coworkers noticed, I just told them that it was my prescription from the doctor. My ankle didn't hurt. I was doing great. If I took the pills more frequently than the doctor's suggestion, so what? Dr. Leah told me that I could adjust my own dosage to "manage my pain threshold" and stay comfortable.

When the prescription was almost gone, I realized I had another week before I could go back for a refill. I panicked. The long days without my medicine stretched out in front of me. I felt nauseated. How would I get by? I picked up the phone and, with shaking hands, dialed Dr. Leah. Luckily, the receptionist was able to get me an appointment for the next day—for an extra $100. I was happy to pay that amount out of pocket. Soon I had more pills, and my fear of running out of them went away. Within minutes, the familiar euphoria washed over me and the world felt right once again. I could get back to work, back to life, back to feeling normal.

This prescription was gone in less than two weeks. The next one, even sooner. I couldn't afford an extra $300 per month to cover my early visits to Dr. Leah, so I found another clinic that would prescribe to me. And then another one. I rotated among as many as five pain doctors as I juggled those pill bottles. The whole time, I somehow knew that what I was doing was risky, but I didn't recognize my progression into active addiction. I just couldn't put two and two together. After all, this was my medicine. It came from a doctor. I had pain, and this made the pain stop. I wasn't an addict. Addicts looked different, smelled different, did different drugs. They were shaky and lived in alleys. They weren't like me. I had listened to the D.A.R.E officers. I was sure I didn't know anyone with an addiction, especially not myself. Whenever I started to worry that I might get into trouble, I would take another pill, and it soothed me. My anxiety evaporated. My depression cleared, like clouds parting to reveal a blue sky.

I wasn't the only one coping with this problem. South Florida, where I lived, was the epicenter of the prescription pain medication epidemic. The pill doctors who advertised their practices on the back page, where I found Dr. Leah's clinic, seemed to pop up overnight. Pain pill–specific pharmacies suddenly were everywhere. They appeared in strip malls, wedged between laundromats and 7-Elevens. Their signs lit up with bright neon, the colors of a billiards hall. I should know: I visited them. I sat in their crowded waiting rooms, sweating, waiting to pick up my scrip.

Looking back, those "clinics" were nothing more than pill mills. I was one of thousands of drug-seeking zombies. It was an open market for opioids, with hawkers in physicians' white coats on every corner. They pushed OxyContin like snake oil, as if it were the elixir of life.

What many people fail to understand about addiction is that, for many people, the negative consequences of the drugs don't show up immediately. The symptoms do not sync up with the progression of addiction. This is important because when we think of the word "disease," we think of overt, tangible symptoms like fevers, blisters, and tumors. Addiction progresses in an asymptomatic way, and that is what makes it so dangerous.

I used prescription pills for a long time, and although my behavior was beginning to change, I wasn't truly suffering yet. If anything, I was doing really well. Seems backward, right? But anyone who has experienced addiction or seen it up close knows that there's often a period where everything seems to be OK for the addict. We can handle it, for a minute. We don't realize that, while we're handling our addiction, we're actually digging our own graves.

I kept using pills, through the stressful times and the good ones. They were my safety net, my security blanket. I worked on one political campaign after another. I landed multiple senior-level staff positions within the Democratic Party. My star was rising. Sometimes I used being so busy as my excuse for needing the prescriptions.

My rationalization skills developed with ninja-like precision as my addiction progressed. I justified my usage and need by focusing on any excuse in my life, real or imagined. It sounds hokey, but I really did have a devil on one shoulder and an angel on the other. And over both of their competing voices, I heard the message of the pills, loud and clear: *You need more! You need more now!* Sometimes it was clear to me that the only reason I took them was that withdrawal was so horrible. Those feelings, hard to ignore, were easily masked by more medication.

As my addiction deepened, I continued to excel professionally. Part of the problem with the classic prevention model I grew up with was that it used scare tactics. It told impressionable children that drug use had immediate negative consequences. This is simply untrue. It's not really how addiction unfolds.

Pills or not, I was great at what I did. And I wasn't the only one who thought so. It seemed like my dreams were coming true. I was living on my own, running my own consultancy business, paying my own bills. I genuinely enjoyed the excitement of working so closely with policy makers, legislators, and people I'd idolized for ages. Finally I had earned a seat at their table. I could feel in my gut that this was where I was meant to be. I was surrounded by people like myself—which turned out to be a double-edged sword.

Although I spent the better part of the next five years networking, campaigning, lobbying, and assisting policy leaders, I was still suffering in silence. Alcohol was part of every social function. There were work lunches at the brew pub around the corner from my office. Cocktails for networking events. Champagne toasts at every campaign win. If my first drug of choice came with a prescription, the second one, alcohol, was culturally embedded and used to celebrate at every turn of events. Was I supposed to "just say no" to alcohol too when I encountered it every day? The substances I used were hardly illicit drugs lurking in the shadows. They were fixtures of everyday life, championed by authority figures and people I looked up to. The D.A.R.E. prevention model simply wasn't relevant in this context.

I was also exploring my sexual identity and finding my footing in the LGBTQ scene very discreetly. My identity added another layer to my already surreptitious drug use. I'd been lying about who I was for so long that it started to feel hardwired into my brain. I was already practiced at concealing that I was gay. My addiction was another thing to hide, from my family, my employers, and even some of my friends. I now realize that, on some level, I was already trained by society to be ashamed of myself. I had internalized the message that who I was was unacceptable, unlovable, bad, wrong, and unnatural. These directly transferable coping skills made me adept at hiding. Drugs relieved the troubling feelings that went along with all of it.

Did my sexual identity predispose me to addiction? I don't think so. But I do believe that we are only as sick as our secrets, and even before I swallowed that first little white pill, I already had a huge, scary secret that I was hiding from the world. The anxiety and depression that went along with growing into my sexual orientation did present a vulnerability to addiction. LGBTQ people experience addiction at much higher rates than non–LGBTQ people, although we're more likely to seek help for our problems with drugs and alcohol.[4] I've learned that the people who achieve long-term recovery, no matter what their identity is, have found a way to manage and deal with the underlying anxiety and depressive issues that trigger pathological cravings. For me, these triggers happened to be related to being gay. For other people, issues can be related to any part of their lives. After all, it's not *what* happened to you; it's *how* you deal with it.

Coming out and living openly as a gay man after the AIDS crisis was a mixed blessing. It was the late 2000s, when the stigma of homosexuality was still a serious one, even in "progressive" circles. (Remember, gay marriage wasn't legalized until 2015.) HIV and AIDS had taken many lives in both gay and straight communities. Although the number of HIV cases fell by almost 20 percent from 2005 to 2014, talking about it was still taboo.[5]

Identifying myself as a gay man felt risky, especially in my circle, where the emphasis was on "being professional." I left my identity at the door when I went to work. Although I'd worked up the nerve to come out to my very Christian family, my professional life was another thing entirely. I kept my lip zipped. I'm not complaining about this; it's just the way things were.

Now I've learned how important recovery is for someone who's at high risk for HIV. No more needle use could mean the difference between life and death. AIDS, we were told, was a "gay disease." I was gay, and in order to feel accepted and safe, I stayed in the closet. I didn't have a partner, and I didn't really seek deep, intimate relationships in my community. It was too much for me. The farthest I was willing to go was to come out to my family—on the phone, in 2009. I don't remember what I said, but I do remember hanging up the phone and feeling like I'd somehow disappointed them.

Although I could deny to the outside world that I was gay, it was getting harder and harder to hide my addiction. I could fake being straight indefinitely. But I couldn't fake being sober forever. I thought I was fooling my employers, but I lost jobs and burned professional bridges, and ended up resorting to "staying with friends" when I couldn't pay my rent anymore. I was actually homeless but never called it that because I was sleeping on someone's couch. My belongings fit in a couple of grocery bags. I could barely afford to feed myself, much less pay for the prescription pills I'd been eating by the handful. The next step, to me, was clear. I was going to have to buy street heroin if I was going to stay well.

As things got worse, all I could think was *I don't belong here.* I grew up in a truly loving family. My mom, Barbara Hampton, is still my rock. She gave my two sisters and me the best childhood she could. We were raised with good Christian values in a neighborhood full of houses with white picket fences. I went to Bible camp, joined the Boy Scouts, and volunteered with my church's youth group. My dad was in and out of my life, and my mother, who's a public school teacher, raised us almost singlehanded. We stuck close together, and I remember feeling that, no matter what was going on with our family, it was important to be happy. To seem happy. Luckily, most of the time it wasn't an act—we really *were* happy.

My mom's spirituality was a godsend when I plunged into full-on substance use. She was no fool. She knew that I'd experimented in high school with a few things, mostly marijuana and a few drinks at parties. But she had no idea that I was getting hooked on pain pills until I was in over my head.

At that time, we knew even less about addiction than we did about HIV. Drug education was limited to tired slogans and trite cartoons, long since proven ineffective. We were taught that people who used drugs had low self-esteem or were just plain self-destructive. We were told it was a choice. At first, my mother believed this messaging. She thought that when I showed up loaded to Thanksgiving dinner, or called

AMERICAN **FIX**

to "borrow" another hundred bucks that I wouldn't be paying back, I was choosing to hurt our family. I'm so grateful that she has since learned that addiction isn't a choice at all. If it was a choice, I wouldn't have chosen it. I would never want to hurt my family, especially not the incredible, strong, compassionate woman who poured everything she had into me.

I know I'm lucky, not only because I survived addiction and made it into long-term recovery, but because I've been able to keep my relationship with my mother healthy and strong. Even when I was at the absolute bottom of my drug use, couch surfing and broke, she still loved me. She'd take my phone calls even when she wouldn't allow me in the house. She made me Tupperware containers of home-cooked meals and brought them to wherever I was sleeping at the time, so that I could have something to eat. She knew I was sick—and I'm beyond grateful that she recognized my addiction for the illness it was. One time I called her in a state of absolute madness. She answered the phone and listened to me babble incomprehensibly for several minutes. When she finally interrupted, I could hear the tears in her voice.

"Ryan, son," she said. "Let's just pray together."

I was silent, and we prayed. When we were done, she told me she loved me and then hung up. She loved me, even though she couldn't help me. In recovery, I've met so many parents like my mom—who feel powerless to help their kids. No matter what, my mom believed in me, and her faith in me made all the difference.

In fact, my mom is the one who gave me the last little bit of money I needed when it was time for me to check into rehab. I'd been trying to find a bed for a month, with no luck. Either I couldn't afford the treatment center or it was full.

Frantic, I called multiple treatment centers, only to be told that beds weren't available and likely wouldn't be for weeks. Apparently, that's the norm: The wait time for access to public facilities typically exceeds thirty days.

Being placed on waiting lists and knowing that my window of willingness to keep fighting for help was waning by the hour were some of the most terrifying moments in my entire life. I knew that my addiction would be lethal if I didn't get treatment. But finally I got a call from a treatment center in Pasadena, California. I confirmed that I could be there in a couple of days and immediately started making calls. I needed money to get help. The rehab was able to give me a scholarship for 50 percent of the cost, but I still had to raise the rest. The last person I called was my mom.

"Praise God," she said when I told her what I was doing. Even though it wasn't my first treatment center, and even though she'd seen me fail to find lasting recovery before, she gave me the money, and her blessing.

Every day I think about the incredible privilege, luck, and help I've had in order to get into long-term recovery. It took a lot to get me here. It makes me wonder: Why should recovery be a privilege? Shouldn't our basic health needs be considered a human right? What if my friends and family hadn't had money to share with me? What if I'd overdosed before finding a treatment center? So many people are in exactly the same position I was. One in three Americans is affected by addiction. Fewer than 10 percent of them will receive any kind of medical help for their condition. I'm one of the lucky few who made it through the net.

At this point, I'm not asking "Why *me*?" I'm asking "Why not *all* of us?"

I've made it my life's mission to challenge and break

through the barriers that keep people like me from surviving addiction. Recovery is a gift, sure, but the path to wellness should be open to everyone. Recovery belongs to any person who wants it, regardless of income level, race, ethnic background, physical or mental ability, spiritual beliefs, family, sexual identity or orientation, political views, or gender. If addiction can affect anyone, treatment and recovery supports must be available and accessible to *everyone*.

Yet, if you ask ten people on the street a few basic questions about recovery, they do not know how the process works. Most have experienced the havoc and pain of addiction in their family. Most will say they've seen treatment fail for someone they cared about.

If you ask ten doctors how much addiction-specific training they had in four years of medical school, they'll probably tell you they got a one-hour lecture. Not even a full credit. Addiction medicine isn't even a full medical specialty; it's just a certification. This is in spite of the fact that overdose is the leading cause of accidental death in our country. We don't educate people on how addiction works, and we don't train doctors how to treat it. Why is that? The shame surrounding addiction and the industries that profit from it are the only culprits.

You may notice that, throughout this chapter, I refer to myself as an *addict* and I talk about my substance use disorder as an *addiction*. I'm using those words to qualify myself and explain my past experiences with the limited vocabulary we have to talk about substance use. Now that recovery has entered the mainstream, recovery advocates are working on destigmatizing the condition of substance dependency. Instead of *alcoholic*, *addict*, *user*, or *abuser*, we now say *a person with a substance use disorder*. This helps keep the emphasis on the person, not the disease. After all, I am a person first. I was a person before I picked up my first prescription, I was a person when I injected heroin, and I'm a person now. I'm also an advocate, a brother, a son, a friend, and a writer. I love my dog. I sing in my car. I'm a *person*. I also happen to have a life-threatening, terribly misunderstood chronic brain illness commonly known as addiction. I nearly lost my life to this disease, and I'm tired of seeing it kill the people I love.

Any other social problem on the scale of the opioid crisis would result in revolution. I'm beyond furious that hundreds of people die from drug-related causes every day, yet America continues to turn a blind eye. By the time you've finished reading this chapter, four more people will be dead as a direct result of this crisis.

I'm fed up, and I'm not the only one.

2. TOO SICK TO GET WELL
From Barack Obama to Black Tar Heroin, the Double Life I Led Was Killing Me

ON FEBRUARY 23, 2012, I was supposed to reunite with Barack Obama. Of course, I woke up dope-sick. I was already running late: It was ten in the morning, and the lunch started at one. I rubbed my eyes, trying to make a plan. Squid, the mutt I shared the couch with, licked my face. A skateboarding video played in a loop on the burner laptop we kept on the coffee table instead of a TV. In three hours, I was going to be shaking hands with the forty-fourth president of the United States and meeting with people I hadn't seen in years. But first, I needed my medicine.

"Star," I called. "You up?"

She was. I could hear her moving around in the bedroom with Horse: her boyfriend, my dealer. In the 400-square-foot apartment where I was crashing, we could practically hear each other breathing. I didn't mind, though. Being homeless and sleeping on my dealer's couch with his dog was better than the street.

The night before, excited to see President Obama again, I'd stayed up later than usual with Star. Her boyfriend was a low-level prescription pill dealer in his mid-twenties. He'd lost a leg to a gunshot wound and was a prime candidate for pill clinics. His amputated limb made my "sore ankle" look like a joke. Horse and Star went to different pain doctors, picking up prescriptions and then selling the pills. That's where I met Star—in the waiting room of yet another doctor's office.

Star was tiny, barely five foot three, and covered in freckles. When I met her, she was wearing little half-glasses, like a grandma. A massive, black star tattoo was visible through her shirt; it covered her entire chest. Her hair was a bright, natural auburn; huge curls stood out from her head in the Hollywood Beach humidity. She looked like Little Orphan Annie, if Annie had been a stripper.

At this point in my life, all I did was work and get high. And work while I was high, and get high while I was supposed to be working.

For work, I had exactly one nice shirt: a pale yellow button-down and a tie that still looked professional. I had one pair of khakis. This is what I planned to wear to lunch with the president. It was the same outfit I wore to every business function: The state representatives I worked with never saw me in anything else. I didn't notice that my pants were getting baggier, or that my shirt looked dingy from never being dry-cleaned. I thought that, as long as I showered, shaved, and showed up on time, nobody would think there was anything wrong with me. I was going to know almost every person at this lunch, so I needed to look good.

But now it was ten in the morning and we needed a wake-up shot. Star and I had used all of the dope from the night before, even though we promised ourselves we'd save just a little bit. Instead of a morning shot, I woke up feeling like my veins were full of salt water. Horse was out too. He started making calls, trying to see if someone would front us some drugs. *Nothing. No luck.* Every time he hung up, I felt my stomach lurch. Instead of just pacing back and forth, I borrowed Star's smartphone so that I could check the headlines and see if there was any breaking political news.

The delivery came while I was in the shower. I hadn't had money for a haircut in a while, but it was too late to worry about that now. I shaved with an old disposable razor. I cleaned my nails, hoping the track marks on the tops of my hands wouldn't be too obvious. When I came out of the bathroom, Star and I got high. *I could breathe again.* I had this whole thing under control.

I had asked Star to be my date to the lunch for one reason only: She had transportation. The bus ride from Hollywood Beach to the Biltmore in Coral Gables would have taken four hours, and there was no way I could sit still for that long. Star, however, had a scooter—not a moped or a Vespa, an eyesore of an actual *scooter* that was painted neon stripper pink—that could hold both of us. She stepped out of the bedroom jingling her keys.

"Ready to go?" she said, practically wiggling with excitement. She'd put on a full face of makeup, as if she were going to work, and she was wearing the same six-inch, sparkly stilettos she wore when she was dancing. To meet the president, she'd selected her favorite dress: a fishnet body stocking that revealed every freckle.

I adjusted my tie. "Let's roll."

The ride to Coral Gables took forever, even going at the scooter's top speed. We had to stick to the side streets: Loaded with both me and Star, the scooter couldn't go faster than twenty miles an hour. It was February, but the South Florida heat was almost unbearable. By the time we arrived at the Biltmore, we were both covered in sweat and road grime. I could feel my skin tingling from the sunburn I knew I'd have to peel off later. Under my shirt, the abscesses in my arms were throbbing. I grabbed a pair of plastic star-spangled sunglasses from a bowl of fundraiser swag. They were printed with the words OBAMA BIDEN. I didn't care that I looked ridiculous; they were dark enough to hide how dilated my pupils were. I put a big grin on my face and walked into the ballroom with as much confidence as I could muster.

The lunch, a reelection campaign fundraiser, was packed with people I had worked with since I was fifteen and volunteering on local campaigns. After all, even though I was a full-time heroin addict, I was still managing to hold my career together. I'd been able to find a $15,000 donor who was excited about Obama's prospects for a second term: That's how I got the invitation to the lunch. I was still fundraising, doing some contracting, and working with a few members of the Florida legislature. I made sure that I was always put together when I had a meeting, but it was clear to everyone, as I walked in with Star on my arm, that something was very wrong with me. Who brings a stripper to formal lunch with the president of the United States of America? *Seriously.* I was an absolute mess, and deep down, I knew it.

A few of the other guests came up to shake hands and ask me how I was doing, but their tone told me that they didn't really want to know. I didn't read deeply into what they were saying. I didn't see anything strange in my behavior or the choices I'd made: It was my new normal, in active addiction. Yet, at the same time, I felt a deep, sick disappointment in myself. Hiding behind those red, white, and blue sunglasses, I couldn't even meet their eyes.

Eventually, many of the people who were in that room in Coral Gables ended up supporting and encouraging me when I came out about my addiction. Seeing my pathway in recovery has helped them understand more about addiction. After all, when it's one of your own, your perspective changes. The heroin crisis wasn't abstract anymore: It was real, sitting in their offices, meetings, and fundraising galas. Many of the people I saw at that lunch are now part of the broad coalition of people facing addiction, *and they're just as furious as I am*. I will never forget the way they looked at me when I was still sick: concerned, afraid to say something. I heard their whispers. *He's killing himself. He'll be dead in a year.* I had lost almost everything, but I couldn't see it. That's how insidious my illness was. I thought I'd fooled them all, but nobody was buying it.

Then it was time. This wasn't my first meeting with the president, but this time was *different*.

Other people have compared Obama to Lincoln, but that's only partly accurate. He is very tall, sure, and when he spoke with me, he leaned down. He listened. He made me feel like I was the only person in the room.

The other thing that not many people mention are his hands. They're massive: the hands of a basketball player or an orchestra conductor. When he shook my hand, he didn't just shake it. He *held* it. We talked for maybe three minutes, and he held my hand the whole time: my hand, which was dirty and had needle marks and bruised veins. My skin was cracked and hard. I could feel how very soft and smooth the president's was.

This handshake made an indelible impression on me. I was

on the verge of needing another shot, about to get dope-sick again, but this man treated me with kindness and respect. Shaking hands with Barack Obama, I realized how long it had been since someone had touched me in a loving, caring way. For those three minutes, I had his undivided attention. For those three minutes, I wasn't a heroin addict. I was a person.

And then I was back on Star's scooter and back to Horse, Squid, the couch, and the life I was used to.

The name "Hollywood Beach" started to feel like a cruel joke the longer I lived there. It wasn't glamorous in the least, and certainly not somewhere I wanted to be. I ended up there completely by accident.

In 2009, I was about three weeks sober and fresh out of my third Florida treatment center. I was desperate to stay away from opioids, so I went to multiple AA meetings a day and spent almost all my time at a clubhouse where people in the recovery community gathered. My mom, God bless her, drove me to these meetings and waited outside in her car for me. One day, as she dropped me off, I told her that I was worried about finding a place to live.

"Why don't you ask about it while you're in the meeting?" she suggested. "The people in there are great. Someone will help you."

So I did. I raised my hand and said that I was newly sober and afraid that I'd relapse unless I was able to find a safe, supportive, sober home. After the meeting, a guy named Jason pulled me and one other newcomer aside. He had a thick Brooklyn accent, which grated on my ears. He told us that he ran a sober living house and we could move in the next day.

Mission accomplished. For the first week, things were fine. I filled up my meeting attendance card in record time. I stayed away from pills, even though I was itchy with cravings. Then, suddenly, Jason wasn't around. I asked about it, trying to find out where he was, and learned that he wasn't what he seemed. A sheriff showed up at the door one night and told me he had been using heroin. He'd stolen a car, committed grand larceny, and was in jail. The police were investigating his case. The sober living home where I'd landed was a trap house. I fell right through the floorboards.

Things quickly went from bad to worse. I relapsed on pills, but nobody cared. There were no rules except to pay the rent on the first of the month. I was working full time, but my entire paycheck went toward my prescription pain pills— which, of course, I needed in order to work. The other people in the house were getting high too. The guy who lived in the room next to mine was shooting heroin. He encouraged me to try it, telling me it was cheaper and more effective than the pills I was spending my paycheck on. I told him no. After all, heroin was a *real* drug. It didn't come in a little orange bottle with my name on it.

Up to that point, I had been using pills exclusively. I kept up my rounds at the pain clinics and spent more than I earned on pills. I just couldn't stay well, no matter how much I snorted, so I started cooking and injecting the pills. I remember thinking that if I was smart about it, injecting couldn't hurt me. So I started by doing some research. I watched YouTube videos about how to shoot up. I practiced tying off my arm and watching my veins rise and throb out of my skin. I learned how to gently pull the plunger once the needle was in, to make sure I'd made contact with my bloodstream. I think it's a mark of the insanity of addiction that I did this with the same collegiate attitude I had toward writing a term paper. I was gathering facts, that's all. I didn't think about the horrific consequences. That's how addiction works. Years of drug education was saying "Just Say No," but my need to get high was saying "Why not?"

I went to a pharmacy and asked for some clean syringes— the kind people use to inject insulin. They were small, slim plastic tubes with long orange caps. I took them home in a bag. I had a spoon, a lighter, a cotton ball, and these sterile syringes. I crushed the pills, put them in the spoon with some water, and heated it up.

Let's see what happens, I thought.

I followed the instructions. They worked. And just like that, my addiction completely took over my life. Before, there might have been a sliver of me still left, still fighting, still believing that I was a normal drug user. But once the needle went into my arm, there was no turning back.

The shots left marks on my arms, but I didn't care. One day I went to one of my pain clinics, run by a woman named Dr. Sullivan. She was a former methadone clinician. The receptionist took my payment for the visit, which cost $150 a pop and didn't include the cost of the prescription. Then a nurse in the back took my blood pressure. When she rolled my sleeve up, she saw the track marks on my skin. Our eyes met.

"The doctor will meet with you in her office," she said, as if nothing were wrong. *Safe.* I thought it would be fine.

But Sullivan was furious with me. She accused me of drug-seeking, called me a "junkie," humiliated and confused me. *Hadn't she been giving me the prescription?* She threatened to put my name into a database of pill abusers, so I wouldn't be able to get any more prescriptions. She told me that what *I* was doing was criminal and that *she* could lose her license.

I was scared of being cut off from the pain clinics. Despite what Sullivan called me, I still couldn't stop. How could I, when I was just taking what the doctor prescribed me? Every doctor I'd seen made it clear that dependence on the medicine did not equal addiction and that I wasn't in any danger, so how could something be wrong with me? I just had a high tolerance. It didn't make sense.

Sullivan 86ed me from the clinic and told me that if I ever came back, they'd call the police. When I got back to the trap house, I was starting to feel sick again. I didn't have any pills left. My neighbor, seeing the condition I was in, offered me some of the heroin he had in a piece of foil. This time I didn't turn him down. I snorted what he gave me, then caught the bus to buy new syringes at the pharmacy. When I returned home, I locked myself in my room and prepared my first shot of heroin. *Easy.* The first time I missed my vein completely. But the second time I got it. I *really* got it. I felt immediate relief from my stress, shame, and sickness. As I felt my new reality take hold, I was already planning on how I could score again.

I had officially leveled up to IV heroin. Game over. In many ways, it was the perfect solution: It was cheaper than pills, easier to get hold of, and a quarter of the cost. Most important, nobody was tracking us in a database. I didn't have to worry about being reported and cut off.

However, I did have a housing problem, because soon the trap house was shut down. As I transitioned from pills to heroin, I'd been spending more and more time with Star and Horse. When the trap house closed, I packed my belongings in two garbage bags and moved in with them. I was stuck in Hollywood Beach for good.

Star and Horse's apartment was right across the street from a homeless shelter that offered hot meals twice a day: breakfast at five-thirty in the morning and dinner in the evening. So many people lined up to eat that there was a rule that you could only go once a day. I started out as a breakfast-only person but soon got friendly with the shelter's director, who let me come back for dinner. So, most days, if I wasn't too sick, I got two simple meals: usually a plate of industrial scrambled eggs and a Subway sandwich for dinner. That wasn't all I ate there. Once I found a loose methadone tablet on the floor and swallowed it. I mean, why not? It was there, and I had lowered my standards as far as they would go.

In between my two meals at the shelter, I had to find enough heroin to stay well and keep from getting sick. There was a Shell station four blocks down Federal Highway from the apartment, and after breakfast, that was my next stop. I went to the station every morning to panhandle for change so that I could buy dope. I told people my car had broken down up the street and asked for gas money. I made fifty cents at a time. The hours stretched out like a desert. I was a professional fundraiser; in retrospect, I probably would have made the money faster if I'd just told people I wanted it for drugs.

After a few hours of begging, I could afford a wake-up shot. I'd go use, go home, sit on the couch with Squid, have dinner at the homeless shelter, and fall asleep. Rinse and repeat. Every day was almost identical to the one before it, except for the ones where I put on my yellow shirt and tie and headed to a work meeting somewhere across town. Ever heard of a functional addict? That was me. After all, I had a roof over my head, even if my name wasn't on the lease and all my belongings fit into two garbage bags. I had something to eat, thanks to the homeless shelter. I was working, even though my drug use was burning my professional bridges one at a time. I had friends, if you could call Horse and Star my friends. Squid liked me. And I had a cell phone, which my mom paid for every month.

My mother, through all of this, was absolutely my best friend. Addiction is so hard on families of people who are in it. Unlike cancer, diabetes, and heart disease, addiction is a disease that also hurts everyone around the user. Cancer doesn't steal from your parents. Diabetes doesn't neglect loving relationships. Heart disease doesn't lie to your friends and employers. Addiction does, and that is why it's so hard to treat: Its symptoms take a fierce toll on all those who truly care about you. The fear of not knowing where your kid is, or if they're safe, or if they're even alive, is maddening. Every day, I am grateful that my mother stuck with me through the absolute darkest times of my heroin use. Without her, I know I would be dead. Somehow, she knew that I was a sick person who needed to get well, not a bad person who needed to become good.

By now, she knew better than to give me money, which I would have spent on heroin. Sometimes she brought me a hot meal when she knew I was struggling. She didn't buy into the "tough love" line of thinking that so many other parents felt like they had to adopt. I'm lucky that she didn't. Knowing that my mother didn't want me out of her life, and that she loved me no matter what, kept me going. She never knew where I would be, or what I was doing, or if I was safe, so she paid for my phone. It was the only way for her to keep tabs on me and make sure that I was OK.

It was a pre-paid Walgreens phone. I remember picking it out: I chose it because it was the one that looked the most like a real BlackBerry. It was a knock-off, so it could only handle text messages and phone calls, but I thought it looked convincing. I really wanted to impress people. It was crucial that I fit in. Did I actually convince anyone? Probably just myself.

I don't want anyone to think that I was using heroin because I wanted to or because I enjoyed it. I didn't. That period was long gone. It's ironic to me that the prescription I took to ease my pain brought nothing but pain into my life. I'm talking *physical* pain. Unless I had a certain amount of drugs in my body, I felt miserable, both physically and mentally. I felt like a failure. My back ached, my bones throbbed, and I felt nauseated. I could barely concentrate on the simplest tasks, and my attitude was terrible. Sometimes it felt like I'd been bitten by fleas, my skin itched so badly. My mouth was dry and my eyes were glazed. I couldn't even look in the mirror. My skin, even with constant exposure to the sun, was pale and yellowish. I didn't tan but burned a deep, bloody red that accentuated the deep creases in my face and neck.

And that's just the physical stuff. Few people experience the psychological torture of active heroin addiction. There's nothing worse. I wouldn't wish it on my worst enemy. This is beyond the symptoms of physical dependency: It's in your mind. You feel hopeless, hated, alone, and undeserving of anything good. You know you are no match for the ferocious cravings that come on or the withdrawal pangs that erupt if you don't put the fire out with a fix. You feel like a hamster on a wheel of self-hate and defeat. You wake up each day telling yourself that today will be different, but within hours you are back to scoring, using, nodding off, and crashing down.

This kind of insanity is really hard to describe. I didn't get a sense of what active addiction was like until I got into recovery in 2014. Until then, my life was a cycle of obsession, shame, and self-hatred. From the minute I woke up until the instant I fell asleep, heroin was the only thing I thought about. The obsession eclipsed everything else: family, friends, employment, hygiene, and basic needs like food and housing. Whatever needed to get done could wait. I didn't answer phone calls from my mom. I skipped work deadlines, giving ridiculous excuses for why I was going to be late on a project. I didn't eat. When I scored, I got a break, but it didn't last long.

Deep inside, I knew that what I was doing was hurting me. It killed me to hear my mom's voice on the phone.

"Ryan, Ryan," she pleaded. "Please, please, stop." She never used my name unless she was dead serious. Sometimes she would call and just repeat my name over and over, as if that would get me back.

I was invited to family gatherings only for the holidays. I felt deeply ashamed of myself. In a perfect world, I remember thinking, I would have it both ways. If I'd been able to use every day and still function, I would have. *That's how it started.* But as soon as I put heroin into my body, I lost all control. As soon as that itchy, nagging feeling came up, I was frantic.

It's not as if I didn't try treatment. In my decade of active addiction, I tried many different treatment centers. I signed up for quick five-day detoxes, sought out sober living situations, and tried to get into rehab. Nothing worked for me. My drug use was to the point where I needed safe, medical detox to help me get off heroin. I also needed significant support beyond detox. I learned this the hard way: by failing. The reality of addiction treatment is that it is an acute care model delivered to treat a chronic disease. I didn't understand the implications of this and blamed myself when treatment didn't help me. Once, I was put on methadone, with the promise that I'd be transferred from the spin-dry weekend detox to a long-term facility. It turned out that was a lie, and I used my entire methadone prescription in addition to heroin within hours of leaving.

Over time, I learned what treatment I needed because I was painfully aware of what worked and what did not, through trial and error. The other thing that I was learning was how difficult it was to find the treatment I needed, even if I was motivated and actively seeking help. I was only aware of treatment centers whose ads I saw on television, billboards, and flyers that seemed to paper every town in Florida. Swimming with dolphins and walking on a sunset beach? Sounded pretty nice to a homeless heroin addict. There were endless luxury facilities—those cost a fortune. I couldn't afford to get in, and I didn't have insurance to cover a twenty-eight-day visit. Their doors were always locked for me. Public assistance was something I didn't know even existed. And my experience with Jason and his trap house had soured me on any help I might find in 12-Step meetings. Who could I trust? I didn't want to be taken advantage of again. I simply couldn't afford to take the risk. I was bankrupt physically, mentally, financially, and spiritually.

Toward the end of my heroin use, I was waking up sick every day. I was dying and I knew it. It was only a matter of time. There were only two things I cared about: the bag of heroin on my glass-topped coffee table and the cell phone next to it. They were my two lifelines. After a decade of abusing opiates, I couldn't just stop using heroin. I was psychologically, physically, and emotionally dependent on it. My phone, too, was an absolute necessity. It linked me to my network—which I'd started building as a young, ambitious White House staffer. On the last day of my drug use, I stared down at the table. To my left, the baggie. To my right, the phone.

I was desperate enough to try anything, even the treatment centers that were out of my zero-dollar budget. I'd been calling rehabs, detox programs, and treatment centers for a month. *Can you come up with anything? Try tomorrow.* A solid month, multiple calls a day. Some places suggested I sell the car I didn't own or ask family to pay my way. I tried rehabs that were out of state, out of my budget. I spent five days in a methadone detox, but that didn't work. It wasn't enough time; I needed more than a mere five days of treatment. I kept trying. Every day I called, and every day I was told the same thing: *We can't help you.*

One day I walked from the place where I was sleeping to an LGBTQ-friendly rehab where I could go to a free support group. The walk was only a couple of miles, but by the time I got there, I was soaked from the rain. I sat in that support group crying because I wanted help so badly. *Nobody could help me.*

After the group, a counselor pulled me aside. She saw how desperate I was and how much I wanted to get away from heroin. "You should talk to the director," she said. "Maybe he can do something for you."

After I told the rehab director my story, he nodded. They wanted to help me: They might even have a bed available, at low or no cost. Finally. I nodded as the director talked about the treatment program they offered. It was a perfect fit. *This could be it,* I thought. I felt a sense of relief. Maybe this was my reprieve.

Then he pulled out a thick, ringed binder. It was so heavy that it made a *thud* when he put it on the desk.

"What's that?" I asked.

"This is the waiting list," he said. "We can put you on this list, and when a bed opens up, we'll call you." He opened the binder and started turning the laminated pages inside. "If we have an available space, we call through this list, in order. Once someone answers and says yes, the spot is theirs. No answer, we go to the next person."

He explained that, some days, they called only one or two people before filling the space. Others, it was thirty or forty people, practically half of the binder. He turned to the very last page and pointed to the empty space in the back of the book. "Write your name and number here," he said.

My hope dissolved. I gave him my information anyway, but when I left the treatment center, I knew I was a dead man. Some of the people on that waiting list had been on it for months. How many of them were still alive? How many of them had died while they were waiting for that call? This treatment center was wonderful, supportive, and progressive, but when it came to helping people—people who were desperate for help, like me—its hands were tied. My only option was to keep using and keep making those phone calls.

By this time, I had relocated to Los Angeles. I thought that a change of scenery would fix my problems, but as the saying goes, no matter where I went, there I was. The problem with any geographic cure is that you always wind up bringing yourself with you. Soon I was right back where I'd started: homeless, broke, and still using heroin. This time, however, I was able to find treatment. I was lucky: The program happened to have space for me and thank God it was willing to accept me without a lot of cash or a flashy insurance card.

It felt like my last chance—because it was.

But even after I started my new program, I couldn't forget the waiting list I'd seen. And I couldn't stop thinking about the thousands of people who were just like me but hadn't been as aggressive about advocating for themselves. What if someone's phone was shut off for too many missed payments? What if they simply didn't answer? What if they were already dead?

It was clear to me that there were not enough beds for everyone and that the longer sick people had to wait, the more likely it was that they would just fade away. What we called the "treatment system" was really a deadly game of musical chairs.

The place where I finally went, in Pasadena, California, was not necessarily the fanciest rehab in America. My bed was paid for by my mom, plus a partial scholarship. The place didn't have a pool or "extraordinary view of the Los Angeles skyline." It was a simple rehab, with all the basics: detox; counseling sessions; three meals a day. I knew if I was going to survive, something had to change. Even though I wanted to get better, I knew the odds were stacked against me no matter where I went. For the first time in my life, I actually felt like I deserved a second shot at life. I clearly didn't land at the best place in America, but I finally felt safe.

However, I learned that there were costs associated with recovery, too. The flip side of getting help was the staggering cost of treatment. A twenty-eight-day treatment center could charge tens of thousands of dollars, and then what? The people returned to the exact place where their addiction thrived, but with monumental depression and anxiety surging, in unsupported early recovery. Although clients weren't guaranteed lasting sobriety, many rehabs sold that empty promise. In fact, patients might relapse only hours after leaving treatment. It's not that hard to understand when you realize that releasing someone from a twenty-eight-day model is essentially abandoning their care. It's the medical equivalent of stopping dialysis treatments midway and wishing patients well as they writhe on the floor in convulsions.

The longer I stayed sober, the more eerily similar stories I heard: After frantically trying to find treatment, the person shelled out thousands of dollars for a program that claimed to provide the most cutting-edge, state-of-the-art, top-of-the-line treatment. These places often offered similar perks, like a pool, acupuncture, yoga, art therapy, organic meals, and meditation. Some of them were really beautiful facilities too, with linen napkins in the dining room and private suites for patients. Yet none of this seemed to keep people from relapsing once they left. What were people really paying for? They paid ten times what a month at the Four Seasons Hotel cost and left with nothing to show for it except a thirty-day chip.

Once I realized that my addiction was going to require months, if not years, of "treatment," the dangers of the treatment industry and the way it sets people up to fail became glaringly obvious. There were Jasons everywhere, eager to take advantage and line their own pockets.

In Pasadena, I left treatment and headed to yet another sober living home. I entered the world of recovery. No matter what the advertisements said, it wasn't all puppies and sunshine: It had a seriously dark criminal underbelly. That criminal element knowingly took enormous amounts of money from desperate families, fully conscious that the patient remained in harm's way and likely would fail. This nefarious business model thrived in plain sight and was completely legal. Yet death rates were skyrocketing. Why? Because society didn't really believe people could recover. There was a general belief that if someone died from drug addiction, it was their own fault. That is wrong. It is actually lack of effective treatment, exorbitant costs, and ridiculous twenty-eight-day vacations disguised as medical help, fed by patient brokers who run a completely legal, high-end human trafficking cartel to push tens of thousands of patients through the broken system. Once I stopped my daily drug use and could think clearly, I saw this exploitation and felt overcome with despair.

What really scared me was that there was no way to tell the difference between good and bad rehabs. They both spent millions of advertising dollars to make themselves attractive to new consumers. They all said the same things, included sunny pictures of their facilities, and charged similar prices. How could anyone know whom to trust and who was out to fleece patients?

The predatory recruiters used to find new patients really freaked me out. It turns out that many rehabs participate in this form of human trafficking, even though it's illegal in some states. The recruiters were kind of like pharmaceutical company reps: young, good-looking, newly sober, and excited to evangelize for whatever facility had hired them. They reached out to people who were scared or struggling, offered to "help," and then delivered the people—their marks—to rehab. Once a person was checked in, the treatment center paid the recruiter thousands of dollars. The recruiters weren't helping people shop for the best treatment program or providing the kind of support a social worker might offer in navigating recovery resources. This was headhunting, plain and simple; in fact, it bordered on abduction.

Recruiters took advantage of a person's shame and fear. Under the guise of "helping them get sober," these traffickers put suffering people in the hands of negligent, unqualified facilities whose only goal was to milk them for every insurance dollar they could get. Some of these recruiters actually believe they are helping, sure, but they all drive new BMWs too. Now *that's* sick.

There was no limit to how low these recruiters would go either. They found people who were sleeping on the street, found out if they were eligible for Medicaid or a preferred provider organization (PPO), and then dumped them in whichever facility would take them. Or they recruited patients for out-of-state centers and essentially kidnapped them, refusing to let them contact their friends or family until they were through the intake paperwork process and "safe." This happened to a friend of mine named Jeff, who was brokered: caught by a patient broker and essentially trafficked into rehab. He'd relapsed after treatment and vanished shortly after. His mother called me, panicking. I offered to help and started making calls. I tried contacting Jeff's previous rehab, but they said he'd just disappeared.

"Disappeared? How the hell is that possible?" I said.

They couldn't answer me. I persisted, but as the days went by, I started to lose hope. I was certain that he was dead in a hotel somewhere and that he'd turn up in a morgue with a tag on his toe.

Then Jeff's mom got a call from her son; he was in Fort Lauderdale. A broker had caught him while he was in the middle of his relapse. Instead of offering support and help, the broker had capitalized on Jeff's shame and his illness and gotten him a one-way ticket to this rehab in Florida. *Florida!*

Jeff was calling his mother because he wanted to go home, but the facility wouldn't release him. Every time he tried to walk out, the treatment center would use the Baker Act, which allowed them to declare Jeff a medical risk and "commit him" involuntarily—to the same place he was trying to leave. He was essentially a prisoner there. Furthermore, this treatment center billed Jeff's insurance for the days when he was held there against his will. He was able to escape only because his parents got involved.

Jeff's story is not an exception; rather, I'd say it is the rule. Patient brokering is illegal in most states, and it hurts the most vulnerable person in the transaction: the person who needs help. Recruiters and greedy treatment centers rob patients of thousands of dollars and set them up for a potentially lethal relapse. The punishment for doing this is a slap on the wrist, compared to the consequences of the crime. If brokers are caught by the police, they go to jail. The treatment center they work for might pay a small fine, but it's rare for anyone higher up the food chain to serve time. And if the people they're "helping" relapse again, or die—well, they were hopeless anyway. If they're lucky, they end up back at square one. If they don't, we find them on the obit page.

Even some of *my* people—members of the recovery community—are willing to look the other way when it comes to recruiting. After all, it's often people who are newly sober participating in this exploitation. Are they at fault? Do they even know what they're doing? It's hard to explain to a twenty-four-year-old that it's wrong to take a $2,000 reward for "helping" someone find their way to rehab.

The money is extremely tempting, especially for people who are starting their lives over and don't have resources of their own. Some of them hand out their business cards in AA meetings. They call it "relapse insurance" and offer people $1,000 to come to a particular treatment center if they fall off the wagon. Though this is predatory, it's routine. Likewise, there are people like Jason who grab newcomers in meetings and "help" them with high-priced housing in unregulated, dangerous living conditions. Some recruiters move farther up the ladder and start their own "treatment centers," adding to the number of bad actors in the industry.

I've met people who chose to work for treatment centers or laboratory groups, selling lab contracts to rehabs. They own massive homes, paid for by the thousands of dollars they make every day. They can say that they're "helping," but really they're just helping themselves. These bad actors never seem to stop to ask themselves what they're doing. They don't see the role they're playing in feeding the toxic relationship between rapacious treatment centers and their victims: people just like I was, last-gasp heroin addicts who were desperate for help. They give lip service to recovery and just cash their checks.

Two other young men I know, newcomers to recovery, opened a sixty-day sober living "program." They're not professionals: Six months earlier, they'd been flipping burgers. They require their "patients" to have private insurance. The facility has zero services—and I mean *zero*, unless you count the raft of Top Ramen the kitchen is stocked with. The rules require residents to attend outpatient treatment of some kind so that they can bill insurance as an outpatient provider. Residents take urine tests three times a week, paying a hefty fee for each test. Essentially, all the operators do, besides housing newly sober, gullible people, is put them on a bus and collect their AA meeting attendance slips—and they make money hand over fist. This kind of corruption is much worse than just taking a job promoting unnecessary lab services because *it kills people*. Bad actors do absolutely nothing to help the people they're housing. They're working a system that is designed to put insurance money into the pockets of the greedy. Would you hand a fragile heart attack patient over to an unqualified money pit, run by a former gas pump jockey? Absolutely not, but families do this unwittingly every day.

We ignore the selfish greed of bad actors like this because, at the end of the day, we're still blaming people who need help for their addictions. Instead of shielding suffering people from predatory recruiters, treatment centers, and housing, we throw them into the deep end. Once you've been through the chaos of treatment or tried to advocate for a loved one as he or she was trying to enter recovery, it's not surprising that so many end up dead. We have no way of telling whom we can trust. There is little regulatory oversight, and the American public lacks compassion and outrage.

This kind of exploitation happens every day, in every city. It kills people.

The way the treatment industry is set up, our insurance cards become carcasses for the industry's greedy to feed on. It wasn't meant to be like this. It drives me crazy. Leaders in this field, lobbyists, and well-intentioned policy makers have worked for *decades* to do the right thing and bring attention to unethical treatment practices, but the number of overdose deaths is breaking records every year. Obamacare, for example, provided a mandate for substance treatment. It should have helped get millions of people into treatment; that was the intention. However, it wasn't the outcome. Instead, more unscrupulous treatment centers opened, sensing there was money to be made. The mandate just dumped money into bad care and cultivated a new crop of predatory operators who developed new scams to lure patients into their facilities. Then they charged exorbitant amounts for necessary services, like medical detox, medicine, urinalysis, and inpatient treatment that never occurred. These rehabs were set up specifically to suck as much money from people as possible.

The greed of the operators of these facilities doesn't affect just people with substance use disorder but *all Americans*. Rehab clients don't get the life-saving help they need: how can they, in facilities that are just run to suck them dry? Insurance companies, legally bound to provide substance use treatment, have to pay higher and higher prices as rehabs increase in number and raise their rates. What happens next? It's simple: Premiums go up, care becomes limited, and fewer people can access treatment or other medical services. Insurance companies, acting in their own interests, create arbitrary barriers to treatment.

All of this is done under the auspices of "saving lives." Treatment centers, like the young people they hire to recruit for them, can point to the fact that they're supposed to be helping people. They can pretend that the industry they're in is a moral one or that they have some ethical foundation that supports choices that are in fact deeply selfish and self-centered. Something has to change, as I'll discuss later in the book. I know many treatment center owners, and some are genuinely good people. But they all live very comfortably. They all drive luxury cars. They travel half the year. Their children go to exclusive boarding schools. Where is that money coming from? No matter how "good" someone is, we need to see the receipts. Charging your patients $3,800 for a urine test, three times a week, so that you can take your family skiing in Aspen for the weekend is just plain wrong.

Until we drain the treatment industry swamp, we won't really know who's in it for the money and who's taking advantage of desperate people and their families. I shudder to imagine parents handing their children over to some of these rehabs, whose aim is only to fleece them by committing insurance fraud. That should never be the outcome of any medical treatment, especially not for a life-threatening condition like substance use disorder. New laws and enforcement of ones that are already on the books are needed, as are universally agreed-upon quality standards and metrics. Standards in advertising must exist. A universal definition of what actually constitutes "recovery" must be established. Badges, the power to subpoena, and the fortitude to turn over every single rock in this industry are required. Communities need to build independent authorities that can ensure that fraud is not committed, that patients are receiving reputable, safe care, and that rehabs aren't gaming the system. Conventional medicine must be involved in *every* part of addiction care, just as it is in mental health care.

This kind of change won't come from within the industry, though. We have to fight for it ourselves. Bad actors don't want to change: Why should they? They're doing well financially, and aside from some patient deaths, there really aren't too many complaints about their services. They partner with pharmaceutical companies and labs to make money from the people they "serve." They want to look good, write good op-eds, play the heroes when a client makes it into long-term recovery. They don't want to write a check to an advocacy group that might undermine their existence.

The harder we push for reform, the harder the industry pushes back, and the more people die.

Remember, recovery *is* an industry, and its "raw materials" are patients looking for help to get sober. With so many people in need of aid, there isn't a lot of incentive for treatment centers to focus on helping an individual patient who's struggling. If one drops out of the program, walks out of inpatient, or leaves the sober living house, so what? There's a long waiting list of people who are desperate to take that available bed. The fact that the math is in the favor of treatment center owners creates real job security for them. Think about this. If you had a job where you couldn't be fired; where your income would increase astronomically, year over year; where you could charge each client $24,000 or more per month for your services; where you didn't have to provide a standardized treatment modality but could make up your own program; and where you had a never-ending, guaranteed source of clients, no matter how badly you ran your business, would you be passionately focused on improving your program and helping as many people as possible? Or would you do the bare minimum and continue putting hundreds of thousands of dollars in your pocket every month?

Patients and their families shouldn't have to guess about a treatment center's ethics and commitment to recovery. Community oversight, and more regulation, is the answer for clients and families: It provides peace of mind, not to mention industry standardization. If we can find a way to provide treatment for *everyone* that is safe, effective, and accessible, we are well on our way to fixing this industry.

When we turn a blind eye to the treatment industry, we're killing people. An immediate overhaul that touches every part of addiction and recovery is required.

We deserve to know who's treating our kids, parents, and friends. We deserve to know what we're really paying for. We have the right to transparency. We have the right not to be trafficked. We have the right to live.

3. NOT ANONYMOUS

How the Misinterpretation of "Anonymity" Perpetuates the Stigma of Recovery

"TAKE THE COTTON OUT OF YOUR EARS and stick it in your mouth."

If I had a nickel for every time I heard that in a 12-Step meeting, I'd be rich enough to own my own treatment center. Insane, right? I've been told to shut up so many times that I'm numb to it. *Another* person wants to silence me. Big surprise. *I will not be silenced, shamed, or invisible.* What I have to say challenges the status quo, and some people just don't want to hear it. Let me tell *you* that the status quo is alive and well, north, south, east, and west. It's in the recovery world and right smack dab in the middle of your own community.

The entire culture of recovery and sobriety starts with the concept of "anonymity." Think of a game of telephone: What the term "anonymity" is meant to mean and what it's used to mean are totally different. Some people have used this word to mean that, if you're sober, you must be silent. That you have to hide and never speak of your experience to someone who isn't in the "club." This misconception has infiltrated the mainstream. The misinterpretation of anonymity is so ingrained in our collective archetype of recovery that if you asked ten people on the street what they knew about the field, almost all would mention AA. Even laypeople are familiar with the idea of anonymity and its origin: the iconic Alcoholics Anonymous program, started in 1935 by a salesman named Bill Wilson.[1]

The field of psychiatry and addiction treatment didn't exist in the 1930s, when Bill was struggling with his own alcoholism. He used his own life experience with peer support and how it helped in his own recovery to write the famous 12 Steps. He was influenced by other spiritually based temperance groups of the time, including the Oxford Group. Bill's program was essentially a self-help tool developed when no other scientific or public health field was offering any solutions. *Cutting edge, for 1935.* It adopted the idea of anonymity for very practical and sensible reasons: At the time, people with alcoholism or substance use disorder were considered the scum of society. They could be put in jail for being symptomatic. They could lose their jobs. They could be thrown out of their homes, forced to divorce, and be separated from their children. The concept of pathological chemical dependency had not been discovered yet. The general belief in 1935 was that, if you kept drinking or using drugs, you were immoral, with appallingly weak willpower. Some people still believe this today!

These myths have endured, even though they're wrong. The good news is, we can change what we believe about addiction and, more important, recovery. We don't have to keep buying the lie. Our misconceptions are killing people. Just think: At one time in human history, the astronomer Galileo

Galilei was banished for proving that the planets revolved around the sun. Charles Darwin was ridiculed and almost ex-communicated for writing his theory of evolution in *On the Origin of Species*. Today we understand that their theories are right. In 1935, saying that alcoholism and drug addiction were diseases was progressive. It still is; it busts a myth that costs people their lives and keeps them silenced.

I found my voice in recovery. It's unique to *me*. Nobody can silence me, shut me down, or tell me that I don't have anything to offer. I have to speak up, because if I don't, *people that I care about may die*. Currently, more than 1,000 people a week die from drug-related deaths. In late November 2015, one of those people was Bear, one of my best friends.

His real name was Greg, but everyone called him Huggy Bear. *Bear.* We met in treatment. I actually hated his guts while we were in there together. He was loud. He was full of life, and, boy, did he let his opinion be known—about *everything*. He rubbed me the wrong way at first, but eventually we became friends: We knew the same people. Our sober living community in Pasadena was small, and almost everyone knew everyone else. Bear was big, goofy, and sharp as hell. He was twenty-four, and he was one of my first real friends in recovery. We'd actually discussed traveling together, checking out the East Coast, maybe doing a road trip. We argued about what music to play in the rental car, picked a list of places we *had* to see together, and bragged about who could eat more pit barbecue. (Bear always won that argument.) He used to make me laugh so hard that I'd cry. He'd tell jokes and I would laugh until my eyes burned. Over the holiday months of 2015, we kept in touch, checking in. I was in Florida, visiting my family for Thanksgiving. He was back home in Texas. He was excited because he'd just won an all-expenses-paid vacation to Miami in a trivia competition.

"We should meet up," he texted me on my last day in Florida.

I said that sounded awesome. That was on Friday. It was the last time we had contact.

I got back to California the next Monday. Home was a four-apartment sober living. The carport had been converted into a deck, with a television, smoking area, and a few chairs. Of course, I'd immediately claimed the recliner. I was out there on Monday night, smoking and shooting the shit with the other guys who lived there. They had become like family. During the ten years of my life I was using opioids, I never had a real friend. But once I put the drugs down, I started to find my people. That's how it is in recovery. We make friends quickly. We know what it's like out there. We've all survived the same nightmare.

That night, I'd just talked to my mom. She was making sure that I'd gotten home safely from the airport. Everything was going well: I was sober, safe, and making progress. After we said our I-love-yous and hung up, I checked my Facebook app. Immediately, something didn't feel right.

> I can't believe this.
> Miss you, Bear.
> Gone too soon, hope you find peace.

"What the fuck," I said. I put my phone down. All of a sudden, the carport was silent.

"I think Bear's dead," I said. No, I didn't think, I *knew*.

"Bear's dead."

"What?" someone said. But that was it. The others nodded and said a few words. Then they went back to their cigarettes and card games. There was a sense of acceptance. A lot of us had lost friends before, and all of them had dealt with the death of someone they cared about in early recovery. Bear was just another face to some of them. Another casualty.

He wasn't a number to me, though. He was my *friend*. He'd been doing exactly what I was doing: sober living, AA meetings, trying to change. And just like that, it was game over. *Dead*. The reaction I sensed from the people around me was, *his death wasn't a big deal*. Bear's death, and the way people responded to it—or *didn't* respond—was a very big deal to me. It was unacceptable.

> That's what you get when you use.
> I guess his bottom was death.
> Some have to die so others recover.

People actually say that stuff. What if Bear had died in a car accident? Would people have said "That's the risk you take when you get on the road"?

Hell no. The response would have been totally different. Bear was dead. I can't change that. Nobody can. But saying that he deserved it, or was asking to lose his life, is the damn lie we're told every day about addiction.

I checked Bear's Facebook profile obsessively, clicked on his pictures. I swiped through his posts, wondering if I'd missed something. Was this really happening? All I saw was my friend. It was real. Within a day, Bear's page became a virtual tombstone. The comments poured in, friends and family members all saying how much they loved Bear and how much they'd miss him. I didn't mean to, but I always ended up there. It just didn't seem real. Over time, the sympathy posts got fewer and fewer "likes," and it seemed as if I were the only one who couldn't forget him.

What the hell was I watching?

No matter how much we missed him, nobody was actually *doing* anything. We were just watching. Watching each other die. We accepted overdosing as part of the risk of finding recovery. We talked about relapse like it was inevitable: If you hadn't relapsed *yet*, it was just a matter of time. People died all the time. That was our normal. Our friends died. We grieved. And then we woke up the next morning, brushed our teeth, got dressed, and went back to business as usual. Outside of a small group of people who truly loved Bear, nobody cared. Even within our group, people did their best to act as if he never really existed. Bear's actual cause of death wasn't clear. But *we* knew.

No one expected people like me and Bear to survive. We weren't set up to succeed. If we relapsed or died, it was just another disappointment. If we made it to long-term recovery, well, it must be luck. And on top of it all, *we were trained not to talk about it*. I heard people in AA meetings jokingly refer to the 12-Step programs as Fight Club. The first rule of Fight Club? You don't talk about Fight Club. There was a culture of silence, which I now know compounded a deep sense of shame. It was slowly strangling us. The things we weren't talking about were killing us. *Secrets keep us sick*, right?

At that moment, I knew something needed to change in the way that our culture treats and views addiction. I could no longer be silent and live in the shadows while my friends were dying. I couldn't keep living in shame. I was ready to kick down the closet doors and shine a light on recovery.

I felt something inside me turn, as if a loose screw had just been tightened into place. I no longer wanted to suffer in silence. My perspective had changed. I no longer believed the lie. Death should not be the acceptable, "natural" outcome of substance use disorder. We can be better than that. We *have* to be.

Two weeks later, searching Facebook for recovery groups, I met Greg Williams, who ran a nonprofit called Facing Addiction. I'd seen his 2013 documentary *The Anonymous People* and was impressed by the scope of his vision: a world where people like me were treated like human beings, with equal opportunities and equal rights as everyone else. I saw a live stream of a Facing Addiction rally in DC, with tens of thousands of people on the Mall, calling for change. This moment represented a glimmer of hope. What I saw was a revolution waiting to happen.

This excited me. I practically cyberstalked Greg. Eventually, I called him on the phone and got him to listen to what was happening in my community. I said I was sick of watching my friends fade away. We talked for an hour. I learned that there was an underground movement of people *who weren't anonymous* using their voices to fight for social justice and end the drug epidemic. It gave me hope. I wasn't the only one who felt like what was happening was wrong. There were thousands of us. We were all over: in sober living homes, classrooms, boardrooms; behind cash registers; in jury boxes and voting booths; carrying the mail—*everywhere*. I had to meet them. I didn't want to stop talking, actually—Greg finally, very politely, told me that he had another meeting. I didn't know it at the time, but he would become my friend, my mentor, and my teacher.

Greg Williams, who had entered recovery as a very young man, had decided he was not going to hide the fact that he was in recovery. He confronted the tradition of anonymity that is part of the 12-Step doctrine, arguing that it was never intended to keep people from disclosing their recovery status. What did hiding one's recovery really achieve, at this point? Clearly, keeping silent wasn't reducing the number of those struggling with addiction or dying from it. It wasn't 1935 anymore, it was 2015. Everything had changed. We had a black president. HIV was a treatable illness. Gay marriage was legal. Yet, when it came to addiction, we were still stuck in the days of Prohibition.

Greg challenged this idea in *The Anonymous People*, which is told from the point of view of a person in long-term recovery. Whether Greg realized it or not, he kicked off a pride movement for people who struggle with addiction, people who find recovery, and their families. People like me. *People like you*.

As more people came out about their recovery, the public conversation about the need to dispel shame took on new urgency. We had nothing to be ashamed of. Someone who survived addiction shouldn't be condemned to linger underground. Nor was it right that, when someone died, nobody cared. We were taught in recovery to resign ourselves to despair: to believe that no one cared about what happened to us, except us. In that moment, the paradox of anonymity was so crystal clear. How can we expect anyone to believe we are worth saving if we engineer our lives to be anonymous?

Greg Williams helped me to see that the future was a lot bigger than just stopping the deaths and overdoses. He pointed out the need for equality and inclusion with the rest of the world. Some of us had hidden behind anonymity, and because we hadn't put a face on our recovery, we'd allowed horrible, negative, and demeaning stereotypes to thrive. But Greg had challenged those in recovery to be accountable for everyone's survival. There was a bona fide revolution happening. And I wanted to be part of it. I had to be, for my own survival.

Two months later, in January, President Obama made his final State of the Union address. I had to fight to get it on our home's TV. I am a huge political nerd, but I was totally outnumbered. I had to record the speech to watch by myself later. (Seriously, nobody loves watching *COPS* more than a bunch of dudes in sober living. I don't know where this deep love comes from, but I know it's real.)

After everyone else had cleared out of the carport, I settled into my recliner and played back Obama's last address. "Mr. Speaker, Mr. Vice President, members of Congress, my fellow Americans . . . We need to work together to help people who are battling prescription drug abuse and heroin abuse."[2]

Holy shit. The president of the United States said the word "heroin."

He said it. I heard it. The drug epidemic didn't get another mention after that. Obama went on with his speech, sticking closely to his script. I know because I checked the White House's website immediately after: The speech Obama gave was already online, but the "as delivered" version hadn't been transcribed yet. Heroin and prescription drug abuse weren't in the prepared remarks; it was an ad lib. Obama talked about the crisis not because it was part of a larger agenda but because it was on his mind.

It was on my mind too. Following my friend's death in November, my life felt like a series of falling dominoes. One thing after another seemed to show me that my instincts were right. If I wanted change, I could no longer hide in a church basement. I couldn't stay anonymous "at the level of press, radio, and film," as AA dictated. Saving my life, and the lives of others, required action.

It was time. When I heard Obama's State of the Union address, I took his mention of the heroin crisis as an *invitation* to walk the walk. I was probably the only one inviting me—but I was ready.

At first, all I knew was that my friends kept dying.

Bear. Nick. Jeff. Nicholas. Mica. Tyler. Chris. Brian. Justin. Kelsey. Jeremy. Holly. It seemed like, every month, someone in my recovery community was gone. *Blip.* Erased, as if they'd never even existed. The month before Bear passed away, one of my roommates from sober living overdosed and died. He had been picked up by the local police for loitering while high and taken to a hospital for evaluation. He wasn't admitted and was found dead the next morning a few blocks from our home.

A few weeks passed and I learned that another friend, a young and vibrant aspiring actor, died alone in his room from a heroin overdose.

Every time I lost a friend, I got the same message. People in AA told me to work on myself: "Learn to tie your shoes." I took the advice, learned how to handle daily life without heroin, and was clean for a while. But it wasn't enough. I was savvy, professional, and connected, but when I mentioned my interest in the recovery movement, people looked at me like I was an idiot. I felt a deep sense of social injustice that no amount of self-care or 12-Step meetings could erase.

I was absolutely confounded by the systematic, legal discrimination against people like me. We could be jailed if we relapsed. We could lose custody of our children if we became symptomatic again. Despite our country's antidiscrimination policies for everything under the sun, an employer could fire us for the risk we posed. We could be subjected to random drug tests at work, with or without cause. We could be denied life insurance policies for admitting we'd gotten treated for substance use disorder. We could be denied commercial drivers' licenses. We could be forbidden to teach, coach, or hold other positions of community leadership. Yet many of the people I met who were in long-term recovery didn't seem to care. They just shrugged, as people all around them continued to die.

I talked about this a lot with my best friend, Garrett Hade. We stayed up late, smoking in the carport, discussing what was really going on with addiction and recovery. If new information came up about policy changes or programs, we hashed it out. But where were the voices of people who were actually affected by these policies? Where were *their* stories? All that was written about policy, funding, and even scientific discovery seemed to quote everyone *except* those in actual recovery to give a first-person account and an opinion. No other societal problem or disease existed where the people who were affected were so conspicuously absent from the discourse. Other people did the talking, and we were left holding the bag.

Then, one evening in April, I caught an article in the *Sacramento Bee* that said the California primaries were coming. The elections for delegates to the Democratic National Convention were planned for early May. Any registered voter could throw their hat into the ring. At the end of the article, it said you had a better chance of being accepted to Harvard than winning a seat as a delegate.

I looked at Garrett. I had always wanted to go to Harvard.

"How many people do you think are in sober living homes in Pasadena?"

"We can look it up," he said.

In my past career, I'd worked on plenty of campaigns. I'd called Democrats to register to vote, helped in run-offs, and participated in conventions. However, running my own campaign was something totally new to me. First things first: I needed to register to vote in California. I did. The same day, I filed to run for delegate. Unlike previous campaigns, in this one, all I wanted to talk about was heroin and the opioid crisis. It was the leading killer of young people and the nation's number one health problem. Yet no one from the recovery community was represented in this national election, let alone in my district.

"What if we just registered people who were in recovery from heroin addiction?" I said to Garrett.

Insane, but doable. So we decided to do it.

We went door to door, organizing in sober living communities. I registered people to vote—many of them were very young, in their early twenties. They'd never even seen a ballot. Many of them had turned eighteen while they were homeless, in jail, or kicking. They were like me: newly sober, and scared of losing more of their friends.

In AA meetings, if there was a call for non-AA related announcements, I mentioned my campaign.

"Something needs to change," I said. "To do that, we have to get loud."

What started as a whisper became a roar. Over time, I got bolder about mentioning the election. I thought of Greg Williams, the recovery rally I'd seen online, and Bear. I raised my voice in meetings. Considering that I hardly said a word in the groups, this was a big step for me. I wasn't able to speak for myself, but the thought of losing more people to this disease spurred me on.

Sometimes people with decades in recovery pulled me aside after I'd made this announcement. Instead of telling me to put a cotton ball in my mouth *again*, they shook my hand.

"Never seen anything like this," one man said to me. "Keep it up."

"What you're doing is important."

Of course, not everyone agreed with what I was doing. Some still invoked their twisted interpretation of "anonymity." They used it to mean that anyone who actually survived our disease should quietly behave. But we all know what happens when we let people without lived experience make policies that affect *us*. When someone told me to "respect anonymity," I pointed out that the addiction crisis was exploding. This was a health crisis, worse than AIDS. Although connecting with my peers, drinking coffee, and talking about moral principles helped me get sober, I was way beyond that. Too much was at stake. It couldn't just be about me and my sobriety. Hoping that a politician who was totally ignorant about addiction would magically make the decisions that were in our best interests was insane. We wouldn't get better access to public resources, treatment, anti-overdose medication naloxone, or social justice by just hoping that leaders would do what's right. Recovery wasn't an issue of one person's spiritual wellness; it was a pandemic.

I was on a mission. Running for convention delegate on a platform about heroin had never been done before. Nothing in my life ever felt more right. I also knew that we were being ignored. We were a huge population of people, but we were being silenced by our own elected representatives. That sense of opposition fueled my fire. We needed a collective voice, and I knew I wasn't the only person who felt this way.

In fact, I felt confident that many other people were just waiting for *their* invitation to get involved too.

Running for office was one in a string of revelations that kept me going. In AA, I'd learned to show up, follow through, and not overthink the outcome. I could do that with my campaign too.

May came: election day. In running earlier campaigns, I'd learned that the hardest thing to do was get people to actually show up and vote. *I was so fucking nervous.* I got pancakes, asked my friends and the people I registered to meet up at my place, and said we'd carpool over to the voting site. I actually overdrew my bank account buying food, Lyft rides, and enough coffee for everyone. Although the election didn't kick off until noon, friends started showing up at eight-thirty that morning—twice as many as I'd expected. Many brought friends. It turned out that most of them had never voted either. We ate, we organized, and we headed over to the election site.

"We're here for Ryan," I overheard someone say to his friend. Maybe I had a chance after all.

Or maybe not. I didn't realize it, but there were seventy-odd candidates on the ballot. They were judges, Democratic Club presidents, lawyers, and city commissioners. And me. I flipped through the ballot guide, checking out my competition. My name was the only one with nothing next to it. Ryan Hampton: *blank*. Walking into the labor union headquarters where the election was to be held, it was clear to me that everyone there knew each other already. *Seriously.* They were associates, professionally and personally. I saw a lot of handshakes and slaps on the back. I was the outsider. I felt a wave of fear and closed my eyes and paused. As stupid as I felt, and as absurd as this campaign seemed, I was still going through with it. My friends piled out of their cars and went to stand in a line that snaked out of the building and down the street, already wrapping around the corner.

I was the only candidate not covered in swag. Since this was an election for the Democratic National Convention, the other candidates were wearing their Hillary gear. They were duded up in crazy outfits, handing out slick brochures, and offering buttons and stickers to voters. Some lady even had her face imprinted with Hillary's on a lollipop. Me? I showed up with nothing but my halfway house crew. Honestly, it was intimidating. I felt invisible: nothing next to my name on the ballot, nothing to give. I felt like a "heroin addict"—empty-handed and worthless.

However, I knew I couldn't let my friends down. I looked at the line of voters and realized that, based on the numbers, I would need everyone who showed up with me, plus a lot more votes, to win. I gathered my group together and we organized a strategy.

"Just tell people why you're here," I said. "You don't have to tell them your story unless you want to."

We started at the front of the line and worked our way back. I was scared, expecting to be rejected or insulted. It was hard walking up to a stranger and telling them I was in recovery from heroin addiction. I did it anyway, one person at a time.

"Hi, my name's Ryan Hampton and I'm running for delegate. I'm in recovery from heroin addiction. I'm not sure if you're aware, but a lot of people in our area are dying of overdoses."

A lot of people just thanked me and shook my hand, their minds already made up. But about every third person opened up—like, *really* opened up. They shared their experiences.

They knew someone who was affected by addiction. A grand-kid, a friend, a coworker. They told me their stories. When I called addiction a public health crisis, they nodded. It seemed like they'd been waiting to talk to someone about the burden they were carrying. Now they had a chance. My friends and I gave them permission. We opened up people's hearts and listened while they told us about their loved ones and friends. Many of them said it was the first time they'd ever admitted out loud, to a stranger, that something was wrong.

The entire state of California—over 39 million people—only had 317 district-level elected delegates for the 2016 convention. Delegates vote on behalf of the community they represent at regional caucuses and the national convention. They endorse party candidates, ballot measures, and resolutions; in so doing, their primary focus is representing their community. I knew who my community was, and I was finding that there were more of them than I anticipated.

After the ballots were cast, all of the candidates sat in one big conference room for the results. There was a massive whiteboard on one wall, with our names and a running tally for our votes. I sat in my chair with my phone in front of me. Everyone who'd come with me had gone home; it was just me. The other candidates had their wives with them, official-looking campaign books, and calculators for keeping score. I opened a note on my phone and started marking my votes as they came in.

Every voter got to choose three candidates. If I was going to get a seat, I needed to be in the top two *out of more than seventy choices*. The campaign staff brought in bag after bag of votes, huge sacks of paper, and began to read the results.

Hampton. Hampton. Hampton. I heard my name over and over. The other candidates laughed; they thought it was cute.

The heroin guy's getting votes. I assumed that the first batch of votes had all come from my friends. But then they opened the next bag. And the next one. And the next one. *Hampton. Hampton.* It was no longer cute; it was real. Once we got to the seventy-vote mark, I knew I was beyond my group of friends. The votes kept coming, and I kept counting.

I won. By a *lot.* It was a landslide.

I was overwhelmed with gratitude. I had followed through with something. The results spoke for themselves: People really wanted to hear my message. I was speaking, and they were listening.

I almost crashed my car on the way home, I was so excited. I was bumping "0 to 100" at top volume, grinning like a fool. I couldn't get home fast enough to call Greg Williams and tell him the good news.

"I can't believe a junkie like me won," I said.

He stopped me. "You're not a junkie, Ryan. You're a person in recovery. You deserved to win; this is what we do."

For the first time, I really understood what he was saying to me.

I wasn't a junkie. I wasn't doomed. I wasn't worthless. And I had a voice. The next morning, I sat down and wrote my first op-ed about the addiction crisis. My *Huffington Post* article, "Why I Started Facing Addiction Out Loud," got an incredible response. The election results were still unofficial; they had to do a recount, then certify the outcome. But I didn't care. When momentum is at your back, you don't hesitate. I was ready to kick my activism into high gear and see where it took me. I had something to say, and I was ready to grab the mic.

I talked about why I ran for delegate, what I wanted to do, and how I wanted to do more. My experience sharing my story with those voters—people who were outsiders, not in recovery, and who we *weren't* supposed to mix with—showed me that our message wasn't just for people who had substance use problems. It was for everybody. Addiction affected us all. So did recovery. In those interactions with voters, I saw measurable outcomes.

Finally, I knew I wasn't alone. There were people who felt exactly like I did, who wanted to get involved and were *desperate* to be heard. We were all tired of being silent. We were ready for change. I saw, clearly, that I was just one among millions. I just needed a way to amplify our voices. I needed allies. It wasn't hard to find them.

Later that month, following the election, I was at an event in Compton. Bill Clinton was there, mingling and shaking hands. When it was my turn to talk to him, I told him my story. I was fourteen months sober. When he heard that, he put his arm around me.

"That's very brave of you," he said. He told me that he couldn't go to events without someone sharing an experience like mine. Many of his closest friends had lost their kids to addiction-related causes, and it affected him profoundly. For that reason, the opioid crisis had become one of his top issues. He shook my hand, promising to keep in touch.

Clinton. Obama. Bear. I had my mandate. It was time to speak up. We'd heard plenty from the Dr. Drews and Dr. Phils of the world, the self-proclaimed addiction specialists and talk show doctors whose only advice was rehab or AA. The same people soaked up all the airtime on the subject, and none of them had anything new to share except that things were getting worse.

Yet when I went to the 2016 Democratic National Convention, I understood why advocates hadn't made a lot of progress in the political world. I showed up feeling so hopeful. I had no doubt that the leaders in this space were sincere. How could you not be, when your community was literally dying in front of your eyes? But I soon realized that, for most people, especially those who weren't directly affected by the crisis, addiction was just another buzzword. Walking into the convention, I felt that I was drowning in a sea of words. All around me, I heard talk—the other delegates were chatting enthusiastically, shaking hands, pushing their agendas. I realized I was a very small fish in a large, loud pond. When I brought up recovery, the response was condescending.

"People are dying," I told more than one of my fellow delegates. "We need to overhaul Medicaid and ensure that everyone has access to treatment on demand."

They smiled and nodded, said a few inspirational words, and moved on to their own agenda. I felt like I was being dismissed with a pat on the head. This deadly epidemic was being treated like a sound bite, not a serious issue. It didn't make sense to me. My election made it clear that people were ready to vote in support of this *one specific issue*. People affected by addiction wanted change, and to accomplish it, we needed representation. But political activation wasn't enough. We needed a *lot* of people working on this issue. It was clear to me that making life-saving changes to fix our broken system was going to be an uphill battle. Taking on apathy in the political arena was just the first step.

We'd heard the talking points. The media kept recovery off the radar, mentioning people like me only once they were in body bags or six feet under. I started to pay attention to the news—*really* pay attention. I noticed that most of the news coverage about addiction was overwhelmingly about opioid addiction and the acute portion of the crisis. In one day, I might see stories about another cluster of deaths caused by fentanyl, a scary statistic that was on the rise, and another celebrity getting sent to treatment. There really was no discussion of *recovery*. Nobody talked about how to treat the long-term, chronic nature of this disease. There were no national 5K races for recovery, like there are for breast cancer every October. There was no ice bucket challenge for recovery. No one focused on positive outcomes or success in treatment. The media kept pushing scare stories and the "Just Say No" propaganda distributed by an unsympathetic government. This approach just didn't work.

Where were the people who were fresh off drugs and discussions of how they had survived the crisis? The few voices I heard in the recovery community, mostly at 12-Step meetings, were all "old-timers": people with many years of sobriety under their belts. They were comfortable; they'd moved beyond the early, uncomfortable stage of recovery. They'd gotten careers and families and houses but didn't seem to be concerned about changing things on a national scale, by raising care standards in treatment, making better policy, and fighting discrimination. Similarly, the general public had no sense of urgency about the issue, just more of the same. More deaths, more bad news, and more useless "help."

Although a few people were "out" in the media and raised awareness by telling their stories, they all followed the same pattern. They emphasized how sick they'd been and how twisted their addiction made them. They talked about how ashamed they were. Their stories were about a long, dramatic fall from grace and then a miraculous rescue. How long they'd been in recovery was really anyone's guess. How they did it was also a big question mark, in my mind. There is no road map to recovery. The stories made it sound like once someone was on the other side of acute, inpatient treatment, they were "cured." *How?*

Most of the people I saw who were "out" about their recovery were white, middle class, or wealthy, and had access to private insurance and all the medical care that goes with it. I'm sure that had *something* to do with their survival. Some of the people who told stories about addiction were rich and famous, celebrities who were trying to sell their tell-all memoirs. *Nicole Richie. Robert Downey Jr. Carrie Fisher. Alec Baldwin.* I didn't hear my story, and I didn't see people like me in the media.

I never heard any of them talk about the desperation of trying to find help. They didn't have to cobble together recovery supports, yet they *all* ended up in 12-Step meetings. Most people I knew recovered with a combination of self-care, 12-Step meetings, support groups, and sober living homes. The people who talked about their path to redemption from addiction on daytime TV seemed to have it all figured out. I doubt Nicole Richie ever had to walk two miles in the rain to get on a waiting list for rehab. Or that Anthony Hopkins panhandled for change and ate Subway at the homeless shelter. Maybe they did, but we sure as hell never heard about it. It seemed like, for the rich and famous, as soon as they wanted to stop using, the pieces of the puzzle all fell into place. These stories were incredible, of course; I'm not knocking them. I read them, I heard them, and I was inspired by them. I just knew that my path was different. I didn't identify with people who'd gotten out so easily.

I didn't understand how they'd escaped addiction and still had all their friends.

The parents of people who had lost their lives are, in my opinion, some of the strongest advocates for this cause. But their voices are isolated. For every mom or dad sharing their story, where was everyone else? Where were our people? Where were *we*? One person out of every few hundred might say something, but shame and stigma effectively silences the rest.

Coming out as a sober person is huge—a very personal decision. I remember taking my first step over the threshold, dropping my anonymity, and truly sharing my story with someone who had never gone through what I did. It was terrifying. Yet I knew that if I was going to help change the fate of millions of Americans, I had to get over my fear. If even one person out of every 2,500 people is willing to be a loud, proud voice, seismic shifts can be made.

I'd seen this work in other civil rights movements. For example, when ACT UP was born to fight the AIDS crisis in 1987, not everyone living with HIV took to the streets—but some did. The few brave souls who engaged in activism with ACT UP got enough media coverage to force the conversation around a taboo subject. Larry Kramer, Ann Northrop, Spencer Cox, and others changed our nation. I'd come of age during the fight for marriage equality, ending the AIDS epidemic, and equal treatment for the LGBTQ community. I still remembered a time when people thought that HIV was a "gay disease" and that you could catch it just by touching someone's skin. I'd seen pictures of Marsha P. Johnson, the black trans woman who threw the first brick at Stonewall and set a radical, sweeping revolution into motion. I'd seen the pride parades, where same-sex couples held hands in public, unafraid. In college, I'd read Harvey Milk's "hope" speech that called for reform.

I knew what it was like to dream of a more equal and just world, where there was room for everyone. I also knew what it was like to be on the other side of that struggle. Now the vast majority of Americans, regardless of party affiliation, agree that gay marriage is a human right. Coming out is not only encouraged; it's celebrated. Discrimination against the LGBTQ community isn't just extremely unpopular; it's illegal. A handful of activists gradually changed hearts and minds. I want to do that too. I believe that it is possible. Furthermore, the lives of millions of people with substance use disorder depend on it.

We don't need *everyone* to speak out. We only need a few.

What we are fighting for is social justice, just as the African American civil rights movement and the suffragettes did. In each case, people are standing up and speaking out against a culture that marginalized and oppressed them. Women deserve equal rights to men. They deserve the right to vote, hold property, work in the same industries for equal pay, and make their own medical decisions—all the things that men have the right to do, under the law.

Icons like Martin Luther King Jr. insisted that black people be given equal treatment. Black Americans deserve equal opportunities and access to the same schools, restaurants, swimming pools, and neighborhoods as white Americans. They deserve to marry who they love, regardless of skin color. They deserve equal pay for their labor.

More recently, gay and lesbian Americans have been dealing with similar types of discrimination. Some people won't sell homes to gay couples. Some break the windows of gay businesses and throw their children out of the house for being gay. Outside of semi-accepting industries, like fashion, entertainment, and cuisine, some people won't hire gay employees. You can still be shipped off to gay conversion therapy camps and given electroshock treatments against your will, to zap the homosexuality out of you. Some pastors still tell their congregations that gay people are immoral and evil, "choosing" a lifestyle that is unholy. If you leave the house looking too gay, you can be threatened, assaulted, or even murdered. Gay and trans people can't find beds in homeless shelters.

I see the same kinds of discrimination within our community toward people who struggle with addiction. It's very real. People with substance use disorder are treated as second-class citizens. We're shunned if we talk about our addiction. In some cases, transparency costs us our jobs, homes, and custody of our children. At the doctor's office, we are treated like drug seekers if we say we're in pain. We can't donate blood if we'd ever used a needle or had sex in exchange for drugs, even if we are 100 percent healthy. We are given housing only on condition of abstinence from substances and then evicted if we relapse. We represent a shockingly high percentage of the homeless population. Our insurance cards take longer to work, and most of the time we're denied life-saving care because we have relapsed following inadequate prior treatment. It's impossible to get a life insurance policy. If we are caught with narcotics, we end up locked up. We are treated as if we were dirty or undesirable: "Filthy junkie" is the insult I hear the most.

But we have the right to change and the right to participate in society as equals through access to treatment and the power of recovery.

Many people truly believe that we deserve to die. They assume we are hopeless and aren't worth saving.

They are all wrong. *Dead wrong.*

I did hear people who talked like me in 12-Step meetings. For years, especially during the times I struggled to find a treatment center that would take me, I went to AA. I met people who used drugs like I did, who felt the way that I did. I heard the same desperation I felt. Their moms sat in the parking lot, waiting for them too. They'd been homeless. They'd used a needle when they didn't have any other choice. I didn't feel out of place in those meetings. I told my story, and I felt connected.

However, a big part of 12-Step groups is this narrow idea of *anonymity*. That's defined as a spiritual principle: the basis of recovery. In addition to the famous 12 Steps, which are behavior instructions for someone in recovery, there is also a companion doctrine called "The 12 Traditions." These can best be described as the "rules of order," and they outline how individuals and groups should relate to one another and the outside world. These commandments are essentially a policy manual, but they are called *traditions* instead of *rules* because of the self-defeating attitude that those in recovery are inherently uncomfortable with authority and rules. To be fair, there is a lot of truth to that approach.

The Twelfth Tradition reminds members to "place principles before personalities." People use the word "anonymity" in different ways, depending on their own experiences. For some people, it symbolizes equality: Nobody is more important or less important than anyone else. For others, this principle explains why people in 12-Step programs don't use their last names to identify themselves and don't "out" their recovery status unless they're in a meeting.

What I was taught is that, pretty much universally, *anonymity* prevents discrimination from happening. By staying quiet, we could "pass" for nonaddicted. We could hope to live normal lives.

That was a huge problem for me.

What does *anonymity* mean in practice, anyway? I was ridiculed in some 12-Step meetings for telling my story outside of the groups, yet we all knew of famous people who were sober and out about it. It seemed to me like, once someone got sober, they got a bad case of holier-than-thou and became eager to police other people's choices. I didn't play that. Had it not been for celebrities like Eminem being public with their recovery, I might never have heard of AA in the first place. People I didn't know normalized the issue for me when they talked about recovery. I needed that; I'm sure it saved my life.

I attended AA while I was also telling my story about winning the election on a nonanonymous platform. I thought I was making good progress. I was sober, had a sponsor, was working through my resentments and getting my self-esteem back. I went to meetings, helped out other people in recovery, and took suggestions from people who had been sober longer than I had. I thought I was checking all the boxes.

Then, one day, Scott P. pulled me aside after a meeting. "Dude, have you ever heard of anonymity?" he said.

"What are you talking about?" I asked. I mean, I wasn't exactly standing on a street corner with a megaphone, screaming about my recovery. *Not yet, anyway.* I was just writing about my story and finding other people who'd shared my experiences. It didn't seem that different from what we did in the meetings, honestly.

"First of all, if you break your anonymity, you put yourself at risk for a relapse," Scott told me. "And second, it shows that lack of humility. You need to change your behavior, or you might go out."

He was absolutely serious. I am pretty sure my mouth was hanging open by the time he delivered his ultimatum. *Here we go again.* If I told my story outside of our secret club, I was going to use again. I might as well just put the needle back in my arm right now. It was a threat, plain and simple. Keep your mouth shut, or you'll end up where you were. I looked at Scott closely. He'd been brainwashed; he totally believed what he was saying. He was telling me a lie, and it was a lie that could kill me. It was a lie that cost hundreds of lives, because it reinforced the social status quo and kept people silent and suffering.

Did I listen to his advice?

What do you think?

And no, I haven't relapsed either.

We're the Millennials, the Gen-Xers, the ones with the world at our fingertips. The algorithms we've created literally run the world and transform the way we send and receive information. We're more connected than any generation before us, and we are using that technology to change the world. Yet transparency and honesty aren't always celebrated.

> Go kill yourself.
> You don't deserve to live.
> You did this to yourself.
> Junkie.

I will spare you the private messages I get every day.

That toxic culture keeps so many people from seeking help. It creates stigma, and shames people who are dying from a treatable medical condition. Can you imagine if we had the same attitude toward other chronic illnesses that we do toward addiction? Imagine shaming someone for having cancer. Or asthma. Imagine shaming someone for developing multiple sclerosis or finding out that they're diabetic. We would *never* do that. So why are the rules different with addiction?

The stigma that surrounds addiction really does have the power to kill. I believe that the culture of shame and silence around this disease is lethal. Fewer than 10 percent of people with substance use disorder *ever* get medical help.[3] That means that 90 percent of this population—over 20 million Americans—are trying to handle this deadly disease on their own.

So, 10 percent of people like me are the ones making calls—to treatment centers that don't have beds available or charge sky-high prices; to ERs that patch us up and put us back on the street; to shelters that say housing is conditional on our ability to stay sober without assistance; to detox centers who give us tranquilizers and methadone and no long-term plan. The more I learn about the way people like me are treated in this country, the more outraged I am. Honestly, I'm amazed that the people taking advantage of us have been getting away with it for so long. It's sick and wrong, a tacit genocide that goes on right under our noses.

If we're going to save lives, we need to be speaking up, *all of us*, and making as much noise as we can. We must call out the industries, institutions, and prejudices that directly contribute to the deaths of hundreds of thousands of people every year. Activism, at its core, is about change. It's also about anger and, in my case, grief. It's about recognizing something harmful and uprooting it for good. It's not about making friends.

The truth doesn't change, no matter who doesn't want to hear it. And the truth is, we are complicit in creating a toxic culture by silencing ourselves and conflating humility with shame. The truth is, millions of Americans are affected by addiction. As you're reading this, people in towns across our country are dying. Many lose their lives without ever seeking help, because they are ashamed and don't know where to turn.

Martin Luther King Jr. said, "A riot is the language of the unheard."

A death by overdose is a sign of someone who was too ashamed to ask for help. It's time for us to rise up. Heroin and other drugs are killing my generation.

Everywhere I look, I see people turn away. They don't understand us: They blame the person who has the problem. Some people deny that anti-overdose drugs like naloxone are helpful, when in fact the medication saved more than 26,000 lives in 2017.[4] This hatred and ignorance exist inside recovery communities as well. More than once, I've seen someone with two or three years of recovery say that we *shouldn't* help people who are suffering. Their reasoning is straight out of the 12-Step meetings: *The addict has to hit bottom, or they won't stay sober.* For so many people, there is no bottom, except death.

You can't help someone if they're six feet under. Dead people don't recover.

Period.

Maybe a normal person would have given up at some point. *They* might have taken the advice, kept quiet, grieved for their dead friends, and prayed that they weren't next. But I'm not normal. And I'll be damned if I give up on this.

I sought out a different kind of community that supported me, no matter what.

The more people I talked to, the more determined I became. I remembered the powerful actions of the civil rights groups that had come before us. There were millions of people in recovery in America and millions more who were trying to get there. We are separated by shame, by stigma, and by lack of services, but we *exist*. We represent almost

15 percent of the population.[5] We vote. We own homes. We work in every industry. It blew my mind when I discovered that we were *everywhere*.

Our shame silences us.

That's what we need to change.

I'd found my voice, and I want you to find yours. We've suffered enough. Too many lives have been lost. Too many families and communities have been destroyed. It is time to step into the ring and start telling the truth.

This is the missing piece: your voice. Grassroots activists, nonprofit organizations, and lobbyists have worked for over a decade to change the system. But that isn't fast enough. In some ways, playing by the rules perpetuates the same culture of silence that is choking the root of our existence. The agreements made behind closed doors stay there. Who is representing our interests at the table? Are they connected to what is actually happening on the ground or making decisions based on some abstract data that has nothing to do with reality? Who's profiting? The road map, if they have one, isn't available to the people their work affects. Once again, power is taken away from people with substance use disorder, with the reasoning that "father knows best."

Every four minutes, another person loses his or her life to drug-related causes in the United States.[6] It hurts to think that their obituaries won't acknowledge their true cause of death. Their parents mourn them, wondering if there was something else they could've done—when, all along, the only help available to their family comes from a deeply flawed, self-interested system.

Every morning, when I log onto Facebook, I brace myself for the punch. I know what I'll see. Another parent, another family, posting about their child's fatal overdose. Social media is flooded with pictures of kids grinning in their graduation caps—and comatose, plugged into a monitor in the ICU. These posts are sad memorials to the victims of the opioid crisis—and a call to action, to government, Big Pharma, and our communities. These deaths are preventable, and they affect every one of us. After all: *This could be your kid.*

Our kids, friends, and loved ones deserve so much more than a Facebook post. The people affected by addiction deserve to be heard. We deserve help. We deserve a chance to live.

I'm claiming my place with my story. Telling the truth about who I am will save my life and the lives of many others. That's why I'm not anonymous. I take pride in who I am: a person in sustained recovery. I'm a member of a community that is fed up with being ignored, discriminated against, and quietly, systematically eliminated. I didn't become an activist or an advocate overnight. It happened as a result of finally becoming comfortable with who I really am at my core.

I'm not alone. I won't be quiet, and neither will millions of people just like me. We stand up for what we believe in. *We are here.*

4. "WE SAVE LIVES"
The Big Lie Treatment Centers Sell to Desperate People and Their Families

THE MORNING AFTER HER SON, CARTER, sent her his last text message, Liz Berardi said she felt a lump form in her stomach. Her anxiety, which had been on high alert for the last year, intensified. She tried to talk herself down: After all, Carter was in a sober living home. He was being monitored by the staff there and by the therapists at the inpatient facility he'd checked out of only days before. *Everything's fine.* She scrolled through her texts, rereading the final message Carter had sent.

xoxo

She'd already called everyone she could think of, from the treatment center to the owner of the sober living home. She tried the manager. She tried Carter again. No response. She didn't even know the address of the place he was supposed to be staying. She began to panic. The last couple of years had been a nightmare of detoxes, rehabs, and hospitals. Every time Liz felt a glimmer of hope that her son might find recovery, it was snatched away. He wanted to get sober; he tried hard. She was beginning to think that it wasn't her son who had the problem.

The phone in her hand rang. It was Carter's father. Liz answered, although their relationship wasn't good: As Carter fell deeper into his addiction, he had been caught in the crosshairs of their divorce.

His voice said the word "tragedy."

Liz dropped the phone and screamed.

Carter was dead. He'd been found in his room at the sober living home with a needle in his arm. The syringe was the only evidence of drugs: Someone had cleaned up whatever paraphernalia he'd had, made the room look nice again.

Maybe it was the same staff member who had told Liz, "You'll get in the way of Carter's recovery. You're harming him. We have a plan to help your son."

Maybe it was the owner of the sober living home, who told the police that Carter wasn't scheduled to receive care until the following week. "He came on Thursday, and that's the weekend. His treatment plan was supposed to start on Tuesday."

Liz persisted, she said. After a while, nobody would talk to her. They didn't want to be held accountable. When Liz finally got her hands on Carter's full medical records, she began to see the deep flaws in the treatment industry. Her son, in addition to substance use disorder, was also living with clinical anxiety. He was supposed to have outpatient support for both mental health issues, but there wasn't any. Liz said the notation on his medication was way off, to the point that he had to stop taking it if he wanted to get any sleep. There was no continuity of care; handwriting of a dozen providers appeared in the same file. Liz had never heard of any of them. Her son's fate had been in the hands of these strangers. She had trusted them with her son's life.

They failed him. *They failed.*

Liz said she followed every possible avenue, trying to find out exactly what happened. Why had Carter fallen through the cracks? And, more important, why were there cracks in this system to begin with? She said she left messages for the sober living manager, the owner, the therapist at the treatment center, and everyone else she could think of. The silence was deafening. There was nobody to hold accountable. Anyone who was willing to talk to Liz made it clear that they were just a link in the chain: just doing their jobs. Carter entered the treatment industry in good faith, believing the message that he was in safe hands. But he ended up dead, a victim of an industry that cares more about profits and high patient turnover than creating a pathway to long-term recovery.

Carter, like so many other people who seek help, was told that if he relapsed, it was because he "wasn't trying." Sober living homes and treatment centers threatened him with homelessness if he tested positive for substances, saying that beds should be saved for "people who really want to get better." But Liz said Carter *did* want to get better. He followed the rules, went through the process, and lost his life.

Sometimes, relapse can be the result of inadequate treatment. Any treatment facility that abruptly stops care if patients relapse and turn them out into the street puts those people at grave risk of immediate death. Facilities that do this are knowingly committing a sin of omission. Yet no law or other oversight structure takes exception to this. It's done all the time. By evicting patients from treatment after a positive urine test, a treatment center essentially extricates itself from treating the harder cases and improving its own quality standards.

Urine tests, by the way, are a huge money maker for treatment centers.

This is like a cancer treatment center testing patients every day for increased immunoglobulins and throwing them out at the first sign of tumor growth, only for the person to die a couple of days later in an alley. That is what the treatment industry is allowed to do: It's perfectly legal, and we have bought into the myth that those who die from addiction must not want to live. No one understands or cares to understand why someone who makes it through the excruciating, medically supervised withdrawal process begins abusing alcohol or drugs after a short period. To the outside observer, a relapse looks ungrateful, careless, reckless, and insane. But it's no more insane than the erratic behavior people exhibit when they're in diabetic shock or suffering from a concussion.

Considering that fewer than 10 percent of Americans will seek any kind of medical treatment for substance use, Carter's perseverance in getting help is a statistical anomaly. I can tell you that, in my experience, going through rehab *once* is an ordeal. Heck, I barely survived the waiting list process. Once you get in, you hold on for dear life, hoping that whatever they teach you will give you a break from the disease that gnaws your nerve endings to shreds and consumes your every waking moment. I remember showing up to yet another intake session, my possessions in a couple of garbage bags, willing to try again. It was like scaling Mount Everest, only to be kicked down the mountainside and told to start your climb all over again. I attempted the trek over and over, each time with less money and motivation than I had before. I was lucky to survive. Carter did not. Neither did many of my friends.

The problem is, the classic twenty-eight-day treatment model, which is the most dominant type of service available, sets people up to fail. It was never intended to actually help patients enter and maintain recovery. It was created at a time when our behavioral health medical system was rudimentary. Its design was well meant: Doctors were trying to save people who were considered beyond human aid. The development of addiction treatment represented a young scientific field of discovery. For the first time, addiction was isolated as its own disease. The new treatment model was designed to treat a new, enigmatic condition whose pathology was inconsistent with the rest of conventional medicine. But it didn't distinguish between detox and addiction treatment. And it definitely wasn't designed to handle patients with complex medical histories, dual diagnoses, or issues with substances other than alcohol.

Withdrawal, morphine, and opium were known to conventional medicine since at least 1860, when doctors started using opioids as pain medicine and during general surgery. Alcoholic withdrawal was well-known, and had been observed since humans first crushed grapes. Over time, psychiatry blossomed as a medical specialty, and addiction detox came under its purview. Doctors observed that some patients benefited from psychological counseling, and a few didn't relapse after receiving counseling. Based on these results, the twenty-eight-day model became the standard for treatment. The psychologist who is credited with creating this standard model was Daniel Anderson. He went on to become president of Hazelden.[1]

Yes, *Hazelden*. The treatment center.

In the 1950s, Anderson was one of the primary architects of what's known as the Minnesota model. Twenty-eight days or a month at a treatment center was thought to be the minimum amount of time needed to stabilize someone from both acute detox and physical withdrawal symptoms. This was an improvement over earlier methods, where alcoholics lived in locked wards and were released to do farm labor as their outpatient care. The Minnesota model became an industry standard due to Anderson's efforts over three decades. According to Hazelden's website, Anderson "helped incorporate that model of treatment into programs worldwide. Many addiction treatment centers in the United States and worldwide, including the Mayo Clinic and the Betty Ford Center, emulated the Hazelden model of care."

Because of the program's popularity and the good reputations of the facilities that adopted it, the twenty-eight-day model was what insurance companies would pay for. Although there are studies about outcomes of different lengths of stay at treatment centers, there is no consensus on the most effective length for an inpatient stay for addiction. If there is one thing that the US Surgeon General's report concluded in 2016, it's that one size does *not* fit all: Care should be tailored to each individual patient's needs.

Yet treatment centers market the twenty-eight-day model as a cure-all delivered with four-star excellence on their real estate. Why change, when they're making tens of thousands of dollars on each patient—and there's a line out the door of people eager to spend? They have no reason to, because they're getting paid and no one is standardizing quality standards and measuring outcomes. The deadly false paradigm that they have propagated is that if patients relapse or die, it's their own fault. They must have not wanted recovery badly enough. The organic food, soft pillows, and ocean views must not have been *enough* for your son or daughter. The twenty-eight-day model with counseling, trust falls, and van rides to local free AA meetings—the "treatment" that you cashed in your 401(k) to afford—couldn't *possibly* have been inadequate.

Besides, who will their families complain to? Treatment centers are only nominally accountable to loosely enforced rules. Unless someone dies and the family makes a huge stink or decides to press charges, the news barely makes a ripple. It's just another dead addict: another free bed, for the next desperate patient.

At their core, most treatment centers are indistinguishable from one another. They may look different on the outside, or offer a different combination of classes, therapies, and recreational opportunities. The good ones are OK. Humane. Run by people who aren't straight-out scamming their patients. The bad ones look exactly the same but have different intentions. I hate to say it, but good and bad treatment centers are almost interchangeable if you're just looking at the outside. Their marketing is identical. They promise comparable recovery rates, therapy modules, and creature comforts. They may emphasize organic food or horseback riding or meditation or *whatever*, but none of them has reinvented the wheel.

That wheel is twenty-eight days in an inpatient treatment program, followed by suggested outpatient treatment, residence in a sober living home, and zero aftercare. It's a hamster track, spitting patients out as quickly as possible. The fact that it's separated from mental health care and mainstream medical care "has created obstacles to successful care coordination," according to the Surgeon General's report on addiction.[2] It's not holistic. Some of these programs are just cobbled together from bits and pieces of anecdotal evidence, "industry knowledge" that's survived by virtue of being so old, and procedures that insurance companies are willing to cover. If that sounds insane, that's because *it is.*

We can put a man on the moon, but we can't figure out why some people end up with full-blown substance use disorder. At its core, the compulsion to use drugs and alcohol despite negative consequences is driven by a broken receptor for opioids, GABA (gamma-amino butyric acid), or cannabinoids. Chemically addicted patients are unable to restore their brain receptors to a relaxed, at-ease state without drugs or alcohol. This is essentially what drives the classic drug-seeking behavior observed in people in the later stages of alcoholism and drug use. This pathology gets alleviated in detox and withdrawal. But the final, symptomatic phase is only a small part of the bigger complicated picture. If we knew *how* people got to the point of pathological cravings, we could simply treat them at any stage in the progression of their disease—but we don't.

Further, and perhaps what the average person recognizes, everyone has a different threshold for when this "broken-receptor craving pathology" kicks in. Two people can use the exact same amounts of drugs or alcohol for the exact same amount of time, and one will spiral into severe chemical dependency while the other won't. We don't know why there is such a disparity. We do know that genetics, anxiety, and depression seem to contribute, but we do not know to what degree.

Without knowing the elusive root cause of any disease, treatment is a moving target. Medications, therapy, and long-term care support are all built on guesswork. With respect to addiction, all of this means that each patient requires a treatment plan that is unique to the severity and progression of his or her addiction, circumstances, and overall mental health.

Let's consider the way we treat addiction and compare it with another huge public problem: cancer. In this scenario, instead of a comprehensive treatment plan tailored to their needs, type of cancer, severity of illness, and wellness, cancer patients would be given a generic, one-size-fits-all plan that focuses only on the acute phase of the disease: basically, crisis care that is designed to stop any pain or troublesome symptoms. The plan would be for twenty-eight days and would require the sick people to leave their homes, jobs, families, communities, and daily routines and go out of state, to an unfamiliar location. Once at this facility, the cancer patients would give up all their rights and surrender themselves as a medical risk to the treatment center staff.

They wouldn't receive chemotherapy, but they might have to let a staff member shave their head. Their treatment plan would be a series of groups that talked about how to live with cancer; how to tell your friends and family that you have cancer; the many ways that people unwittingly contract cancer through their irresponsible choices, such as going places where there is secondhand smoke or drinking out of plastic containers. The cancer patients might receive some medication, but only to mitigate the intense symptoms of their illness.

This treatment might be carried out in a gorgeous hotel, a place that doesn't even look like a hospital. It might have tasteful decor, wall sconces, high-thread-count sheets with a mint on the pillow, and towels folded into the shape of a dove. The dining hall might serve incredible meals, designed by a four-star chef. But we all know that beautiful surroundings don't cure cancer; why do we assume that they'd heal any other chronic, relapsing, potentially fatal disease?

Imagine that you had cancer, and your doctor told you that your primary goal would be to stop identifying as a sick person. "Once you can't feel the tumor, we'll know we're making progress," he would say. "You just need to change your attitude."

It sounds insane, doesn't it? But this is exactly how people with addiction are treated. What's worse is that treatment centers like the ones I just described are considered highly desirable. *The best.* One of the most expensive treatment centers in America, Passages Malibu, costs more than $60,000 per month. These centers tell patients right off the bat that addiction is *not* a disease, even though every medical organization worldwide defines it that way. They use a sampling of twenty-one different "treatment methods" to help celebrity "guests" get over their substance problems: art therapy, sound therapy, and blood chemistry analysis. They say addiction isn't real. I beg to differ.[3]

Passages doesn't take Medicaid or use 12-Step recovery programs. Can you imagine putting *any other kind of sick person* into this environment and expecting them to get better? I can't. It just doesn't make sense.

And, instead of just being a waste of money, this system creates tragedies like Carter Berardi. The bottom line is, if you don't tell a sick person that they're sick, you are doing them a massive disservice. Cancer is one example, but what if we compare addiction with HIV? People with HIV or AIDS often look, sound, and function just like everyone else. They work, live, and play in every community in this nation. If they were never told that they were sick, would that prevent them from dying? No, but it would keep them from seeking help, getting better, and enjoying their lives. It would reinforce the serious stigma around HIV that prevented so many people from talking about their status when the disease started to pick up steam. We didn't talk about AIDS, and we ended up with a health crisis that killed millions of Americans.

Today, we walk in marches to support people with cancer, AIDS, and other chronic illnesses. We walk for mental health. We work hard to raise awareness about these diseases and ensure that the people who get sick have the best possible outcomes. We focus on empathy, transparency, and courage.

Diabetes is another public health comparison for addiction. Once people are diagnosed as diabetic, they simply *must* control their diabetes, or they will die, just like someone with addiction. There are varying degrees of severity of diabetes, just like addiction. There are many ways to treat diabetes, just like addiction. But *unlike* addiction, treatment for diabetes is adaptive, dynamic. Physicians advise diabetic patients about which tools will bring their disease under control and assess what is working best to come up with a treatment plan using medication, diet, exercise, and other elements. People with diabetes must incorporate new steps and tools into their lives to keep their disease in remission. If managed properly, the chronic condition can be kept at bay and even reversed.

Conventional medicine, by its nature, is self-correcting. If a treatment is discovered that works on a particular infection, the research is published and the protocol becomes standard, to make sure every practicing doctor knows there is a new solution to use with patients. This is routine, normal. Practicing doctors expect to hear about new discoveries relating to unanswered questions in their medical discipline. They deploy a new approach if they think it will help their patients. The same mind-set does not exist in the field of addiction. A group of addiction-certified physicians do share information (more on that later), but *nothing* compels the treatment world to adopt any discovery or conform to any standards whatsoever.

Addiction has been left behind in medicine's push for progress. We don't talk about this illness, we don't have a system in place to help the people who are dying of it, and as a result our morgues are filling up with our parents, children, and friends. Again, we would *never* treat a cancer patient that way—but we have no problem spitting on someone who's literally *dying of addiction*. We have no problem depriving someone of shelter, food, and medical aid when they are on death's doorstep. That's not an exaggeration; it's the truth. The homeless shelter where I ate soggy Subway sandwiches and gluey oatmeal was full of people like me, who'd lost their housing because of their drug use. Once we were on the streets, or endlessly couch surfing, we were really in trouble—even more vulnerable than we had been before.

Would you tell a woman with breast cancer to "just suck it up" and try not to get sick? Would you tell her that, if her cancer progressed, she was going to lose her job and be kicked out of her house? Would you test her for cancer markers before offering social services, like food stamps? Would you tell her that she was no longer your mom, your best friend, your sister, because she was sick? Would you shame her for the expensive treatment she needed that didn't seem to work on her cancer? Would you refuse to take her to doctors' appointments, saying that she needed to "take ownership of her own recovery"? Would you tell her that her cancer had really changed how you saw her and that you didn't feel you could trust her anymore? Would you remind her of all the cancer-inducing behaviors she'd engaged in, from eating nonorganic food to sunbathing? If she got sicker, would you tell her that she had no one to blame but herself?

No. Of course not.

These are the things that people in treatment cope with every day. The shame, isolation, and sense of hopelessness are real. By the time people are sick enough to actually seek treatment—and get in!—they are usually in really bad shape. In treatment, they're given a short break that includes some rest. Maybe some meditation, yoga, or creative playtime. But their real problem, the underlying *medical issue*, is never addressed. Patients graduate a month later and walk back into normal life totally unprepared. Furthermore, they no longer have any physical tolerance for alcohol and other drugs. They are primed for a relapse. After a month, the outcome is likely to be deadly. Shooting heroin after a month-long hiatus practically guarantees overdose. I should know: More than one of my friends have died that way. After a few months or even a few years of recovery, they were more physically sensitive to drugs. They had lived for a period of time in remission, but without a way to address the underlying illness, they were in a more precarious position than they realized.

We expect that people managing diabetes will have days when their blood sugar can get dangerously high. Their doctors give them the tools to manage those days. We need to adopt the same mind-set with addiction. Even after a period of healthy remission, arcane risk factors can make people who have achieved recovery susceptible to sudden, inexplicable relapses. It doesn't make those people bad or good. It doesn't mean they were not "working their program" or didn't want to stay healthy. It simply means their symptoms flared up. Their illness needs to be treated and the cause identified. The cause can be different for everyone, but, most commonly, untreated anxiety and depression are factors in a relapse.

There's a phrase repeated in AA meetings: "Your disease is doing push-ups in the parking lot." I believe it. Addiction continues to progress, even while we're sober. Treatment centers, knowingly or not, give people a false sense of security. Rehab *doesn't actually do anything*. It might buy someone a few more weeks, but that is worthless if it doesn't provide any real skills, tools, or treatment for reentry into the real world. Handing people with a potentially fatal illness a list of triggers to avoid, an AA meeting schedule, and a fake "diploma" isn't going to save their lives.

I think the worst part of all of this is that a lot of treatment centers have the money to change but simply don't want to. They don't invest in research about recovery. They aren't interested in actually *curing* addiction: In fact, most of them would probably say that it can't be done. But we once said the same thing about polio, asthma, and pneumonia. There are millions of dollars to be made by *not* helping people get better.

Am I suggesting that there is a grand conspiracy of treatment center owners colluding in a smoke-filled room, deciding to let people suffer and die? Not at all. I am saying that our business-as-usual treatment is inefficient. False paradigms, clinging to the status quo, and resisting reform are all shockingly lucrative. The treatment industry's lack of transparency costs hundreds of thousands of lives.

Ideally, treatment centers should be working to make

themselves obsolete. They should be working until there are no more patients to treat; adopting new science, measuring and improving outcomes; and making addiction go extinct. No matter what they say about wanting to "help people," they aren't interested in addressing the root causes of addiction or adopting a disease model. Perhaps they are waiting for conventional medicine to take the lead in research, discovery, and new protocols. That would be fair—*if* conventional medicine were up to the task.

There is no reason for them to stop doing what they're doing: offering barely effective "help" with an outrageously high price tag.

As I said, the "bad" treatment centers don't usually get busted unless someone turns up dead. The patients and families entering the industry meat grinder have no context for what "good" treatment looks like. Families in crisis don't know what to look for or expect. Rehabs spend millions on marketing and advertising that pump up their facilities and programs to look like the *best*—whether they're actually the best or not, there's no way to know. There is no Yelp for the treatment industry, though plenty of rehabs spend marketing dollars on fake "reviews" that paint a glowing picture of their facilities.[4] Treatment centers put a lot of dollars into making sure you *can't tell the difference between them*. It probably helps that the people seeking their help are in full-on panicked, crisis mode. Many of them choose a treatment center using a search engine or a review site but don't realize that the listed rehabs all paid top dollar to show up at the head of the "recommended" list.

I'm not exaggerating. Many treatment centers use almost identical website designs, marketing copy, and even stock images. Side by side, their promotional materials all push the same message: *We can help you.* They all make the same promises. In order to make themselves stand out, they pump up their marketing campaigns and spend millions of dollars to get preferential placement in search engine results.

Google AdWords, Google's bid-on-a-phrase advertising service, is big for treatment centers. Centers can buy certain word combinations, such as "alcohol treatment program," that ensure that their ads will appear at the top of a Google search, the first thing someone's eyes will land on. The problem isn't the advertising, exactly: It's that these ads, and the huge amounts of money behind them, turn people into commodities not patients. Some of these ads are run by treatment centers where patients are pumped for insurance dollars, and charged exorbitant prices for urine tests—as much as $5,000 a pop, multiple times a week. They turn their patients into cash machines and bleed them dry.

Urine testing is a recent, well-documented scam that pervades the rehab industry. It's a form of insurance fraud that puts millions of dollars into the pockets of unethical treatment center owners. Here's how it works: Treatment centers buy drug tests at a flat cost—say, $25 per test—then charge patients grossly inflated rates—$1,500 or more. They also make the tests *mandatory*, sometimes testing urine once a day. After a thirty-day stay in a Palm Beach rehab, one patient got a bill for over $300,000 for urine tests alone.[5] A $25 test can net $1,500 or more for unscrupulous, unethical rehabs. The same test can travel through a pipeline of labs, pharmacies, and even doctor's offices, which raises the price tag even more. "More sophisticated," more expensive testing can cost $5,000 or more. There's never a legitimate medical reason to test every day, since traces of drugs remain in the body for up to a month after one use. This scam is clearly designed to do one thing: make money. It certainly does. In 2017, two industry operators were busted for allegedly scalping $40 million from unsuspecting patients.[6] With the help of two dozen doctors, pharmacists, and business owners, they committed complex insurance fraud and put many lives at risk, all in the pursuit of adding another zero to their paychecks.

There's no way for anyone to *know* that this fraud is going on, just from looking at a billboard or TV ad. On the outside, all treatment centers look more or less the same. Bad actors take advantage of that by blending in with the rest of the industry. Scratch the surface, though, and there's a lot of dirt underneath.

Marketers can obscure the true character of treatment centers by soaking up Google AdWords and using targeted phrases to reach potential patients. Hundreds of articles online tell treatment centers how to market themselves using search engines. Keywords, phrases, and better search engine optimization can all be tailored to target very specific audiences while also obscuring other, lower-cost, potentially better options. If a treatment center buys the words "best Florida drug rehab," for example, it knocks all other competitors down in the results. A person searching for treatment probably won't do much research, trusting that Google is providing what they asked for: the *best* rehab. Whether it's actually the best or not is a total crapshoot.

In a list of 384 sample keyword phrases designed for Google AdWords, the word "help" appears nineteen times. One marketing article cautions against using words like "facts" and "hospital," and says treatment centers get the highest click-and-convert rates from location and rehab feature words like "California" and "yoga." Marketers make it seem like centers will meet patients' needs, whatever those are: That's how they convince people to call. Others set up fake hotlines for families and people in need. They are marketed to seem unbiased, 800 numbers that offer basic information. In reality, these phone numbers link directly to the intake desk of a treatment center that refers callers to *itself*. People may think they're calling to get more information about cocaine addiction or to learn about insurance coverage for treatment. Treatment center reps who answer the call are often paid a bonus based on how many admissions they sign up. Many use high-pressure sales tactics on desperate callers, who end up sucked into a system that's interested only in making as much money off them as possible. After less than thirty days, they're spit back out, primed for a relapse.

People with substance problems aren't *people* to treatment centers. We are a market. A cash crop. And business is booming.

The good news is that information gatekeepers, like Google, are taking action against treatment centers that target vulnerable people with these marketing tactics.[7] In September of 2017, my friend Greg Williams met with a policy head at Google to talk about the problem. Greg asked Google to stop selling ad space to treatment centers. Since there's no way to tell who's selling legitimate help and who's pushing snake oil, the simplest solution is to get rid of the ads. Google agreed, releasing a statement later that week that it would allow existing AdWords contracts to run their course. Then keyword phrases like "rehab near me" would no longer be available to anyone.

With a flick of a switch, Google suspended a huge revenue stream for treatment centers: hundreds of millions of dollars.

A single ad click could sell for hundreds of dollars. According to Google's data, 61 percent of people seeking treatment use Google rather than asking friends, family members, or even doctors. Shutting down the scammers is a powerful move that will protect people seeking treatment and hopefully divert them to legitimate help, closer to home. Google made a similar decision for businesses advertising as locksmiths and tech support help because of the high potential for abuse.

The reaction in the treatment industry was immediate. My phone lit up with messages from panicked marketers, treatment center owners, and other industry workers. One treatment center owner had to fly out of the country to see his 12-Step sponsor; he said he'd never been so close to a drink in fifteen years of recovery. He had just tripled his ad spending, trying to bump his company up in Google's search results.

Another person, who works in marketing and development at a treatment center, called me to complain about the change. "I don't understand," he said. "Google didn't say anything to me about this. Did they bring any industry people to the table on their decision? How will this impact people looking for help?"

I told him to give Google a call and hung up.

I got a text message from a marketer's personal assistant, who said that when Google's announcement hit the *New York Times*, her boss collapsed. Physically fell over. The text said: "He finished that article and his lung collapsed. I'm in the ER watching them inflate his lung."

I think it's fair to say that the treatment industry didn't see this change coming. It's also important to note that the actual search engine still works fine. Google results still list where to get help; all Google did was suspend a mechanism for the treatment centers to *pay* for placement on your screen. No-body's access to resources was affected.

The dramatic impact and pushback tells me that, once again, treatment centers aren't used to being regulated. They're used to doing what they want and focusing on profits, not patient care. They assume that they can repeat the same old marketing schemes and subpar programs without anyone making a fuss. Well, *we made a fuss.* And they're losing millions of dollars, because suddenly they've lost access to a massive manipulation tool.

I learned a long time ago that treatment centers don't like change. They resist interference of any kind: legal, political, medical. They *definitely* don't like it when someone challenges their approach to patient care, no matter how irresponsible they are. They're totally invested in seeing themselves as "the good guys," even when their actions are anything but good.

In 2017, the *Boston Globe* printed an exposé of Recovery Centers of America.[8] The rehab giant, which has massive campuses in five locations, has said that its mission is to "save 1,000,000 lives." Fair enough. So, the *Globe* investigated, following the second death at an RCA facility in Massachusetts, and learned that RCA's million-life goal was more like McDonald's "1,000,000 served." A million patients is a lot of money, and RCA was making good on its projections—until someone turned up dead on one of their campuses.

The patient, a middle-age man who was checked into inpatient treatment at the Danvers facility, was the second RCA patient to die that year. According to the *Globe*, "Nine people have died in licensed substance use treatment programs this year, according to the state, and no facility other than RCA Danvers has reported two deaths." The Massachusetts Department of Health got involved and closed admissions to

Danvers, essentially halting its revenue flow. So far, this is the same routine oversight and audit that would occur if a patient died inexplicably in a hospital ER or outpatient surgery center: suspension of services or admissions, pending review. (Danvers has since been reopened and reportedly improvements have been made.)

But there was more. The *Globe* pointed out that RCA was selling services it didn't actually offer. Its false marketing pushed farm-to-table dining and emphasized comfort and luxurious surroundings and top-of-the-line treatment. But, in reality, the company was cutting corners. High staff turnover destroyed any hope of continuity of care. The inpatient facility was basically a fancy hotel, where patients were housed for—you guessed it—a mere twenty-eight days and then pushed into outpatient treatment that was also billed by RCA.

At the time of the *Globe* story, RCA was less than four years old, started by a real estate developer named J. Brian O'Neill, who touted RCA as the "fastest growing addiction treatment provider in the country." It recently had gotten a $250 million cash infusion from Deerfield, an investment fund, where several members had been arrested for insider trading.[9] (Deerfield management agreed to settle charges related to insider trading for $4.6 million.) Clearly, RCA was in it for the money. In principle, profit in the healthcare provider space is a uniquely American phenomenon. We've been functioning under the theory that the free market will spur innovation, discovery, and growth, as well as investment in basic science that benefits patients. This assumption can be fulfilled *only* if providers deliver good, quality, ethical care. Unfortunately, with the amount of money to be made in the private-sector rehab economy, the temptation to cut corners is overwhelming to venture capital wolves.

RCA smelled profit and ran to collect. Lack of strict oversight combined with a mathematically unlimited market created a *gold rush*. The more I followed the *Globe* story, the more I learned about what was really going on inside RCA. Honestly, what I found didn't shock me: It was par for the course, perfectly in line with what many other treatment centers did.

The point is, and I think that even O'Neill would agree with me, RCA was doing *what everyone else in the treatment industry is doing*. RCA is following the same guidelines as every other treatment center. It is advertising comparable services and perks, providing the same kind of programming and therapy, and charging similar prices. On paper, RCA sounds like just about every other facility. It doesn't think it's doing anything wrong, because it's trapped in an echo chamber that tells it it's up to industry par. That's scary. I think that the scandal at RCA is a strong indicator of how this industry is run. If someone dies, the goal is to move on, smooth over any ruffled feathers, and keep running business as usual.

If people die, we have a shitty status quo. Period.

The status quo is the reason Liz Berardi never got a straight answer about who was responsible for causing her son's death. It's why treatment owners panicked when their number one source of revenue, Google, stopped allowing them to recruit patients anonymously through targeted ads. It's because *nobody has taken action against them*. They are not used to being challenged. This industry is not used to having people stand up to it.

Millions of people in America get pushed through the revolving door of a rehab every year. We are a huge population, yet we are left vulnerable and unprotected when it comes to medical treatment. We are treated differently from every

AMERICAN **FIX**

other population of people with an illness. We need the kind of compassion and medical support that cancer patients receive, but we're treated more like we have Ebola or leprosy.

Unless we get involved and demand sweeping, industry-wide change, the deaths will continue. We've got to make it known that *creature comforts do not lead to lasting recovery*. We need research that backs healthy pathways to recovery. We need legislation that enforces a code of ethics and higher patient safety standards. We need transparency. We need regulation. And we need it now.

5. ONE NATION, OVERDOSED
Our Real Problem Isn't Political Differences; It's Big Pharma and Its Addiction to Profits

BILL MAHER IS ONE OF MY FAVORITE things about Friday nights. I'm a total political nerd, so I usually warm up with the evening news first, then switch over to HBO when it's time for Maher's show. Usually his opening monologue gets me laughing so hard that my stomach hurts. He skims a few of the week's headlines, impersonates Trump, and then gets into the interviews. On this particular Friday, I settled onto the couch just as Maher was taking his first bow.

It was two days before Hurricane Irma hit Florida, and the images of the storm moving across the Caribbean Islands were getting nonstop news coverage. Maher started talking about the storm, climate change, all that stuff. I nodded, laughing. That same week, I'd done a ton of fundraising for groups that could help people with addiction issues in the areas affected by the hurricane. I remembered going through withdrawal during Katrina: Nobody should have to suffer like that, especially in disaster zones, without access to food, water, or any kind of medical help if something went wrong. Maher mentioned the many climate change denier Republicans whose beach houses would probably be swept out to sea.[1]

"The right-wingers are still saying that we can't blame climate change," Maher said. "My theory is, it has something to do with Hillary's emails."

I laughed right along with the studio audience. *But her emails.* That was never going to get old.

He went on. "Rush Limbaugh has been telling his listeners all week that Irma is a liberal hoax to promote their 'climate change agenda.' But then he had to evacuate his house! Which, for Rush, has got to be a hard pill to swallow, but if anyone knows about swallowing pills—"

Maher gave his signature shrug. The audience roared again. I felt my stomach crumple, as if I'd been punched. I groped for the remote and turned off my TV. Sitting in the sudden silence, I closed my eyes. I was physically nauseated. I had to leave the room to clear my head.

Once an addict, always an addict. Maher was bringing up a news item from more than a decade ago: Limbaugh's addiction to opioids. Yet, the way he talked about it, it may as well have happened last month. Limbaugh was busted for prescription pill fraud in 2006 and admitted he had a problem with opioids. He was caught after an almost three-year investigation revealed he had received about two thousand painkillers, prescribed by four doctors in six months, at a pharmacy near his Palm Beach mansion.[2] Limbaugh had to take five weeks off work to go to treatment and was sentenced to continue getting help for his addiction for two-and-a-half years; he also had to pay $30,000 to defray the costs of the investigation.

I remember when the story broke. I was as surprised as anyone else. Fourteen to 20 million people listened to Limbaugh's show, and I think they were all in shock too. Limbaugh, who'd turned himself in, told the press that he'd started taking OxyContin for back pain following a surgery. At the time, Limbaugh said, "Over the past several years I have tried to break my dependence on pain pills and, in fact, twice checked myself into medical facilities in an attempt to do so."

There was a rash of jokes about him in the media, especially since he'd taken such a hard line against drugs. He mocked Bill Clinton for claiming he "didn't inhale" when he smoked marijuana and said drug offenders should be severely punished. On his TV show in 1995, Limbaugh said, "Drug use, some might say, is destroying this country. And we have laws against selling drugs, pushing drugs, using drugs, importing drugs. . . . And so if people are violating the law by doing drugs, they ought to be accused and they ought to be convicted and they ought to be sent up." According to a later interview, Limbaugh described himself as a drug addict and said that he'd started in 1995 or 1996. He said that he was starting to use pain medication around the time he made the statement about punishing drug users. The news was a bombshell.

It was deeply ironic, to me and many others, that the guy who'd said all drug users should be locked up was revealed as one of the very people he was out to persecute. Sure, he was a hypocrite. But as much as I disliked Limbaugh's politics, I couldn't jump on that bandwagon. I mean, I'm the polar opposite of Limbaugh on just about everything. I'm super liberal, a true blue Democrat. I've been going to left-wing marches and taking part in liberal politics since middle school.

So much of what Limbaugh says makes *no* sense to me. I never suspected we would have anything in common, except our nation of birth. It turns out, though, that we share a problem with pain pills: *addiction*. The illness that dares not speak its name.

Until the news about Limbaugh's fraud case broke, first in the *National Enquirer* and then on every major news outlet, I didn't think I shared anything with him. I definitely didn't expect to feel defensive or emotionally shaken when Bill Maher, bless his heart, made fun of him for swallowing pills. But I did. And it's a good reminder to me that addiction and recovery is *not a partisan issue*. It affects everyone, regardless of their political beliefs or party affiliation.

Rush Limbaugh, the reddest of the red, the insanely conservative talk show host who's even farther right than the Tea Party, had the same problem I did. We started using pills for the same reasons, and probably hid our drug use or ignored the symptoms of dependence for the same reasons as well. At the end of the day, the biggest difference between us wasn't even our politics: It was our financial circumstances.

Limbaugh is one of thousands of Americans who got sober through the court system. He was ordered to go to treatment by a judge, and he immediately checked himself into a luxury facility in Arizona. He had everything that I didn't, when he needed it: access to treatment, insurance coverage, the financial means to try rehab more than once. He had millions of supporters who kept listening *in spite of* his addiction, who told him they still believed in him and wanted to hear his message. He didn't lose his job or his spot in the pantheon of conservative talk show hosts. He kept his massive Palm Beach home. He could afford the fine he was ordered to pay.

His experience with recovery was the complete opposite of mine. I'm not criticizing; I'm glad he was able to get help so quickly. I wish all Americans who faced this difficult, misunderstood disease had the same opportunity.

I have often wondered how my story would have been different if I'd been in a position like Rush's. If I'd had financial means, celebrity, and personal stability, would I have stopped using? Probably not. If I could afford to see a private doctor once a month, pay for all the pills I needed, and have a never-ending supply, I don't think I'd feel like I had a problem. I might consider myself drug dependent, but I certainly wouldn't see myself as an addict. No, in my experience, what made me addicted was not having the means to support my habit and losing my supply. I've met many people who, like Rush, are insulated from the dramatic, tragic effects of their addiction by money, status, or fame. They struggle with drug dependency in other aspects of their lives but don't face the consequences I did. Our illness is the same. Whether or not we both *identify* as having the same problems is anyone's guess. I mean, try telling a white, middle-class, Christian mother of five that she might be addicted to the opioid painkillers she "has" to take hourly. If her idea of an "addict" is a filthy, homeless, skeletal person using dirty needles to shoot up under a bridge somewhere, you'll have a hard time convincing her. Yet I've met women who snorted Oxy off the granite counters in their newly renovated kitchens and hit the white wine as soon as they'd dropped their kids off at school. I've talked to blue-collar miners who were prescribed Vicodin (acetaminophen/hydrocodone) for an on-the-job injury and, three years later, have moved up to prescription morphine to deal with their pain. *None* of these people think they have a problem. They don't identify with someone like me.

Norman Rockwell never painted a portrait of "The Addict," but the archetype persists of the person who looks sick, emaciated, and poor. Everywhere we turn, that archetype is constantly demonized. Angry mobs scream that *addicts should be locked up.* They say an addict is a criminal rather than a person who's suffering. This old cultural myth has allowed addiction to flourish in white middle-class communities, among wealthy people, and in patients with chronic pain.

Honestly, I have an opinion about Big Pharma and opioid medications. To put it simply: They're evil. I know that's not very nuanced, but I want to just come out and say it: Big Pharma is one of the primary creators of the opioid epidemic. *Public enemy #1.* Its greed and unscrupulous behavior has buried many, many people. Yet Big Pharma isn't held accountable for what it's done.

The massive pharmaceutical companies that create, control, and distribute the medications we take every day are at the core of America's drug problem. In comparison, the drug dealers who import opioids and cocaine into our country barely scratch the surface. The real problem is Big Pharma, which has manipulated the medical system to keep the pills flowing. Nobody ever runs out of medicine.

Big Pharma isn't doing that to help *us.* It is doing it to help itself.

It's simple. When we get a prescription, drug companies make money. A *lot* of money. And, much like the treatment industry, drug companies use aggressive, dishonest marketing to push their products to uninformed buyers.

Let's take a trip in the time machine, OK? We're going

back to the year after Rush Limbaugh admitted he had a problem with pain pills.

It's 2007. The air conditioning clicks on in a small, brick courthouse in far western Virginia. It's July, and outside, the humidity is so thick that it gets into your bones. But inside, it's cool and so quiet that, when the judge clears his throat, the whole courtroom hears it. The judge, Judge James P. Jones of the United States District Court, taps the papers on his desk into a neat stack. The room is full, packed with bodies. On either side of the bench, the two teams of lawyers and their defendants stand for the verdict. In the rows of seats behind them are the families who have testified—who have lost children to prescription pill overdoses. The press is there. Everyone is listening to the man in the robe in the judge's seat.

The air nearly crackles, as if the heat outside has found its way in. He reads the judgment, swallows again, frowns.

"I find in the absence of government proof of knowledge by the individual defendants of the wrongdoing, prison sentences are not appropriate," the judge says. And the feeling comes over the people listening like a wave of heat that wilts you inside your shirt. It's the feeling of sweat and disappointment. The prosecution team members look at each other and lower their heads. *It's over.* They've lost. Purdue Pharma, despite pleading guilty to false marketing charges, is getting the softest possible sentence. It will pay $635 million in fines. The three top executives from Purdue Pharma will get three years' probation and 400 hours each of community service in drug treatment programs.[3] And the families? What about the parents of teenagers and young adults who died from overdoses from OxyContin? Though they traveled from as far away as Florida, Massachusetts, and California for the trial, they get nothing. This is not justice; it's business as usual for Big Pharma.

For a company worth more than $14 billion, $635 million is pocket change. Purdue executives took some of the hit, pleading guilty to misdemeanor charges that they misled regulators, doctors, and patients about OxyContin's risk of addiction and its potential to be abused. The charge was "misbranding."

The estimated body count of this "misbranding" is almost 140,000 deaths between 1993 and 2007. Drug overdose deaths continue to rise, and more users, like me, switch to heroin when they can no longer access prescription opioids. This isn't just a case of using the wrong adjective in an advertisement or misprinting a pamphlet. This is *deliberate misrepresentation* of the risks of a deadly drug. There are serious consequences—consequences that a few hundred million dollars can't erase.

Misbranding. Try telling that to a mother whose child overdoses in their home, dying on the bathroom floor. *Sorry, ma'am. It looks like we misbranded that drug.* Try telling it to the police officer who administers naloxone to dying heroin users nightly, or the EMT who has become an expert at keeping someone breathing long enough to make it to the emergency room. Tell it to the patient whose arms are so badly abscessed by intravenous drug use that they'll need a double amputation and months of physical rehabilitation. Tell it to the millions of Americans who switched from pharmaceutical drugs to street heroin, not understanding that they were physically and psychologically dependent until it was too late. Just a little misbranding.

Purdue's "misbranding" was part of what the *New York Times* called "the most aggressive marketing campaign ever undertaken by a pharmaceutical company for a narcotic painkiller. Just a few years after the drug's introduction in 1996, annual sales reached $1 billion. Purdue Pharma heavily promoted OxyContin to doctors like general practitioners, who often had little training in the treatment of serious pain or in recognizing signs of drug abuse in patients."

OxyContin was marketed as a non-habit-forming drug: Basically, the pill had a time-release mechanism that was supposed to slowly release the narcotic into the user's body. But it didn't take a rocket scientist to figure out that crushing the pill, either by chewing it or breaking it up, destroyed the time release and allowed the drug to hit the bloodstream almost immediately. It was a super-powerful, super-addictive high, and millions of users, whether recreational or prescribed, were getting hooked. A staggering number of these new users were young people:

- A 2014 survey in the United States found that 2.6 percent of twelve- to seventeen-year-olds and 4.4 percent of eighteen- to twenty-five-year-olds had abused prescription drugs in the past month.[4]

- Prescription drug abuse causes the largest percentage of deaths from drug overdosing. Fentanyl deaths have increased 540 percent from 2010 to 2013.[5]

- Of the 22,400 drug overdose deaths in the United States in 2005, opioid painkillers were the most commonly found drug, accounting for 38.2 percent of deaths. That number has tripled in the last decade.[6]

- The average age for first-time prescription pill use is now thirteen to fourteen.

Judy Rummler is one of the people affected by Purdue Pharma's criminal behavior. Her son, Steve, was prescribed opioid painkillers for a back injury in the late 1990s. He had searing, electric-shock pain that shot up and down his spine and into his skull. He wasn't able to get a diagnosis for this condition, and since it went undiagnosed, traditional medicine had little to offer in terms of pain relief. The family doctor gave him OxyContin.

When the prescription ran out, Steve simply got a refill. The doctor had been trained by the pharmaceutical company: It was commonly assumed, at that time, that "if you are genuinely in pain, you won't be able to get addicted." As if the drug were a magnet, picking up pain like metal shavings inside Steve's body. Nothing could be farther from the truth. That's not how pain works, and that's not how the human body works. Steve's body and brain adapted to the OxyContin dose he was on, and soon he needed more.

Judy reached out to this doctor multiple times, but he assured her that everything was under control. However, Steve knew that something was wrong. He was smart: He knew how to get more pills, and was beyond self-medicating with them. He told his mother that he was addicted and needed help. They tried a leading pain rehabilitation clinic in Minnesota, which was helpful in weaning Steve off the pills as well as treating him with physical therapy and teaching him skills to cope with his pain. He was his old self when he came home, Judy told me, but he started using again shortly after.

He wasn't able to get his drug of choice from the family doctor anymore, so he found a pill mill doctor. His habit came back, hard.

His family, along with Steve's fiancée, staged an intervention.

After a twenty-eight-day stint at Hazelden, Steve was in great shape again. It was 2011, about fifteen years since he'd first used opioids. Hazelden, which Judy described as the "bastion of abstinence," didn't offer medication-assisted treatment like Suboxone, but Steve seemed to be OK. He'd graduated from Hazelden's program, endured physical detox, and was ready to give recovery another try. He was doing what thousands of other people with substance use disorder try to do every year: live a normal life, with ridiculously insufficient support and coping tools. He was doing what I did, over and over. He was doing what my friends did. We were all on the same track, from detox to treatment to sober living.

Steve didn't make it. Forty-five days after leaving Hazelden, he overdosed. He'd run out of prescription pills and, just as I had, used a needle to shoot heroin. It was the only time he'd used heroin and the only time he'd injected. The person who was with him when he overdosed ran away and didn't call 911. Steve lost his life that night, and Judy lost her son.

"By the time he got out of Hazelden, the pill mill doctor had been under investigation and surrendered his license," Judy said. "But Steve was able to just go to his pharmacy and get more pills. Hydrocodone was still misclassified as a Schedule 3 substance at that time, and all of Steve's refills were on hold at the pharmacy. He had no supervision at all with these pills. He could just walk into the drugstore and get it from the pharmacist."

Hydrocodone, one of the most addictive substances on the market, was being distributed through pharmacies, with automatic refills. Opioid addiction was being treated with outdated, non-substance-specific programs that set patients up to overdose after they were released. Medication-assisted treatment can work wonders helping opioid addicts through the early stages of recovery, but treatment centers like Hazelden didn't offer it then. The center's program was designed to treat alcoholism, and at the time they felt that medication-assisted therapy with Suboxone or methadone was inconsistent with the program's abstinence-centric dogma. Can you imagine being diagnosed with lung cancer, then being sent to a clinic that only treated breast cancer? Or being told that "our hospital doesn't believe in chemotherapy?" Ten years ago, this was the common experience of opioid addicts searching desperately for healing. The help just wasn't there.

The epidemic was growing, but still, nobody was talking about it. Prescription pills got about as much oversight as antibiotics. Unlike antibiotics, however, Purdue Pharma knew that it was sitting on a gold mine with Oxy. There's little profit in antibiotics or other medicines that are taken for only three to ten days. Patients take them for the prescribed course and then, voilà, they're done. The medicine has done its job and patients are normal again. That's why there isn't a lot of research on medications like antibiotics: There's no money in them. Medicines for hypertension and diabetes, in contrast, can be taken for decades. These life-sustaining medications make billions for the companies that manufacture them. And pharmaceutical companies have put billions of marketing dollars into convincing all of us that OxyContin is no more dangerous than a few amoxicillin tablets.

They did this by pushing the lie that *opiates aren't addictive*. In 1980, that was the gospel of American medicine. Today, in the midst of the worst drug epidemic in history, we know that isn't true. For every person who is injecting, snorting, or smoking street drugs, there are a dozen more taking their substance of choice out of a prescription pill bottle. Prescription pill use doesn't "look" like drug addiction. Many people think that, if it's a prescription from a doctor, they aren't in danger. The pills are made in a lab, distributed through pharmacies, and come in different doses. They look safe, and pharmaceutical companies have gone to great lengths to make people believe that they *are* safe. But they're not. I think they're lying. That lie is killing people in record numbers.

The lie originates from a one-paragraph letter in the *New England Journal of Medicine* by Hershel Jick, a doctor at the Boston University Medical Center, who came to the conclusion that addiction is "rare in patients treated with narcotics." No history of addiction probably meant no risk of addiction, Dr. Jick concluded. It was a throwaway paragraph— even Dr. Jick has said so—but its implications would shape the way we treated substance use for decades.

This is the letter in its entirety:

> Recently, we examined our current files to determine the incidence of narcotic addiction in 39,946 hospitalized medical patients who were monitored consecutively. Although there were 11,882 patients who received at least one narcotic preparation, there were only four cases of reasonably well documented addiction in patients who had no history of addiction. The addiction was considered major in only one instance. The drugs

implicated were meperidine in two patients, Percodan in one,
and hydromorphone in one. We conclude that despite
widespread use of narcotic drugs in hospitals, the development of
addiction is rare in medical patients with no history of addiction.

That's it. The whole thing. The study, if you can call it that, was done with a control group of patients receiving narcotic medications in a strictly regimented hospital setting. Dr. Jick's letter was based on observation in the field, not a designed study that deliberately gave narcotics to patients who may or may not have needed them. Dr. Jick did *not* conclude that opioids are safe for chronic pain, or for home administration, or for higher, unlimited doses. Opioids were designated for end-of-life care and acute pain.

Yet, over the next decades, the pharmaceutical industry would use this letter to justify its case that opioid medications like OxyContin weren't addictive—even though everything we know proves that, in fact, OxyContin and other opioid medications are just as dangerous as heroin, if not more so. After all, pills were "normal." It's not like you were buying a baggie from a dealer downtown. The pills looked safe, and pharmaceutical reps went to great lengths to convince doctors that they could prescribe at high dosages without endangering their patients. Drug companies repeatedly lied about the effects of the pills they were selling. Their greed endangered the patients who used the medications, and many of them, like me, became addicted.

Dr. Jick's study was taken out of context again and again, amped up, and misrepresented by source after source. Big Pharma worked with state medical boards to change the way opioids were prescribed. Companies paid doctors to contribute to informational pamphlets that said opioids weren't addictive and that high doses were appropriate for long-term chronic pain. These marketing materials became the "gospel truth," and since almost no research on opioids was available, what the pharmaceutical companies put out there became the leading source of information.

That's like tobacco companies claiming that cigarettes don't cause cancer and that smoking has plenty of benefits and no long-term risks. It sounds crazy, but they once used the same techniques that Big Pharma is using now. What happened? They got shut down. It's time to take the same steps with Purdue Pharma and every other drug manufacturer in its cohort.

Dr. Jick's five-sentence letter was blown out of all proportion and became academic canon. The "findings" in the letter were taken as God's own truth. Nobody stopped to question the study or look closely at its findings. Ridiculously, even *Time* magazine called this letter a "landmark study" that demonstrated that the "exaggerated fear that patients would become addicted" to opiates was "basically unwarranted."

That letter did more damage to Americans than an atom bomb. It gave pharmaceutical companies carte blanche to advertise, market, and push highly addictive, dangerous drugs while claiming that the medications weren't habit forming. Even as people started to get hooked on their products, these companies deliberately ignored the negative effects of their actions.

Furthermore, Purdue Pharma's insistence on holding up Dr. Jick's five-sentence letter from 1980 perpetuates the deadly stigma that blames drug users for becoming addicted.

They hid behind that letter, stating that opioids aren't addictive—therefore, if people develop substance use disorder, it must somehow be their own fault. They must be morally bankrupt, or selfish, or weak. They must have done it to themselves. That's the logic that pervades our culture, and believing it is killing us by the thousands while at the same time lining the pockets of pharmaceutical companies.

Purdue and other companies have effectively washed their hands of the hundreds of thousands of prescription drug–related overdoses, deaths, and hospitalizations. They continued to perpetrate the lie that opioid medications aren't addictive. And they continue to profit by turning regular patients, like me, into addicts.

Does that sound crazy? It's not, and we have the data and the court decisions to prove it. This isn't just my personal experience: It's happening all over our country, right now. More than 15 million people in the United States abused prescription pills in 2007. Also in 2007, the Drug Enforcement Administration found that fentanyl killed more than 1,000 people in the United States. Today, after 2017, that figure is more than 20,000 people every year.[7] Don't tell me we don't have a problem. We do.

From 2004 to 2012, seventeen pharmaceutical companies were prosecuted for off-label promotion, kickbacks, fraud, and poor manufacturing practices. The total payout has been almost $20 billion in court settlements. Currently forty-one attorneys general are considering action against opioid manufacturers. Seattle, Tacoma, Miami, and other cities are suing the companies. This historic turn of events is very similar to the multistate lawsuits brought against Big Tobacco in the mid-1990s. The CEOs of those companies eventually appeared before Congress, disputing science that proved nicotine was addictive and smoking killed. It was revealed that tobacco companies had conducted their own studies and had known for decades that cigarettes caused lung cancer. The chain of events in the opioid crisis is a direct parallel. There is legal, cultural, and moral precedent for holding the corporate perpetrators accountable. Justice is on its way. However, none of that will bring Steve back.

I wonder how much money Big Pharma made off Steve Rummler's addiction. I wonder how much more the company would have made if, instead of overdosing, he became a lifelong pill user. Hundreds of dollars a month, for decades, adds up. Yet it's clear that those pills weren't *helping* Steve at all. In fact, they were directly responsible for putting him into the ground.

Since her son's death, Judy has gone on to become an advocate for reform. She lobbied her state government in Minnesota to pass Steve's Law, which extends the Good Samaritan law to people who report an overdose.

"Steve might still be alive today if the person who was with him hadn't been afraid to call 911," Judy said. She also participates in naloxone trainings and helps people learn how to identify and stop an overdose.

In 2012, Judy formed a coalition with several other parents called FedUp! No other major group really existed in the field at the time, but parent groups and communities had started the work of taking action against the opioid epidemic. This determined, passionate group calls for federal action and an end to the opioid crisis. It is unique in that it focuses only on opioids, instead of trying to tackle the full spectrum of addiction. Unlike many other nonprofits, FedUp! doesn't take donations from pharmaceutical companies. It's crucial, Judy says, to be able to call out who's responsible and not feel like the group will lose financial support because of it.

Purdue Pharma's annual revenue hit $1 billion shortly after OxyContin was introduced to the American public. The company owed its success to the drug and kept marketing it. Purdue Pharma singlehandedly created a new generation of people with substance use disorder and caused the deaths of countless Americans. These were people who, like me, woke up in their early thirties wondering what the hell happened. That is, *if* they survived.

I didn't set out to "catch" substance use disorder. Nobody does. I picked up that first pill not knowing what an excruciating, humiliating experience I was headed for. Nothing could have prepared me for the incredible pain, shame, and hurt I endured while I was in the grips of active use. I watched my career disintegrate, lost my stability, and, worst of all, hurt my family—all because of a little white pill. And the whole time, I blamed myself. I fell for the big lie, that my substance use was my fault. I was weak. I had no willpower. I could point the finger at myself, my childhood, workplace stress, my identity as a gay man. I never thought to put that blame where it belonged: on the pharmaceutical companies that were doing their best to deny and hide the deadly effects of the drugs they were selling.

Every grieving parent I've talked to says the same thing: "My son was a good kid. My daughter was so smart." Yes, they were good. They were smart. And Big Pharma killed them.

To find out where the drug epidemic comes from, all you have to do is follow the money. It's simple: Pharmaceutical companies planted and watered the seeds of the drug epidemic, all in the name of profit. They created a medically sanctioned golden goose: protected by the government, aided by medical professionals, and commercially distributed by pharmacists. In 2015, almost 300 million pain prescriptions were written in the United States.[8] That's a lot of revenue for Big Pharma, and the companies are doing everything they can to keep pushing pain pills to unsuspecting patients.

Here's how it works: Even if opioid prescription pills are taken as prescribed, people can develop a physical and psychological dependency in as little as two or three days. The patient will finish the prescribed drug course and then go back for another prescription. Although the patient thinks she's just following the doctor's orders, she actually is heading toward drug dependence and possibly addiction. Take that medication away, and she'll go through withdrawal, the same as any street heroin user.

People used to blame people with substance use disorder, saying "They chose to become an addict. They got themselves addicted." That couldn't be further from the truth. Nobody chooses the life of constant sickness, unemployment, homelessness, hospitals, jails, institutions, isolation, and death. Nobody. Yet people say that since someone chose to use a particular addictive substance the first time, they've chosen to lose everything to this deadly disease. That's the stigma of addiction, and it punishes the people who need help. At the same time, this blame-the-addict game protects the real culprit: pharmaceutical companies. And in the case of prescription pills, you can't really say that someone "chose" to use them the first time. Usually the drug comes in a prescription pill bottle, from a trusted physician, for something like a minor sports injury or a dental procedure. Are people "choosing" to get addicted because they took pills doctors gave them? Of course not. They're not signing up to overdose and die. And yet, thanks to unethical, greedy vampires like Purdue Pharma, they are unwittingly signing up to lose everything, even their lives. How are pharmaceutical companies getting away with this? There's never been a successful civil suit against Big Pharma. The government has sued, sure, but the parents, families, and friends of the many people who have lost their lives haven't had their day in court. *Yet*.

I feel certain that that day is coming soon, though. Parents like Judy Rummler are standing up and speaking out. Mike Moore, the lawyer who beat Big Tobacco, is taking on the opioid industry. We won't be pushed around for a profit anymore. We're starting to see through the lies that have been sold to us. We refuse to live in shame.

Misinformed or not, conventional medicine is partly at fault. They are the gatekeepers of this epidemic. No doctor with a conscience would prescribe pain medication at high doses, without serious cause, knowing that every pill could potentially create a deadly addiction in their patients. Yet, instead of educating themselves about addiction, doctors are working with information provided to them by pharmaceutical companies. Doctors are not educated about addiction; on average, they get a one-hour lecture about it in medical school. That's it.

This ignorance isn't universal, though. Surgery simply cannot be done without opioids like fentanyl, which are used under the supervision of an anesthesiologist in the operating room. When these powerful medications are medically necessary, it's standard to bring in a doctor whose sole job is to manage both the pain and the drug used. That's how seriously doctors who are familiar with opioids take them. Strict medical and legal protocols surround every second that ticks by in an operating room and every directive in aftercare post-surgery.

But Big Pharma wasn't reaching out to emergency room doctors, trauma surgeons, or orthopedic doctors, who might be familiar with opioids from surgery, know how to prescribe them, and understand pain management. Its reps went to primary care physicians: The doctors who are supposed to treat *everyone* for daily ailments. These were average physicians, like the Rummlers' doctor. These doctors were wined and dined by pharmaceutical representatives, treated to high-end experiences and "informational conferences," and offered bonuses for opening clinics that carried Purdue Pharma's products.

At its core, the opioid crisis is a huge pyramid scheme built on dead patients' bodies and supported by greedy, gullible medical professionals. If you want to know who was responsible, just look at the revenue stream: Purdue Pharma's revenue continues to grow exponentially year over year, keeping pace with the opioid crisis. Until overdose deaths finally reached levels that could be described as epidemic, with almost two deaths every fifteen minutes due to drug-related causes, Purdue Pharma's profits kept piling up.

Big Pharma has a history of lying to people about the potential side effects of its medications. One such example is Merck, which was forced to pull the anti-inflammatory drug Vioxx from the market after an investigation showed that the company knew for *three years* that Vioxx tripled the risk of cardiovascular death.[9] Companies like Merck use "on-treatment" analysis of their drug trials, which is much less effective than the industry gold standard "intent-to-treat" analysis. "On-treatment" analysis means that data is collected from a sample of patients who are already using a prescribed medication. "Intent-to-treat" is a controlled, unbiased study of how the medication works *before* it's on the market. No patients are excluded from the dataset, even if they drop out of the study. This is important because people who have a serious issue with a medication, such as negative side effects or drug interactions, tend to drop out. "Intent-to-treat" analysis records this and counts the person in the final dataset. "On-treatment," in contrast, censors data.

Why would Merck cut corners in the lab and hide lethal side effects from the public? Money. Because the company cared more about making money than about conducting business in an ethical manner. Because annual revenue is more important than human life.

McNeil Pharmaceuticals did the same thing when it fought the US Food and Drug Administration's warning label on its products. Tests showed that some over-the-counter pain medications, such as aspirin, acetaminophen, ibuprofen, ketoprofen, and naproxen sodium, cause liver damage when taken with alcohol. McNeil put a warning label on its product Tylenol, but it wasn't explicit and it didn't follow the FDA's guidelines. McNeil, along with the Aspirin Foundation of America, an industry group, pushed back against the FDA proposal on the grounds that all competitors needed to be bound by the same "black box" warning. It was well-known that acetaminophen, which McNeil had discovered and patented as Tylenol back in the 1960s, could cause liver failure. Once again, money was more important than letting people know what they were really taking for their pain. Although McNeil resisted, it eventually lost in court and the black box warning had to appear on all Tylenol packages. The FDA extended the black box warning to *all* over-the-counter nonsteroidal anti-inflammatory analgesics, but not before a fight. Legal fights like this are routine in the pharmaceutical industry. The battles are lengthy, expensive, sophisticated, and serve stockholders at the expense of patients' health.

The implications of this fight over a warning label are staggering. What's even more frightening is how blind we've been, as a country, to the role of pharmaceutical companies in destroying American families, communities, and homes. It's not unlike the role of Big Tobacco in the last generation. There is a larger parallel with Big Pharma and addiction than in other corporate conspiracy cases like Big Tobacco, auto manufacturers, and environmental pollution cases, but the average person is unaware of the connection. Some pharmaceutical companies have gone to great lengths to hide, misrepresent, and lie about the consequences of some of their products. As overdose rates continue to rise, we can no longer ignore the all-too-obvious connection between those deaths and the people profiting from them.

We also can't ignore the millions of dead and dying Americans. We can't ignore the crowded jails and prisons, which are full of people whose only crime was possession of a substance they're physically dependent on. We can't ignore the astronomical amount of money—billions of taxpayer dollars—that we're spending to try to arrest and convict our way out of the drug epidemic. We can't ignore the skyrocketing prices of naloxone, the "anti-overdose" medication that can revive someone who has overdosed. Whether people are overdosing or desperate for more opiates, the pharmaceutical companies are making money. What starts with pain relief turns quickly into substance dependence and leads to more medical needs. Demand continues to climb, and pharmaceutical companies keep supplying without being challenged, feeding the deadly cycle.

Now we are at the tipping point. Advocacy is making a difference. Some groups, like FedUp!, are taking on Big Pharma and calling it out. Backed by private funding and citizen leaders, these groups work with lobbyists to spread the truth about who's really responsible for the opioid epidemic. It's revealing that the FDA, which is supposed to protect Americans from tainted, dangerous, or poor-quality food and drugs, has done so little to fight back. Government regulation requires extensive testing, including human subject tests, to ensure safety, efficacy, and minimal side effects. It can take the FDA a decade or more to say that a drug is safe for the market. How did it miss the fact that drugs like OxyContin are not only *very* unsafe but also highly addictive?

If the FDA really knew what OxyContin could do to people, why would it approve this drug for children as young as eleven? The FDA made that decision in August 2015—well into the opioid crisis, when the death toll had soared and over 2 million people were struggling with an addiction to pain medication. That same year, drug overdoses for the first time killed more Americans than guns and car accidents combined. The opioid epidemic was making national news that year. The FDA had already required special labeling for OxyContin that indicated its "risks of addiction, abuse, and misuse." And yet this drug was deemed safe for children. Considering that prescription pill overdoses are a leading cause of death for young people, this decision could only be described as reckless.

Dr. G. Caleb Alexander, an internist and a director of the Center for Drug Safety and Effectiveness at Johns Hopkins

Bloomberg School of Public Health in Baltimore, told the *New York Times*, "Manufacturers don't pursue regulatory approvals simply to provide prescribers and patients with additional information. This approval allows Purdue Pharma to market and promote this product for use in children, and the obvious concern is this approval will change the pattern of use."[10]

Having FDA approval on the drug's label, warning or not, gives Purdue Pharma carte blanche to continue targeting younger and more vulnerable populations. It also reinforces the idea that prescription pills, because they're "regulated," are somehow safe. Setting limits on prescriptions, such as five-day supplies of pills, gives the illusion that opioid medications can't hurt patients or create long-term problems like physical dependency. An FDA recommendation is just that—a *recommendation*—and its approval looks a lot like an endorsement.

Even smart, sympathetic doctors write prescriptions that end up leading to overdoses. It's the result of misinformation, not motive. Big Pharma has a hand in that too. Although the Purdue Pharma "misbranding" case did cause some increase in restrictions on marketing, good-looking pharmaceutical representatives still make the rounds to doctors' offices and hospitals every day. They treat medical practitioners to lavish meals and offer perks in exchange for prescriptions. Big Pharma has dug deeply into the medical industry, and the corruption it's created is so well-known that major news outlets now clarify whether doctors have financial ties to makers of painkillers when quoting them. Yet, again, there is no outrage. Parents, desperate to help their children, take them to oncologists and pediatricians who have been groomed for *years* by pharmaceutical companies. Parents are effectively putting their children's health into the hands of people who are misinformed about the long-term effects of the drugs they're prescribing. Decades later, what's happening to these kids? They're at a higher risk for developing full-blown substance use disorder and eventually overdosing. That's an incredible price to pay for giving your kid a couple of Vicodin after they get their wisdom teeth removed.

However, I don't think we can let these doctors completely off the hook for their part in causing these kids' deaths. It would be really easy to say that Big Pharma is the one at fault: In fact, many doctors hide behind the corporations whose products they prescribe. Yet, how could any doctor claim to be innocent? The drug epidemic has been going on for *decades*. This is not news. I find it hard to believe that highly intelligent, educated people who work directly with sick and suffering people could *possibly* miss the correlation between opioid painkillers and addiction. When a patient shows up pale, sweaty, and begging for pills, doctors should recognize that something is wrong. Yet it seems like many in the medical profession have chosen to bury their heads in the sand and keep blaming people with substance use disorder. And, meanwhile, doctors keep handing out those poisonous pills.

Doctors even can set patients up to become long-term users of opioid painkillers. A 2017 study published in the *New England Journal of Medicine* showed that some emergency room doctors were three times as likely to prescribe painkillers for their patients as their colleagues. Doctors use dramatically disparate prescribing rules, even within the same emergency room, on patients with similar ailments. So what's the problem? The patients who were treated by frequent prescribers were 30 percent more likely to have become long-term opioid users within a year of their visit.[11] Furthermore, another study found that doctors from lower-tier medical schools were more likely to prescribe opioids: nearly three times as many per year as doctors who graduated from highly ranked medical schools.[12] Thus, doctors who are not well educated are more likely to give opioid medications to patients inappropriately, and those patients are then more likely to develop a potentially life-changing or lethal addiction. It's clear that not all doctors are created equal, and just because someone wears a white coat doesn't mean he or she is a reliable gatekeeper.

Worse, overprescription is an industry-wide problem. Almost *all* doctors overprescribe narcotic painkillers, with 99 percent of doctors giving prescriptions that exceed the federally recommended three-day supply.[13] It's just easier to give painkillers than take an alternate route. In 2010, doctors wrote enough prescriptions for hydrocodone to give every American adult a one-month supply, according to a report by the US Centers for Disease Control and Prevention.[14] That's shocking . . . but not that surprising. Dentists, in particular, tend to be irresponsible with painkillers, as I learned from experience.

At the end of 2017, I went to the dentist for some serious work that included a couple of extractions. On the intake form, I indicated that I was allergic to opioids. Almost three years into recovery, I knew better than to mess with painkillers. While I was sitting in the chair, I said that I *really could not have* pain medication and that I needed something other than opioids.

The doctor nodded, did the extractions, and finished up. Of course, my jaw ached, but I kept calm. After the appointment, the nurse came back to my exam room and handed me a prescription. It was for Tylenol 3, which contains a combination of acetaminophen and codeine. An opioid. This is *in spite of the fact* that I had really clearly said, both verbally and in writing, that I couldn't have medication of this type. Multiple times! I tore up the prescription and ended up treating my pain with ibuprofen and ice instead.

What scares me most is my sense that the nurse didn't know that Tylenol 3 is an opioid. Maybe, in her mind, it was just a stronger anti-inflammatory. How many medical professionals are making decisions based on that same misinformation?

The progress made in continuing education about addiction by groups such as the American Society of Addiction Medicine doesn't reflect the amount of change we need from the medical industry as a whole. It's no longer acceptable for a prescriber to say "I didn't know my patient was abusing those pills," or "It's easier for me to refill the prescription instead of suggesting alternative treatments like physical therapy and acupuncture." Continuing education and certification, especially in addiction medicine, is crucial. Doctors, after all, share the same biases and prejudices that many of us harbor about substance use disorder. They see people with substance use disorder as dirty drug seekers, junkies, and criminals. They don't understand that substance use disorder is an illness. Their ignorance has the power to kill us. Furthermore, some patients do cope with serious, chronic pain. They shouldn't be lumped in with people who are suffering from substance use disorder. It's two different issues that share a common symptom: a physical need for painkillers.

In late January 2018, the news broke that musician Tom Petty, who died in 2017, lost his life to an accidental overdose. Petty was recovering from hip surgery and had been given a large prescription for painkillers. Under normal circumstances, that would be totally appropriate: Hip surgery is major, just like a C-section or back surgery. However, Petty was very open about the fact that he had serious problems with substance use. He'd been in rehab multiple times. A doctor nevertheless decided to hand him a prescription for painkillers anyway, because Petty's history didn't cancel out his need for painkillers or create stricter prescription guidelines. It's the perfect setup for an overdose, and that's exactly what happened. And that's a *normalized* outcome: According to a 2016 study, 91 percent of overdose survivors were still able to get another prescription for opioids.[15] That means that doctors, who should be treating patients according to their needs, are blatantly disregarding their needs, wishes, and personal safety. Whether it's based on ignorance or apathy, the outcome is the same. It's killing us.

A good doctor manages a patient's problem, even if substance use disorder is in the picture. Every one of these losses was preventable. The problem isn't just lack of medical oversight. It's an attitude that's prevalent in conventional medicine: Physicians are product delivery systems, not care providers. Big Pharma uses doctors to connect future customers—patients—with their highly addictive products. Tom Petty's death is an example of what happens when Big Pharma gaslights the medical industry and obscures the true nature of the painkillers it sells. Good doctors are out there, sure, but they're outnumbered by the rest. One bad doctor can poison many patients—at three times the rate.

Limiting prescriptions is one way to turn the tide, but it's not the only answer. Michael Lyons, a researcher and emergency medicine doctor at the University of Cincinnati, said, "What we really need is research to know whether this particular patient should get opioids. Then it would become possible to guide high-or low-prescribers to a common standard."[16] We have to hold doctors accountable to a better standard of care. We have to ensure that their education on opioids *isn't* coming from drug manufacturers. We have to make sure they're actually *listening* to patients, especially those of us who self-identify as being in recovery or having substance abuse disorder. But eliminating a lazy approach to treating pain is only half the battle. To win it, we have to keep our focus on the real culprits: opioid manufacturers like Purdue Pharma, which should include body counts with their quarterly revenue reports.

Big Pharma makes money whether people with substance use disorder live or die. The companies profit directly from the drug crisis, but as long as they keep lining their pockets, it doesn't matter to them how many bodies pile up. When the last person overdoses from prescription pills and there is no one left to sell these deadly medications to, then maybe they'll care. But until then, they chase down more revenue by convincing doctors to prescribe more and more powerful drugs to younger and younger patients. Who's going to stop them? Not the FDA; it's complicit. Not doctors; they've been fooled into thinking that these medicines are less dangerous than they are, less addictive. The task has fallen to normal, everyday people like you and me.

In 2017, OxyContin manufacturer Raymond Sackler died at the age of ninety-seven. The same day, ninety-one other Americans died due to lethal overdoses of the pill that made Sackler a billionaire. Sackler died in comfort, in a hospital bed, with the best possible medical care, "following a brief illness."

How did the ninety-one people killed that day by opioids, including Purdue Pharma's best-selling product, die? Who knows? Maybe they died alone, or at home. Maybe they died in the backs of ambulances, while EMTs tried to give them a life-saving dose of naloxone. Maybe they faded out on their parents' couches and never woke up. Maybe they died in their cars, parked in front of their places of business. Maybe they passed, never knowing exactly what was wrong with them and why they couldn't seem to feel right without the white, green, and blue narcotic pills their doctors gave them.

Sackler is survived by his wife and two sons. Who is standing at the graves of the other ninety-one people who died on July 17, 2017? Sackler, whose company is estimated to be worth $13 billion, was buried with dignity. His life was celebrated by his friends, associates, and loved ones. We can't say the same thing about the dead Americans he built his fortune on. OxyContin robbed families of their parents, children, neighbors, and communities. As of 2017, this medically sanctioned genocide has put more Americans in the ground than the entire Vietnam War.[17]

OxyContin created a drug epidemic that is now the leading cause of death for people under fifty.[18]

I'm reluctant to speak ill of the dead, but Sackler was no hero. He was a businessman whose greed poisoned our nation and directly contributed to the deadly drug epidemic that's killed millions of Americans. Kentucky Attorney General Jack Conway said, "Purdue lit a fire of addiction with Oxy-Contin that spread across this state, and Kentucky is still reeling from its effects." That fire is still burning today.

Raymond Sackler died with American blood on his hands. He got to live over ninety-seven years on this earth. As he was laid to rest, he was remembered as one of the primary actors in creating a health crisis that will have unknown, frightening consequences for generations.

Because of Sackler and pharmaceutical companies like Purdue Pharma, people who should be enjoying their retirement are going back to work and struggling to raise their children's kids. Treatment centers are overloaded with people desperate to find recovery. This is the world Purdue Pharma built through decades of pushing lethal narcotics into the American healthcare system: narcotics that it insisted were generally safe to take.

Thirteen billion dollars. That's what the deaths of hundreds of thousands of men, women, and children were worth to Sackler. It was never about helping people. It was never about medicine. It was all for revenue.

May God have mercy on his soul.

Because Big Pharma certainly has no mercy on us.

6. END THE WAR ON DRUG USERS
How America Can Recover from Decades of Prejudice, Injustice, and Ignorance

I HAVE FOND MEMORIES OF THE 1980S. I mean, I think I do. In 1983, I was still a toddler, running around in a pair of blue Velcro shoes. My mom wore her hair in an aggressively bobbed perm. "Billie Jean" was on the radio all the time then—you'd hear it drifting through the windows of people's Datsuns as they drove by. It was a weird time to be a kid. Pee-wee Herman, He-Man, and *Fraggle Rock* paraded across our family's TV screen. I was insulated from the moral panic that whipped adults into a lather: The Reagan administration had launched its War on Drugs, with a special focus on keeping kids away from harmful substances.

In a 1983 speech to kick off National Drug Abuse Education Week, President Reagan said, "No longer do we think about drugs as a harmless phase of adolescence. No longer do we think of so-called 'hard' drugs as bad and so-called 'soft' drugs as being acceptable. Research tells us there are no such categories; that the phrase 'responsible use' does not apply to drug experimentation by America's youth. And as far as the recreational use of drugs is concerned, I have never in my life heard a more self-serving euphemism by those who support drug use."[1]

Reagan didn't distinguish between types of drugs, the reasons people had for using them, or a casual drug user and a person who was addicted. He also segregated drugs in their own category, away from alcohol, although alcohol *is* a drug and can lead to severe addiction problems. All drugs were lumped into one category, labeled *bad*. There was only one way to keep kids off drugs, Reagan said, and that was to physically separate drug users from the rest of society. At the same time, Reagan used the media and kid-friendly communication tools like comic books to stigmatize drugs and drug use for very young people. Kids like me, who were barely out of diapers, were seen as the most vulnerable and were targeted with the most messaging. The Keebler Company, America's largest cracker and cookie manufacturer, worked with media giant Warner to make antidrug ads that were specifically aimed at kids.

Those messages definitely got my attention. Even though I barely understood what the president was saying, I was engrossed. By the time I was six, I was combing my hair *just like him*, watching his speeches on TV, and absorbing every word. Drugs and Reagan. Let's just say I was an early adopter.

In the late 1980s and early 1990s, while the AIDS crisis claimed countless lives and the crack epidemic swept urban centers, the message from the White House was clear: "Just Say No." It seemed simple at the time: Don't use drugs, and you won't get high. Don't get high, and you won't get hooked. Avoidance was the method of prevention. It's not so different from "abstinence-only" sex ed. Three decades later, however, we're in the firm grip of an addiction crisis that claims nearly 350 American lives per day.[2] And yet we're still being told to "Just Say No," even though evidence increasingly shows that it doesn't work.

Reagan pulled the ultimate "think of the children" move. He created a generation of people, like me, who were taught that all drug use is the same and that all drugs are bad. By painting drugs with a broad brush, he helped encourage the terrible stigma of addiction and spread misinformation about it that persists to this day. It wasn't just after-school scare cartoons either. Reagan criminalized drugs and built the case for locking people up for using them.

In scores of states, laws were passed with mandatory minimum sentences for drug offenses, requiring that judges send those convicted to jail for years, with no obligation to provide treatment. Removing judicial discretion is generally a bad idea, but imposing mandatory minimum sentencing for those who violate drug laws created a very practical mathematical problem—hundreds of thousands of people in desperate need of addiction treatment were converted into prisoners. This created overcrowding in our jails, so much that new jails had to be built. The fundamental principle of criminalizing the disease of substance use disorder was profound and deep and activated an entire branch of government.

Realistically, if we locked up everybody who used or misused substances, every town would be a ghost town. Every college campus would be practically abandoned: 96 percent of college students, ages eighteen to twenty-two, use alcohol on an average day. More than half of them use marijuana.[3] Those substances aren't legal for underage use. Should we just put these young people in jail, to scare them out of developing substance use disorder? What if we locked up every Wall Street banker who ever tried cocaine or every stay-at-home mom who popped a pain pill when her kids got on her nerves? Every coal miner who had too many beers after work, mixed with prescription drugs from an on-the-job injury? Who would be left?

Let's consider what happens when we take drug users, even casual or recreational ones, out of the system. Imagine if every person who used substances in a way that was noncompliant with federal or state law was charged with a crime for misuse and sentenced to serve time. What would happen? Being convicted of a drug-related crime has far-reaching consequences for both individuals and society. With a drug conviction on your record, it's harder to find housing, buy a home, and get a job that pays a wage that can support a family. The more serious the offense, the harder it is to find work: Many people simply go back to their former lives, because of the lack of better options. Inmates lose their right to vote, effectively taking them out of the democratic system. That may sound just to you, but it's not. Drug use is criminalized, sure, but it's more illegal for *some people* than for others. If Reagan's antidrug laws were applied equally to everyone who misused substances of any kind, for any reason, regardless of their race or income, we would see dramatic changes in society. Whole generations of people would suddenly disappear behind bars and exit the criminal justice system unemployable, unable to vote, and dependent on social services for healthcare, food, and housing. We've turned a blind eye to this because drug laws primarily target the black community and reinforce the systemic racism that targets nonwhite people in America.

Recent statements from the federal government regarding recreational and medical marijuana have made that racism ultra obvious. Although marijuana has been legalized in some states, the federal government still considers it an illicit substance. States' rights prevail for the moment, thanks to an Obama-era policy of noninterference in state laws. However, in January 2018, Attorney General Jeff Sessions issued a memo to rescind the hands-off approach and unleash federal prosecutors on states to crack down on substances and substance users. Sessions's memo said, "These principles require federal prosecutors deciding which cases to prosecute to weigh all relevant considerations of the crime, the deterrent effect of criminal prosecution, and the cumulative impact of particular crimes on the community."[4] Well, it's been shown that criminal prosecution doesn't deter people with substance use disorder from using illegal substances. And it's also been shown that treating people who struggle with addiction like criminals makes it very, very difficult for them to heal from their illness. We need to repair this broken system, stop ignoring the deeply racist bias that punishes people of color, and stop using drug laws to create a subclass of Americans who can't work, vote, or contribute to society. We can start by releasing all nonviolent, low-level drug offenders and using the money we would've spent on incarcerating them on their treatment instead. We need better treatment programs for people who enter recovery through the criminal justice system. We need to use our anticrime resources on *actual crime*, not on policing a bunch of sick people.

Furthermore, we need to look at the tax revenue that states receive from legalized marijuana. Oregon's first payout of recreational cannabis tax money in 2017 was $85 million to schools, public health, police, and local governments. The state allocated a mere $1 million for drug and alcohol abuse prevention, the state's youth marijuana prevention campaign, and drug and alcohol use data collection.[5] Tax revenue can be invested in research, recovery support, and evidence-based treatment. Decriminalizing substance use kills multiple birds with one stone: It frees people who aren't criminals, adds to our workforce, reduces the expense of policing people with substance use disorder, empties prisons of nonviolent offenders, and declutters the criminal justice system. Oh yeah, and it helps fund *life-saving programs* for people who are at the bottom of their addiction. Sounds like a no-brainer to me, especially because those changes truly benefit *all* of us.

One thing that I don't think people really understand about addiction is that *we are all at risk*. Every person who *ever* touches a substance is at risk for substance use disorder. No one is immune. It may take some people longer to get there, due to their substance of choice, genetic makeup, or psychological traits, but we are all susceptible. So let's look at who *is* being locked up for drug-related crimes. It isn't people like me: white, middle class, professional, and educated. Thousands of low-level drug offenders go to jail every year. Many of them are people of color, from low-income families, who have been pushed through the school-to-prison pipeline.

Simply put: We're locking up people who don't deserve to be punished, and we're aided in this by racist, antipoor, inhumane beliefs. A disproportionate number of black men are sitting in prison *right now* for drug-related crimes. Some will serve sentences that send their white, middle-class peers to treatment. Many will spend too many days, months, and years behind bars because they can't afford bail, or because they've been convicted of more than one drug-related offense. An entire generation of black men, trapped in prison, without access to treatment or harm reduction? That's not a coincidence. It's an extension of three very common, extremely harmful beliefs that Reagan exploited in his "Just Say No" campaign:

1. Drug users are morally bankrupt.
2. Black people are dangerous.
3. Addiction is a choice.

None of those claims are grounded in fact. Yet even people who say they don't believe the claims struggle to accept the idea that it's time to dismantle the prison system and treat addiction like an illness, not a crime. We have to do more than keep offering white kids treatment and sending black ones to jail.

Mandatory minimums for drug convictions are a huge part of the problem. When mandatory minimums went into place, the prison population went off the charts, growing exponentially for forty years. Pursuing serious charges for low-level, nonviolent drug offenders is unnecessary and cruel. These unforgiving laws fall especially heavy on black Americans. They waste human potential, taxpayer dollars, and anticrime resources. We spend $7 billion per year on prisons, a quarter of the Justice Department's budget.[6] Yet we're not getting our money's worth, because mandatory minimums and other punitive drug possession laws are ineffective. They crush communities by splitting up families and creating economic hardships. They tie judges' hands and prevent the courts from doing their jobs. Mass incarceration is at odds with our American ideals of justice: Long prison terms don't make things better for anyone. We need to be smart, not tough, on drug-related crime.

Criminal justice reform is a controversial subject. Add addiction to the equation, and things just get crazy. I've met people who think that addicts should all be behind bars. Our government subscribes to strict, punitive laws for possession of any illegal substance. A single grain of cocaine, one marijuana seed, and you're going to jail. Yet it's clear that the presence of a controlled substance isn't the real problem here. Addiction is, and incarcerating people who have substance use disorder isn't going to "cure" them of their illness.

If you're going to argue that "all lives matter," then many of those lives belong to people who are incarcerated. Their lives matter too. We need to reform our laws around drug-related crimes.

News flash: All kinds of Americans use drugs, legal or not, for all kinds of reasons. All of a sudden, any drug user or anyone in possession of an illegal substance was on the government's hit list. All those people had to go somewhere. Suddenly we couldn't build prisons fast enough. It became an incarceration gold rush, with private prisons swooping in to cash in on the criminal justice system's sudden surplus of bodies. According to New Jersey senator Cory Booker, a Democrat, the War on Drugs led to "a 500 percent increase in incarceration in our country, disproportionately affecting poor and disproportionately affecting minorities."[7] Once the prison pipeline was established, there was plenty of financial incentive to keep feeding people into the machine. For that reason, the number of people who are incarcerated increases exponentially, year over year. According to the Sentencing Project, a criminal justice reform advocacy organization, the prison population in 1974 was 218,466. After 2017 it's over

2.2 million people.[8] Prisons are severely overcrowded and cost taxpayers *billions* every year. Yet because drug use and possession carry such unnecessarily heavy punishments, many people never escape this system—especially if they have substance use disorder. Not all prisons offer treatment for the disorder. Many people who are suffering with addiction receive lengthy sentences where they rot in jail and are never offered treatment.

Some jails do offer excellent treatment and have spectacular outcomes in reducing recidivism, but nothing compels uniformity in quality of care in corrections. People who aren't geographically lucky enough to wind up in a jail with a robust treatment program are recycled through jails and prisons, picking up charge after charge. Their criminal record makes it increasingly difficult for them to adapt to normal life and move forward, and their addiction makes it impossible for them to quit using the substance that gets them into trouble. It's a vicious cycle, and the only way to stop it is to find real, achievable solutions to addiction and *stop the war on people with drug problems*.

Let me get one thing straight, though. While I do support decriminalizing drug use, helping people with substance disorder leave the criminal justice system, offering treatment during jail time, and eliminating mandatory minimum sentences for drug convictions, I'm not saying that all people with drug problems should get a free pass on the crimes they've committed. I may be liberal, but I'm not *that* liberal. I'm saying that there's an insanely high correlation between drug addiction and incarceration, and most of the people who end up serving time do not belong in prison. Especially in the case of nonviolent crimes, like petty theft, we need to work to alleviate the symptoms of people's addictions instead of locking them up for having the addictions. People like this belong in treatment. That's one thing that the War on Drugs got completely wrong: It thought you could just scare someone into sobriety by threatening them with loss of freedom. For some people, that may be true. For the vast majority, however, it's simply not possible to stop using just because a judge tells you to.

I find it both hilarious and ironic that I'm a product of Reagan's Drug Abuse Resistance Education program. Seriously. I'm a heroin addict, a former "Just Say No" kid. At my elementary school, a D.A.R.E. officer visited my third-grade classroom twice a week to lecture us about the dangers of using drugs. After school, I saw the same antidrug public service announcements as everyone else. "This is your brain on drugs" was the message, and I got it. I heard it all, loud and clear. Did I miss the memo? No. I became addicted, and, as anyone who's experienced it knows, addiction is *not* a choice.

It's very simple. One definition of addiction is repeated use of alcohol and drugs, despite negative consequences. People use alcohol and drugs to alleviate the negative psychological burdens of anxiety and depression—not to ruin their lives and their families. By the time it's obvious that substance use is causing problems with a person's relationships, employment, school, or the law, chemical dependency pathology has taken over. Real, medically diagnosable cravings are driving the compulsive behavior. It's not because the person is reckless. It's not because he doesn't care. It's not because she wants to hurt herself or others. It's how an addicted brain operates: on autopilot, through a fucking tornado of mismanaged emotions. The wreckage will not stop until there is a supervised withdrawal period, followed by medically managed treatment.

Choice goes right out the window. The brain is hijacked, the same way the body's sugar management is hijacked during diabetes or the lungs are hijacked by tuberculosis. A disease takes its course until something stops it. The reason many people don't perceive addiction as a disease is that its symptoms are behavioral aberrations that seem to be within the person's control. But no rational person would choose to alienate those around him- or herself and ignore the moral compass. When people are symptomatic from addiction, their observable behaviors are a hijacking. Because the behaviors look deliberate, family and friends become resentful. Addiction ruins lives. Cancer doesn't hurt your loved ones. Diabetes doesn't make you a lousy employee or husband. Addiction does *all* these things. That is what feeds the sick person's shame.

For people like me—that is, people with substance use disorder, whether they're in active addiction or not—the government's return to the Reagan era "Just Say No" campaign raises a lot of red flags. The zero-tolerance policies of that era were designed to do exactly one thing: Feed people into America's prisons. In 2016, at a meeting with law enforcement officials, Attorney General Sessions said, "Educating people and telling them the terrible truth about drugs and addiction will result in better choices by more people."[9] If that's true, though, how do you explain someone like me? I had all the information but still started using drugs at fifteen. Just saying no wasn't enough. If this program works so well, why are our prisons full of people with substance use disorder?

"Just Say No," a relic of Reagan's presidency that's still in use today, puts thousands of people in prison for drug-related offenses. Besides the obvious—that someone with addiction needs treatment, not jail time—we now know that D.A.R.E. doesn't work. As early as 1992, a study from Indiana University showed that kids who had been through the D.A.R.E. program had *higher* rates of hallucinogenic drug use than those who had not been exposed to the program.[10] A ten-year study by the American Psychological Association showed a similar result: D.A.R.E. is ineffective and in many cases is even counterproductive because it makes kids curious about these "forbidden" substances.[11] In fact, D.A.R.E. lost its federal funding in 1998 because the APA study showed that D.A.R.E. kids actually had *higher rates of drug use.* Seriously! Clearly, just saying no and working on our self-esteem weren't cutting it.

So, we misinform, shame, and stigmatize drug users, and then arrest them if they have a relapse or show symptoms of substance use disorder. Three-strikes rules and mandatory minimums punish people who need help rather than a heavy sentence. I think a big part of the problem is the myth that drug users have to "hit bottom" in order to get help and that they need a lengthy dive into their illness in order to really "want help." But, as I've said before, that's not a humane or productive method. Jailing someone who's addicted is about as productive as putting diabetic patients into solitary confinement and telling them to "use their willpower" to get their blood sugar to normal levels. The fact is, just like other illnesses, early intervention works with substance use disorder. People respond to it—but they need more than just saying no and subliminal media messaging. I think we can start by acknowledging that drug use is not a black-and-white issue. And guaranteed jail time for drug offenses is counterproductive. Instead of clinging to an outdated antidrug program that is *proven* not to work, let's look at something that does.

REAL, which was designed by research conducted at Arizona State University in the 1990s, works from the bottom up. "REAL," which is an acronym for the program's strategies "Refuse, Explain, Avoid, and Leave," has shown positive results. One reason why? Instead of police officers, the messaging about smart choices and drug awareness is created by kids for kids. High school students make video narratives for middle school–age children about making good decisions about drugs. Peer groups discuss the content and talk about ways to react if they were offered drugs or put in an awkward situation. The program is more like what we do as adults in peer mentor programs. Involving kids, instead of lecturing them, shows good results—because, after all, in the moment of truth, when the blunt or the bottle makes its way into young people's hands, no cop is going to be there to remind them to love themselves. And the odds are good that scare tactics, like the threat of going to jail, won't matter in that moment either.

Once addiction has taken root in people, the deck is totally stacked against them. The laws we have in place to deal with drugs like opioids are designed to protect doctors, not their patients. My own experience is a great example of that. People like me, who become dependent on prescription painkillers, are threatened with blacklisting. I'll never forget the sick sensation I felt when Dr. Sullivan threw me out of her clinic. It wasn't just the humiliation of being chased through the office, out of the waiting room, and into the parking lot while other patients stared at me. She called me a junkie, a *drug seeker*. Damn right I was a drug seeker. I was seeking the drugs that she'd been providing to me on a regular basis! But when she brought up the register of names—the people who were banned from accessing certain medications—my blood went cold. She wasn't adding me to the list to protect me from myself, far from it. Her only concern was whether she'd get caught providing me with the opioids I needed. She was looking out for herself. As soon as I displayed "criminal" tendencies—the track marks that one of the nurses noticed—I was persona non grata. I was shut out of that clinic and added to the list. I was also shut out from receiving clean, FDA-approved opioids too.

Catching someone who's using drugs, or even *misusing* them, doesn't help them. That's not what those lists are for.

The way that we approach these drugs—as if they were totally different, unrelated substances—is completely backward. Prescription painkillers are government-endorsed, clean, highly addictive heroin. Heroin is a cheaper substitute for overpriced prescription pills. The link between the two drugs is obvious to those of us who have switched from one to another and watched substance use disorder destroy our friends and loved ones. Why is it so hard for the government to see the connection and quit treating people with *a mental illness* as if we were criminals?

Fast forward to August 2016. As I stepped into the holding room of the Chesterfield Jail, I felt the temperature drop. Jails are cold places. Even in Virginia's summer heat, this one seem to be permanently chilled. I'm from California: the liberal land of sunshine. I'm used to blue skies. Now I was deep in rural, red, Republican Virginia. The type of place that eats liberals like me for lunch. The land of pickup trucks with Second Amendment bumper stickers, hellfire billboards and church marquees, and no pride parades. I shivered. The prison's cinder block walls, hard cement floors, and industrial architecture made it clear that this was a warehouse for people society doesn't want around anymore. A hundred movie clips played in my head. What was it really like, on the inside?

I was there to learn about the jail's recovery program for prisoners. It was an incredible opportunity, but I couldn't shake my nervous feeling. I kept thinking, *This could have been my story.* I was about to meet with people waiting for trial, most for drug-related convictions. Some were looking at a decade or more behind bars. The link between addiction and incarceration is obvious: 80 percent of inmates are there because of substance use, and nearly 50 percent of jail and prison inmates are clinically addicted. Approximately 60 percent of individuals arrested for most types of crimes test positive for illicit drugs at arrest.[12] I'm not exaggerating when I say that *this could have been me.* These prisoners weren't doing anything different from what Star, Horse, and I had done to get high back in Florida.

My life would have been totally different if I'd been arrested, even once. This jail visit was like a trip into an alternate reality: the life I could've ended up in if I hadn't finally made it to recovery. I was totally disconnected from the criminal justice problem until I actually stepped into Chesterfield Jail and was exposed to it in person.

I was connected with Chesterfield through my friend John Shinholser. John's a big, hearty guy. I loved his Virginia drawl, punctuated by frequent expletives. He was salty, and real, and eager to show me what was happening on the front lines. He called me up and told me that I needed to come and take a look at this program in Virginia.

"You get all these alcoholics pulled up in these jails, and it's like shooting fish in a barrel," he told me. "Judges are screening people. Convictions are part of their budgets: 'honey bun money,' 'telephone money.' Jails don't help an addict. It robs you of your hope and steals your humanity. They're just keeping you in an incubator, you're worse than when you went in. The sad part of it is, being locked up and getting off the street can be helpful, but giving someone a felony will ruin their life."

After that, how could I turn down an invitation to check out Chesterfield? To know John Shinholser is to love him. He's a former Marine who's been in and out of the criminal justice system. He'd been drunk and homeless and joined the Marines at twenty-one. It wasn't a cure for what ailed him. By the time he was twenty-three, he'd been locked up twelve times. Finally, his colonel offered him the chance to go to rehab. John took it, mostly to avoid another trip to the brig. He said, "I learned two things about jail: The food sucks, and the women are fake."

In treatment, he was introduced to the 12-Step program, where he learned how important service work is. "My sponsor said that the only way I'd stay sober was doing H & I: visiting other alcoholics in hospitals and institutions. I still take meetings into jails and prisons, once a week, and I have for thirty-five years. In 2004, we started creating jail programs to help people more regularly," he told me.

During his thirty-five years of recovery, John's made criminal justice reform *his* issue. He's on a mission to visit jails and prisons in all fifty states. He's spent his career screaming that the criminal justice system is stacked against people with substance use disorder. His passion lit a fire under me. John told me that instead of a top-down, policy-led solution, *real* results were coming from recovery programs led by communities, local law enforcement, and family advocacy groups and nonprofits. He told me that one of the best programs in the United States is run by Sheriff Karl Leonard in Chesterfield, Virginia.

After a quick briefing, John and I shook hands with the jail's head warden. We were led through the sliding iron doors to a room called "the tank" where, oh my God, it didn't feel like a walk-in freezer. A few dozen plastic chairs—weirdly, the same kind we had at my high school—were arranged in a semicircle. Forty men in blue jumpsuits were standing around, waiting. When John and I came in, they turned to look at us. I wondered how long it had been since they talked to an outsider. A couple people got up and gave me a hug. *Awkward.*

I settled into the plastic chair, feeling sweaty in my necktie and button-down vest. Were these guys different from me? Were they really hardened criminals? One man, his entire face, neck, and head covered in swirling tattoos, grinned at me. I smiled back and started to relax. When someone made a joke, it broke the ice. John started us off, introducing me, and then we went around the circle, telling our stories. I realized that my story was almost identical to every other man's, except that I hadn't been caught. The only difference between me and these prisoners? I was wearing a tie.

I didn't feel cold anymore. I was part of the group. We joined hands, preparing to pray. No matter where I was, it turns out that I fit right in: We all spoke the language of recovery.

Some of these guys were in for crimes like a dirty UA on probation; others were in for grand theft auto and were awaiting trial. Nobody had killed anyone. Every crime was related to addiction. Soon a big, tall, burly dude walked in wearing a suit: Sheriff Leonard. He went to the center of the circle and asked, "What's the difference between me and you?"

The men chorused, "Right turn and left turn."

Karl meant that he'd made a right turn at one of life's intersections. The inmates had made a left turn. He explained that the choice *he* made doesn't mean he's better than them. It just means he has different consequences. Like me, maybe he happened to get lucky.

The recovery program addressed a problem Karl saw all the time in the prison system. He said he was sick and tired of seeing people come back for the same drug-related crimes. The system didn't rehabilitate these people or treat their underlying issue—addiction. Yet it was immediately apparent that the guys at Chesterfield Jail were benefiting from the support they were getting. When we went around the circle, almost every one of the guys praised Karl and the Chesterfield program. They hugged each other. They sang a fucking song. Honestly, I was blown away.

Chesterfield's program is unique for a lot of reasons. For one, Karl took the initiative to find a solution to the addiction problem in his community. Sick and tired of deaths and high reincarceration rates, he banged down doors to ask for help. Let me be clear: Karl is a conservative, Republican, elected sheriff. He's not trying to legalize marijuana and put a dispensary on every corner. He saw a problem in his community and took matters into his own hands. Despite his efforts, however, he was not able to find funding for the jail. Frustrated, he called John, who runs the McShin Foundation, a recovery nonprofit that focuses on outreach programs.

The next day, John was on-site. He showed Karl what to do, and they started implementing this program. "It's simple," John told me. "Hope is powerful. All we do is go into these jails and say, 'Anyone who wants to stay sober, come in this unit over there.' The girls go with the girls, and the guys go with the guys. We work with them three hours a day. We give them the Big Book, Basic Text, or Bible: You pick one. Every day, we've got volunteers going in who are living proof that the message works. They tell their stories. We get a big-screen TV for them to watch, with recovery-themed movies, documentaries, and videos. We want them chasing their recovery like they chased their drugs."

The fact that the program isn't *mandatory* makes a big difference, especially for people who have been pushed through less-effective programs and served time in the past. People are asked if they want help and if they have a problem with opioids. They don't have to make any changes unless they want to, and they're not forced to adopt any beliefs. John said, "We give them multiple pathways. AA isn't going to be for everybody. Basically, if you can find something else, that's great, but find it so you don't fucking go back to jail."

Putting participants in the same area, using a peer-to-peer support system, and creating a postrelease support network have been key for Chesterfield. Guys who have left the jail who have an urge to use can call 911 and talk to the police dispatcher, and a cop will come pick them up and take them back to the peer group in the jail. The program is built around the recovery group—just like an AA meeting—plus clinicians, therapists, and twelve hours of recovery support every day.

The Chesterfield idea was simple: Instead of isolating people and keeping them away from their families and support network, the jail was open. Instead of "business as usual," it would treat the underlying issues. Inmates' families can visit and take part in the recovery workshops offered through the jail. Volunteers share their stories with the inmates and help provide a support network once they're released. Karl says that including friends, family, and community is key to reducing the rate of relapse and death.

"People forget that addiction is a disease, not a crime," he said. "Everyone is a human being first."

I couldn't agree more. Instead of releasing inmates without support—putting them back on the street and in danger of relapsing—Chesterfield Jail has helped create a network of people in recovery who can offer housing, meals, and fellowship instead of drugs. One phone call can link someone to a ride, a hot cup of coffee, and a safe place to sleep. All they have to do is ask. The jail's doors are open daily to anyone who needs help: Karl says anyone who's interested can come in off the street and take part in the jail's drug education program.

"People think Narcan is the answer," Karl said. "They resuscitate someone and send them on their way, saying 'Well, I saved their life.' But that's not true. You are not saving someone's life. You're only postponing their death. We are taking action to make sure that these people actually get another chance."

What he's doing is working. Karl said that his program has an 89 percent success rate. That's higher than most detox and treatment centers can claim—and at a fraction of the cost. The sheriff is paying for this program from his own budget. He started out without any state or federal funding. That's unacceptable, especially since it costs only about $3,500 a month for forty men, or about $1,050 per person per year, to truly rehabilitate each inmate. Let's compare that to the cost of keeping someone in jail for the same amount of time: $42,000 for one year. One year in jail costs about the same as a twenty-eight-day stay in an average treatment center. And $1,050 for a whole year? That's *peanuts*.

Imagine the long-term economic savings if we implemented a program like this in each and every town and city across the country. According to a study by the academic journal *Crime & Delinquency*, providing only 40 percent of people who are drug addicted with treatment and recovery services instead of incarceration would save the US economy over $12.9 billion per year. Every federal dollar invested in drug court or court-mandated treatment leverages $4.30 in state funding due, in part, to reduced prison costs, reduced revolving-door arrests and trials, and reduced victimization.[13] Safer communities, less crime, and fewer drug-related deaths. It sounds like a no-brainer to me.

The bottom line shows that treating people with substance use disorder is absolutely worth it. People who go to diversion or get some kind of treatment while they're incarcerated show a better recidivism rate. They're less likely to have a second offense and less likely to be arrested again. According to the National Association of Drug Court Professionals, the average recidivism rate was only 16 percent in the first year after leaving a drug court program and 27 percent after the second year. This compares very favorably to recidivism rates on conventional probation, in which 46 percent of people commit a new offense and over 60 percent commit a probation violation.[14] That means that there's real potential in the criminal justice system to break the cycle of addiction and incarceration.

How we define *success* is key to understanding why jail programs work. John said, "There are two things that are a true gauge of success. Five years out of your fucking treatment center, if you have the same sober date, that is one benchmark. In that same five years, even if you relapse, if you're still engaged in the recovery process, that's success too. The real message here is that Karl is committed to helping addicts. He's following suggestions from people in recovery. With all these different stakeholders coming together, when you listen to people with recovery experience, you get better results."

That meeting in Chesterfield Jail changed my life. A year later, I was invited to visit two prisons in Alaska: Spring Creek and another correctional facility in Anchorage. I boarded the plane in Los Angeles, wondering what I was in for. The people I was meeting were incarcerated in *Alaska*, of all places: one of the reddest states in our nation. I was traveling to Wasilla, which was practically in Sarah Palin's backyard. Yet these prisons offered some of the most promising programs in the nation. Their results were significant: better than government agency-designed programs, high-end treatment centers, and hospitals.

A few years ago, Spring Creek wasn't exactly a poster child of compassion and care. An inmate's complaint in 2013 led to an investigation that showed how guards had paraded naked male prisoners in front of the female staff and locked prisoners in cages as punishment for minor infractions. One man was leashed like a dog and stripped naked so that the guards could laugh at him.[15] Seriously, read the report. It's like something out of Abu Ghraib. The new superintendent, however, had cleaned house by the time I got to Spring Creek. The empty cages were still on the prison's grounds, which was creepy, but what I found inside showed me that prison recovery was alive and well in Alaska.

What I saw at the new, improved Spring Creek convinced me that these prison treatment programs weren't successful just because of what they were offering people; they were successful because of what they *weren't* doing too. I noticed an absence of the stigma, shame, miseducation, and silencing that is the norm in our country. Prisoners could talk honestly and openly about their issues with substances without being embarrassed. They got good resources to support their recovery, covered by state funding. They were included in community as much as possible. They were given a lot of freedom, allowed to decorate the inside of the facility, and encouraged to express their feelings in appropriate ways. The programs I saw in action in Alaska followed a lot of the same guidelines as REAL. Participants talk through their issues in groups, use a buddy system of mentors, and actively take part in creating the recovery that they want to experience. Literally nothing is off limits. When I left, the inmates were putting the finishing touches on their meditation room: a cell with no door, a beautiful jungle mural painted on its walls, filled with comfortable seats and plants. They had yoga, mindfulness, and meditation workshops. Imagine that: a room full of hard-core, convicted felons, all doing tree pose, totally peaceful. It turns out that treating people with dignity and offering them all kinds of support gets good results, for the long term. It was the *opposite* of what happens elsewhere in the criminal justice system.

The Spring Creek superintendent, Bill Lapinskas, told me, "We looked at the best practices guide and thought, best practices for who? What's best for one person isn't best for another one. We had to look closer and adapt." He worked with inmates, mental health professionals, and recovery groups to make this new program that focuses on the individual's needs.

Mindfulness, yoga, classes in entrepreneurship, Bible study group, and more help people address their underlying issues.

Just as important is a change in the way prison is used: Instead of unremitting, dehumanizing punishment, prison programs are designed to rehabilitate people and prepare them to stay healthy and sober when they reenter society. By treating people with substance use disorder as *people*, Alaska's criminal justice system is breaking ground. Yet its program is simple enough to be adapted to almost any facility. When will the rest of America catch up?

For many people with substance use disorder, the criminal justice system takes on the role of treatment provider. People are sentenced to thirty days in a county jail to "dry out" or "think about what they've done." I've heard stories about families calling the police on their own children because they think their kids will get sober only under lock and key. They hand their sons and daughters over to uneducated, untrained, and uncaring wardens, hoping that they'll detox in jail and come home sober. They refuse to stand beside their children in court, thinking that the "tough love" of the criminal justice system, and maybe a felony charge, will scare them straight. These poor families, who are so tormented by their children's drug use, are truly caught between a rock and a hard place. They feel that they must take *some* kind of action or else watch their children die.

Putting someone who needs treatment in jail is dangerous. It's not a choice: It's forced withdrawal, without medical assistance. The outcome of this nonmedical detox can be fatal. At least four cases of inmates dying while incarcerated have made national news in the last few years. In 2015, for example, David Stojcevski died an excruciating, slow death while serving a thirty-day sentence for a careless driving charge in Michigan. His cause of death was listed as "acute withdrawal from chronic benzodiazepine, methadone and opiate medications."

That's what happens when we treat people with addiction like criminals.

When someone dies, jails often point the finger at hospitals, saying that the victim should have been in a hospital bed. But we're not sending people with drug convictions to hospitals: We incarcerate them. *We make detox the jail's responsibility because we won't admit that addiction is an illness.* Hospitals aren't much better than jails. They regularly discharge substance use patients within hours of administering naloxone and reversing a heroin overdose, putting them back on the street instead of offering treatment that addresses the deeper issue. People who are given naloxone are in withdrawal, dope-sick, and highly likely to try to use again to alleviate their symptoms. They're the ones who walk out of the ER and immediately get busted trying to buy drugs. They ricochet from hospitals to jails, never getting the help they need. We don't have a law for that.

Jails blame hospitals. Hospitals blame jails. And in the meantime, people are dying because nobody wants to be the "somebody" who does something. Our jails and prisons are full of people whose only crime is being arrested while under the influence, or in possession of, a substance they are dependent on.

Wouldn't it be easier to break that dependence, address the substance use, and teach people the skills they need to stay drug-free and out of the criminal justice system for good? Absolutely. It's more cost efficient. It's more humane. It saves lives and frees up billions of dollars for law enforcement, criminal justice, legal defense, and social services. Yet we haven't made the single, simple change of *decriminalizing addiction* because keeping people in jail generates revenue. The system has been set up to profit off people like us. People with substance use disorder are treated like cash cows and criminals, plain and simple.

Jail time doesn't make substance use disorder go away. Once released, people aren't "cured" of their chronic health issue either. It's clear that we can't just arrest our way out of the drug epidemic. My friend Greg Williams said, "Substance use always has and will be a concern to public safety and public health. But when someone develops an addiction, we need to understand that a law enforcement-centric approach hasn't and will not get us the 'rehabilitation' goal of the criminal justice system if we continue to ignore treatment and recovery support needs for people."

There is no substitute for medical aid and treatment, and incarceration isn't the answer. Neither is using people as slave labor, ostensibly in service to their recovery. Although older models of treatment that predate the Minnesota model released patients to farm labor as "aftercare," I think we can all agree that that's both self-serving and inhumane. Christian Alcoholics & Addicts in Recovery, for example, was exposed in 2017 for essentially enslaving 200 people with drug convictions at the Chicken Farm. CAAIR was supposed to provide treatment for nonviolent offenders but was essentially a cover for a poultry processing plant. The men there were sentenced to work, and they received no wages. Instead of addiction treatment, they spent hours pulling guts out of frozen chicken carcasses. If the inmates slowed down or complained, they were threatened with prison. According to an article in *Reveal*, CAAIR "was started in 2007 by chicken company executives struggling to find workers. By forming a Christian rehab, they could supply plants with a cheap and captive labor force while helping men overcome their addictions."[16] This is horrific, but it's not uncommon in the criminal justice system. Once you're convicted of a drug-related crime, you can be enslaved, shipped across state lines, and forced to comply in any number of barbaric "treatment" practices. You lose all your rights. This is what the War on Drugs has done to our country. But America is better than this. *We* are better than this.

As long as policy makers are hesitant to decriminalize addiction, this destructive cycle that costs so many people their lives will continue. That's not an exaggeration either: Substance use disorder is a health condition that often requires medical treatment, but people who suffer from it are often denied care. This is a violation of the Eighth Amendment to the US Constitution, which protects Americans from "cruel and unusual punishment." Would you lock up emphysema patients without the oxygen tank they need to "train their lungs" until they could breathe normally? Force an asthmatic person to load heavy crates in a warehouse to "work off" the illness? No. That's monstrous. Yet we do this to people who struggle with addiction. People with substance use disorder are treated like second-class citizens, jailed, and discriminated against. And, as a result, we die in record numbers.

Some communities, like King County in Washington, are forming drug-specific task forces to ensure that people are diverted to treatment programs instead of receiving automatic drug sentences. The Heroin and Prescription Opiate Addiction Task Force "recommends a comprehensive strategy that focuses on prevention, increasing access to treatment on demand, and reducing the number of fatal overdoses."[17] Like the program in Chesterfield Jail, the task force runs an open, safe facility where people who are addicted can access medical, behavioral health, and social services. The "supervised consumption site," another word for a safe injection site, is one of about ninety worldwide where people can use safely under supervision, and find resources when they need help. Places like this have been in operation for over thirty years, and were started largely in response to the AIDS crisis. By focusing on harm reduction and early intervention, a supervised consumption site can significantly impact recovery rates. It's one part of a larger strategy to address the opioid epidemic. The other recommendations include preventing people from developing substance use disorders, identifying and treating people who need help, expanding and enhancing treatment options, and improving the health of drug users by expanding the distribution of naloxone to prevent overdose deaths.

Elsewhere, police officers get substance use–specific training that includes basic First Response for overdoses and teaches officers how to identify and assist someone who is under the influence of substances. People with substance use problems are given the option of going into the drug court system and getting help instead of going to jail. New policies in Seattle, Washington, and Portland, Oregon, ensure that, no matter how many times people are arrested, they'll always have the option of treatment. It's in everyone's best interest to keep offering help: It's less expensive, less of a burden on an already stressed system, and better for families and neighborhoods. Programs like these break the tyrannical three-strikes rules that many court systems use to punish people who simply need help getting into recovery.

Harm reduction and decriminalizing substance use are really touchy subjects. The fear is, if we stop convicting people for drug offenses, our streets will be filled with aggressive, dangerous drug users. People will be shooting up left and right, stealing, and robbing to feed their habits. But that fear is not grounded in reality. It's based in the idea that people with substance use disorder are different from you. If you want to know what a real drug addict looks like, go look in the mirror. People with substance use disorder are, for the most part, totally indistinguishable from everyone else. This isn't *Reefer Madness* or some stupid after-school special. Locking people up only makes things worse—for everybody. It's time to change that by treating people with substance use disorder *like people*. We're not maddened criminals with crazy eyes. We look like you: We work where you work, live where you live. We go to the same coffee shops and gyms and parks and schools. We are *not different from you*. Instead of criminalizing our mental illness, we deserve help.

Recovery, not incarceration. That's justice.

7. DIRTY WORDS
The Way America Talks About Addiction Directly Affects Whether We'll Stay Sick or Recover

. . . you stupid little f****** junkies we need to take all these her-oin addicts and kill them they're all a bunch of garbage junkies worthless garbage

You made your bed, now lie in it. No one forced you to become an addict. We spend too many tax dollars on you all already. "Opioid addicts on their way to recovery." No way, more like opioid addicts fixin to lose all their free handout lifestyles.

You do the crime, you pay the time . . . and if that just so happens to be paying with your life, that's a choice you made. Maybe it's God's way of weeding out the weak . . . ever think of that? Every life cannot be saved. No empathy here for criminals, period.

Please do tell us who put the gun to your head and forced you to stick that needle in your arm. Have you paid back all the money you stole so you could get high? Frankly, the biggest mistake I ever made was calling 911 when my ex-husband overdosed; a funeral would have been easier and cheaper than the hell he put me through.

EVERY DAY, I GET COMMENTS like these on my social media posts. Many of them are abusive. They tell me to go overdose, relapse, die, kill myself. Although I'm proudly living in recovery, all they see is an addict. The vicious, hateful way these strangers feel entitled to talk to me is a reflection of how people who struggle with addiction are treated in our society.

I'm comfortable identifying myself as a heroin addict, because I know that addiction is a mental illness and not a crime. It's not a moral failing, and never was. However, I want to take a moment to talk about identity and recovery and why it's so important to use words that point to our progress and personhood. In life, language is everything. Here's why.

In my years of recovery, I've gotten used to the label "addict." I say it in 12-Step meetings, and I say it when I'm in groups of other people who are also in recovery. *Addict*. See? No big deal.

With that said, the extremely negative connotations of the word "addict" have taught me that we need to be really careful with how we talk about addiction. I say "addict" because it's easy, and most people have a basic understanding of the concept of addiction as an illness. Most people use the word "addiction" to refer to a habit you can't break, right?

I've heard people jokingly refer to themselves as coffee addicts, chocoholics, and *Game of Thrones* junkies. They mean that they've got something in their life that they like so much that they want to do it all the time. They love the thing, whether it's pumpkin spice lattes, Sunday football, or *Farmville*. They can't quit doing it. The important distinction between that kind of "addiction" and substance use disorder is that the former type is an attachment, not an illness. It's not a life-ruining, unbreakable obsession that isolates you from everyone and everything. Friends may think that your crazy love of shoes is a little kooky—but they're not going to judge you for it.

The word "addict" is not a degrading term in itself, but it's not useful because it is conflated with ugly slurs like "junkie," "wino," or "crackhead." We use some of those words indiscriminately in our culture, in a euphemistic or joking way. However, when it comes to describing people like me, who actually have the disease of addiction, those words are harmful. I don't mean in a hurt-my-feelings kind of way, though people often use those words as slurs, to insult and demean me. Identifying people with substance use disorder as "addicts" has a massively negative impact on the way we're treated by the many systems we live in. The word doesn't differentiate whether someone is in the throes of active, symptomatic, drug-seeking compulsive behavior and dreadfully sick or has been in recovery for twenty years, with a rock-solid foundation of health and spiritual fitness. There simply hasn't been any social pushback to stop the one-size-fits-all terminology. The old slang words that we use interchangeably represent a lot of demeaning, detrimental baggage and shame.

The negative banner of addiction—a modern version of the proverbial scarlet letter—affects people's lives, and it all starts with that one word: "addict." Although I've referred to myself using this word throughout this book, I rarely call myself an "addict" when I'm outside my community. The terms I use are "person with substance use disorder" or "person in recovery." Now, I know that those terms don't exactly roll off the tongue. To some people, the difference between an "addict" and a "person in recovery" is so minor that it's not really worth distinguishing. But insisting on using this isn't splitting hairs. Nor is it an attack of political correctness. The language we use to describe people who cope with addiction can have a real, tangible effect on their lives. Do we describe a sick person as an "AIDS victim" or a "person living with HIV"? A person who beats cancer is a "cancer survivor" or "living in remission." There's a big difference. One term describes a powerless, hapless recipient of a death sentence. The other is a person living in hope while managing a chronic condition. Both phrases carry with them different emotions and assumptions. We have carved out positive, redemptive definitions in just about every other chronic disease, because we know doing so gives hope and dignity to the person. So why don't we do this for addiction?

As I said earlier, being an "addict" is actually a crime in our society. It's one of the last designations that still triggers legal, accepted, and celebrated discrimination and bigotry. The disease of addiction is criminalized. Once you've been identified as an "addict," you become the target of social and institutional discrimination. That can happen if a doctor puts your name into a drug database as a drug seeker, which creates an obstacle to medical care. It can happen if you end up with a criminal charge on your record. Even if you're not convicted, that charge can affect everything, from custody of your children, to your car payment, to your ability to find housing or a job. If you've been arrested, every potential employer, landlord, or romantic partner is just a Google search away from seeing your mug shot. And yes, you guessed it: There are mug shot publishing companies that put those pictures online and charge a fee to take the image down. Once again, bad actors profit from the stigma of addiction.

Every night, it seems like there's a news story showing

proud police officers and sheriffs at a podium displaying all the "illicit drugs and contraband" they found in a bust. On the TV series *COPS*, you can watch people get arrested for having small amounts of drugs. The narrative that drug addiction and the "addicts" that drive it are the criminal underbelly of our society is alive and thriving. People with substance use disorder suffer from shame and fear of a bad reputation. Society constantly reinforces that prejudice with the images and words it uses to describe us.

Don't believe me? In 2017, Fayette County, Ohio, implemented a policy that allows police to charge drug users with "inciting panic." A person who overdoses can be slapped with this charge, fined $1,000, and face more than 180 days in jail.[1] What the fuck? That's like reviving someone who's just had a massive coronary, then taking them to jail for "disturbing the peace." It's sick and twisted, and doesn't help the person who overdosed at all. An overdose is a life-threatening situation. We don't imprison someone who has attempted suicide. We offer them help, support, and healthcare. Addiction is treated differently because, well, it's addiction.

Also in Ohio, Middletown city council member Dan Picard suggested not offering Narcan to people who have overdosed more than twice. The city's reported overdose rate increased by 300 percent in 2017, with first responders answering more than 600 overdose calls by the end of June. Picard's solution? Let people die. Seriously. According to *The Washington Post*, "Picard's plan calls for the city to issue a summons to people who overdose on illegal drugs. It would also require them to do community service if convicted. Punishments would double after a second conviction. The proposal also calls for the city to create a database of overdose victims who paramedics have responded to."[2]

I'm going to say it again: *What the fuck?* That's the most backward thing I've ever heard! It openly places a value on human life. Picard is saying we can simply discard and snuff out "these addicts" because their health challenges are undesirable. And Picard rationalizes it because he is totally ignorant about substance use disorder. He characterizes sick people as a drain on the system: criminals, just waiting to get busted. Picard said, "An addict obviously doesn't care much about his own life, but he's expending a lot of resources." Well, so do cancer patients, but we don't leave them to die if chemotherapy fails to make them better. It's expensive to get sick, but no sick person, *regardless of the illness*, should be depicted as a drain on the system.

"Addict" is a filthy, hurtful word. It makes my skin crawl. When I hear it, I feel like a second-class citizen.

Picard, like so many others, doesn't see us as people. Once the A-word is in play, it seems like we stop being human.

That happened when I went back to the recovery center where I got sober to meet with former Congressman David Dreier of California. It was July 2017, and I'd been in recovery for more than two years. The congressman and I had an hour to talk about the cause and how he could get involved with advocacy. I walked into the office where he was waiting, shook his hand, and sat down. We chatted for a few minutes. Then he looked at me and said, "Are you really a heroin addict? You don't look like one. All the addicts I know have track marks on their arms and they're down begging by the Los Angeles River. You look really good; are you OK?"

I was shocked but stayed calm. I said I prefer to identify as a person in recovery. David went on to tell me a story about someone he knew who was in active addiction: He said he'd never met someone who was identifying as "in recovery." By the time our hour was up, David was friendlier and more interested in what I had to share. That's why it's important to show people that we are more than "addicts." David didn't expect *me*; he expected some skinny, strung-out guy with a paper bag. I think my humanity surprised him. It certainly opened his mind.

I can't tell you how many times I've introduced myself to someone new, and the first words out of their mouth are "You're a heroin addict? But you look so normal!"

Uhh, yeah. I *am* normal. I mean, I'm awesome, but I'm also a totally ordinary person. I'm a son, a brother, and a neighbor. A friend. A worker. A voter. There are millions of people just like me—living with substance use disorder—in America today. We may not all look the same, but we all deserve to be treated with respect, equality, and dignity. Not excluded from an uncaring society that would rather let us die on the streets than make policy changes that acknowledge us.

Have these politicians forgotten that we are Americans, too? It sure sounds like it to me. When people like Picard start focusing on "addicts" and making laws that push people who need help to the outer margins, they reinforce the deeply ingrained social idea that people who are struggling with addiction are second-class citizens. Add race, class, and gender to that equation, and you end up with millions of people being denied care for their medical condition because they are not seen as human. Would Picard still use that word if it was his own daughter, or his best friend? It takes someone who's close to you to change the way we are perceived and show who we are.

As you're reading this, you're probably thinking about how wrong I am. You're thinking about how people behave when they're in the active, uncontrolled part of their addiction. They hurt others emotionally, spiritually, and sometimes physically. We all know the archetype of the abusive alcoholic parent or the heroin addict who steals car stereos. We know about the havoc addiction wreaks on families and support circles as it rages. This is real, and when we are in active addiction we hurt those around us, even when they are trying to help us. But these are symptoms of an unfolding pathology. It's not malicious. It's not sociopathic. And most of the time, it's not even a choice. Keep in mind that the active pathology of addiction—an aggravated brain receptor in a state of craving—is essentially a hijacking. How do we know this? Once we separate someone from the substance that is driving their addiction, such as opioids, alcohol, or cocaine, their behavior changes. In general, they are no longer destructive to the loved ones in their lives. They stop being socially disruptive. The hijacking is over.

Every person who has achieved long-term recovery will tell you that one of the essential elements to preventing relapse is to repair relationships, make amends where necessary, and focus on humble, healthy, loving behavior and gratitude toward others. This is explicit in the 12-Step literature; most clinical professionals would agree that it's a pillar of treatment. My point is that the disease of addiction directly drives and causes negative, alienating behavior. Think of it like smallpox for your emotions. Treating the disease brings those emotions and behavior under control and can transform someone completely, from a liability to an asset. Sober, the sick person can once again be a friend, loving family member, husband, wife, daughter, or son. This explanation is *not* an excuse, and it doesn't mean people shouldn't take responsibility for their actions. Everyone who has achieved long-term recovery understands that accountability is theirs. My point is, we are not bad people becoming good but sick people becoming well.

The damage we cause when our disease is in full bloom makes it extremely easy to marginalize, demonize, criminalize, and even subjugate us. This is why normalizing recovery and using respectful terms for people at *all* stages of their substance use is so important.

It turns out that calling someone with addiction an "addict" is bad for them. Really bad. Greg Williams pointed out, "Labeling the sufferers of a disease with a pejorative term defines people in a limited way." It's not just abstract limitation: It affects our lives in a real, tangible sense. For example, people who have been convicted of a drug-related crime, such as possession, may lose their right to vote: Since 1996, sixteen states have enacted reforms of their disenfranchisement laws. But in Kentucky, some 128,000 individuals who have served sentences for drug felony convictions are permanently disqualified from voting. Antidiscrimination laws were passed in 2006, when eligibility for federal financial aid was restored to all students with prior drug convictions, and in 2008 President George W. Bush signed a law requiring health insurance companies to offer addiction treatment coverage benefits that are comparable to the benefits offered for other health conditions. Although most people agree that discrimination against people in recovery is bad, their actions don't match their words. A 2004 survey from Faces & Voices of Recovery showed that 27 percent of adults wouldn't hire someone who was otherwise qualified, if the applicant was in long-term recovery.[3] Yet these same people overwhelmingly believed that it was wrong to exclude someone in recovery from opportunities like employment and housing. How does that make sense? One explanation is that the average person is *extremely* familiar with what active addiction looks like: We see it on television reality shows, at law enforcement press conferences, and in our own families. However, the average person really doesn't know what long-term, healthy recovery looks like. That's *our* fault.

I think a lot of the problem comes from how we have allowed that archetype of the iconic drug addict to flourish. That concept dictates the way we think that people with drug problems look, behave, talk, and feel. Where did we get these ideas? Who's put these images into our heads? I think a lot of it goes back to the "Just Say No" campaigns of the 1980s, which depicted people like me as shadowy, dangerous figures with long, grasping claws. They wore dark rags and gathered under bridges and in parks. That shifty-looking silhouette on the Neighborhood Watch sign? That's what an "addict" looks like. It's crude, but that depiction of substance use disorder appears almost everywhere in the media and popular culture. Heroin addicts all look the same in the movies. Have you noticed? Their skin is translucent to the point of looking pale green. Their eyes are too large. They look like something is draining the life out of them, sucking their blood and replacing it with something milky and toxic.

When people ask me what my addiction was like, I know they're comparing my story to a movie they've seen. The media has glamorized the sordid details of active addiction since the motion picture camera was invented. Propaganda films like *Reefer Madness* only fed the intrigue. There are plenty of films about addiction, from classic dark gritty depictions like *The Panic in Needle Park*, to the stylized amphetamine torture of *Requiem for a Dream*, to the outrageous *Pineapple Express*. I saw my addiction reflected in *Magnolia*. That scene when Julianne Moore melts down in a pharmacy? Yep, that was me. *Fear and Loathing in Las Vegas. Jesus' Son. Ciao, Manhattan. Trainspotting. Pulp Fiction.* I've spent my time inside each of them. I never had to look far to find images of a sick, suffering addict: They were on my television screen, in my living room. Addiction is a popular plot device in literature, as much as murder or amnesia. It works. It's provocative. It's salacious. It touches the viewer and reader in a visceral place and triggers deeply held feelings about addiction. It's an effective device, sure. But it also hurts.

Ironically, I watched a lot of these movies when I was using. Doing so assured me that at least my story wasn't a total anomaly. It wasn't until I got sober that I realized there are almost no people in recovery in the movies.

When there are, they're stupid. As if they are only whole in the presence of the substances that animated them. Genius belongs to the doomed ones, the alcoholics who are about to relapse. Or it's the province of artists like Basquiat, who mix brilliance with eight-balls. Sober people are depicted as boring proselytizers. They're self-righteous, to the point of being comical. Marisa Tomei, in *Crazy Stupid Love*, can't stop talking about her sobriety date. It's clear from her behavior that putting the drink down was the only thing she's got to be proud of—and her sobriety is a joke. Rarely is recovery seen as achievable, desirable, fun, and healthy.

The message is clear: People who turned out like me are a joke.

We're also depicted as unreliable. Alcoholics turn up trying to prove that they've changed, like Hal in *Picnic*. Characters may take a break from weed or psychedelics and find that life without hallucinogens just isn't worth it. Or they calmly puff their lives away, like The Dude in *The Big Lebowski*, who is basically a kahlua-seeking missile. The person who is sober, in the movie, is never the hero. They are always fragile. Their addiction is a plot point. It shows up in the first act, like the gun on the wall, and we know that their reprieve won't last. Sex addiction, alcohol, heroin, whatever. When they slip back into their old habits, it's just part of the story. Inevitable, even.

Those images of addiction, and the prejudices toward people with substance use problems, didn't prepare me for life in recovery at all. I had no idea what I was in for. Was I going to become manically cheerful? Was I going to become some kind of super-Christian do-gooder and stand on a soapbox witnessing to people about the evils of liquor? It didn't seem like there was a lot of middle ground, honestly, and that made me nervous. In 12-Step meetings, I heard other people talk about how they'd changed when they got sober, but I had no idea what that really meant.

Our culture is simultaneously obsessed with addiction and in denial that it even exists. That makes it really hard to find positive, realistic role models—which means it's incredibly important to lift up people in recovery. As more and more of us leave anonymity behind, we are starting to see people living with addiction in the public eye. Celebrities like Alec Baldwin, Robert Downey Jr., Gucci Mane, Daniel Radcliffe, and many others have "come out" as being in recovery. In 2017, when Ben Affleck announced that he'd completed treatment for alcohol addiction, I almost lost it.

In a Facebook post, Ben said: "I have completed treatment for alcohol addiction; something I've dealt with in the past and will continue to confront. I want to live life to the fullest and be the best father I can be. I want my kids to know there is no shame in getting help when you need it, and to be a source of strength for anyone out there who needs help but is afraid to take the first step."

Wow. His statement, which was heartfelt and sincere, sounded totally different from the casual, crass statement he'd made when he went to treatment in 2001. Instead, he sounded serious about recovery and wanting to be the best dad he can be. The mask, it seemed, had come off.

Within a few minutes of Affleck's post, thousands of well-wishers sent messages of support. Many people shared their own experiences of seeking sobriety or how they'd gotten to long-term recovery. Reading their comments, I was overjoyed. By showing his true self and being candid about his recovery, Ben sent a signal to the world: He wasn't going to apologize for who he was. His recovery and his struggles weren't a secret anymore. He was done hiding. His honesty gave permission to many people to stop lurking in the shadows and recover out loud. Also, his willingness to talk about his second attempt at recovery is encouraging. There's a common misconception that people are "only as good as the time between their relapses," and that's just not fair. If people have a relapse, that doesn't diminish the progress they've made or discount their advocacy. It just means that their disease has exhibited symptoms.

A few months after Ben's announcement, Brad Pitt also shared that he was in early recovery. That was another moment that I'll never forget. The first time I saw Brad was on-screen—another movie about drugs and bad choices. Brad played Floyd, a long-haired, couch-surfing stoner in *True Romance*. Surrounded by smoke in every one of his scenes, Floyd was a burnout. He smoked a page of an important letter; he was immune to the threats of the mafia. Along with everyone else in the theater, I laughed when he yelled at his roommate to bring home beer—and cleaning products. It wasn't until years later, when Brad's marijuana use made headlines, that I connected the dots. Maybe it wasn't an act, after all.

"Floyd" became a household name after roles in *Thelma & Louise* and *Legends of the Fall*. Brad tried to shake the "heartthrob" image with serious roles, and ended up netting sixty-one acting awards, including an Oscar and two Emmys. He is still one of the most successful, best-known actors in Hollywood. He's gone from big-screen hottie to low-key dad, but it seemed that, like so many people who struggle with addiction, his drinking and drug use followed him to the top.

During his divorce from actress and producer Angelina Jolie, Brad's drinking and drug use got the full media scrutiny. He was seen at the *Allied* premier looking gaunt. Filing for divorce, Angelina said her choice was "for the health of the family," which may have alluded to Brad's issue with substances. Like everyone else, I saw the tabloid headlines and wondered how much of it was true—and, if any of it was true, how long it had been going on.

When I heard Brad's story, I totally related. What started out as a good thing, like a glass of wine, some recreational marijuana to unwind, quickly turned into an unmanageable, destructive problem. "I just ran it to the ground," he told *GQ*. "I had to step away for a minute. And truthfully I could drink a Russian under the table with his own vodka."

Just like Ben Affleck, Brad Pitt's openness and honesty show the importance of recovering out loud. Addiction and substance use thrive in the dark; by opening up and sharing our stories, we not only help other people by erasing the stigma of addiction, we also help ourselves by living our recovery without shame and by treating it for what it is: part of us and part of our lives. We also give other people the opportunity to relate to us and see what addiction and recovery *really* look like. Celebrities in particular can carry the message that they don't want to be put on a pedestal for their recovery. If they happen to slip, it can help normalize the experience—especially if they're not shamed for relapsing. Highlighting the chronic nature of the illness can help lift the stigma and reinforce the idea that *you don't have to be perfect to deserve recovery.*

"For me this period has really been about looking at my weaknesses and failures and owning my side of the street," Brad said. "For me every misstep has been a step toward epiphany, understanding, some kind of joy. Yeah, the avoidance of pain is a real mistake. It's the real missing out on life. It's those very things that shape us, those very things that offer growth, that make the world a better place, oddly enough, ironically. That make us better."

My hope is that more people will share their stories and raise their voices. Of course, not all of us reveal our status as people in recovery by choice. Sometimes we are thrust into the spotlight, as Laurie Dhue was in 2013.

You'd know Laurie if you saw her. She's a gorgeous, statuesque blonde who was a career news anchor. She's the only person to be a news anchor on all three of the major cable networks: CNN, Fox News, and MSNBC. She was also the youngest full-time anchor in CNN's history. She attended press junkets and interviewed notable celebrities and leaders like President George W. Bush. For fifteen years of her career, however, she was also struggling with substance use disorder. She went to great lengths to hide her addiction, knowing that it would cost her her job. Especially in the media, showing any weakness is a huge risk: Being in the spotlight meant that, if she were outed, Laurie would be torn to shreds by the same reporters she worked side by side with on a daily basis. Although she was never drunk on camera, she told Katie Couric that "what you were getting was a hungover person. I would drag myself into work deeply hung over. I thought I had to drink myself into oblivion several times a week. I suffered in silence. I lived in constant fear. On the inside, I was dying."[4]

Laurie didn't set out to become a face of recovery. She told herself that she didn't *really* have a problem, because she was so successful—and because so many other women she knew drank just like she did. A Gallup poll indicated that two-thirds of women drink regularly and tend to prefer wine.[5] As a TV personality, Laurie was also immersed in a culture that glamorizes and promotes alcohol use: Those images are powerful influencers. She struggled to manage her addiction and, at the same time, wasn't really sure she wanted to stop.

Laurie said that she decided to seek help in 2006, when she found out that her sister was pregnant. She reached out, got into recovery, and decided to maintain her silence about what she was going through. Since addiction was such a taboo subject, she thought she should just keep her head down, move past her substance use, and carry on with her life.

Things didn't work out the way she planned. After over five years in recovery, Laurie gave an off-the-record talk at a private prayer meeting in 2011. She spoke honestly about her journey through alcoholism and sobriety and the role of faith in her recovery. There were no cameras in the room, and she assumed that her recovery story wouldn't go any further than the people who were listening to her speak. She was wrong. One of the reporters at the meeting leaked her story—and all its sordid details—to the mainstream press. Suddenly Laurie was making headlines, whether she wanted to or not.

The next day, Laurie was at President Obama's prayer breakfast when her phone started blowing up with texts and messages. "Laurie Dhue is a recovering alcoholic."

Laurie said, "I thought, *It's over; I'll never work again. I'll be a complete pariah. What TV station is going to want to hire me?* But my agent said, 'You know what, Laurie? I think this could be a very good thing for you.' I realized that he was right."

Instead of panicking, Laurie stayed calm. Her recovery status had been disclosed—the cat was out of the bag. There was no going back. She decided to see the event as an opportunity to share her experience, strength, and hope with the millions of viewers who tuned in to watch her every day. She also set strict boundaries with media outlets that wanted to interview her and hear her story.

"I said I would come on the *Today Show* on the condition that this is a message of hope I'm delivering. I'm not going to tell you how many drinks I had in one night. I'm not going to give you any salacious stories. I'm not going to gossip, but I am going to talk about how alcoholism doesn't discriminate," she said. The show agreed, and after Laurie spoke on air with Meredith Viera in a respectful, supportive interview, she emerged as an advocate for recovery.

Laurie said, "One of the biggest misconceptions in our society is that people don't think of alcoholism as a disease. I think the stigma that still very much exists in our society comes from the fact that people don't really get addiction at its core. It's a dirty little secret; it's a dirty little word. I think so many people in our society still think of addicts as homeless people living under bridges, who are wearing trench coats and clutching a paper bag full of whiskey, and that's just not who we are."

Talking openly about addiction has the power to change the narrative around this disease. Instead of shaming and silencing people with substance use disorder, using ugly slurs to describe people who struggle with addiction, and limiting resources based on the misconception that people "choose" to get addicted, we could change our perspective. We could change our words. And we could change the outcomes for people who have this disease. We could turn a disease that's portrayed as a life sentence into the starting point of someone's recovery story. Instead of focusing on sickness and death, we can highlight the fact that people like us *do recover*, in record numbers, when we have the help and support we need.

Luckily, this kind of change has been accomplished before. Remember the massive social biases against people with AIDS? Nobody wanted to be near someone who was HIV positive. Touching someone who was sick was taboo, because we had this idea that it was a "gay disease" that was a punishment for men who had sex with men. It was treated like a moral failing, just like addiction is today. Getting AIDS was seen as a "choice," just like addiction, because people were choosing to have sex with one another. It sounds so backward when you spell it out, but that's really how society behaved toward people who were sick. Because of the stigma of homosexuality and AIDS, hundreds of thousands of people died. We lost so many artists, musicians, actors, and luminaries to this illness, simply because of the taboo surrounding the disease that killed them.

What changed? People started speaking up. Princess Diana famously visited AIDS hospices and talked with people who were sick. She made sure that the media saw her actually touching, hugging, and interacting with AIDS patients; she tried to show that this illness didn't dehumanize someone. The way we treat them *does*. Later, when Magic Johnson came out as a person living with HIV, he became an advocate for awareness, as well. Our nation has spent billions of dollars to find a cure for AIDS. We have AIDS walks and fun runs, art about AIDS, and special fundraisers. AIDS and HIV are a key part of many schools' sex education and public health programs. People who live with the disease are no longer shunned. The stigma has been shattered.

I think we can do that with addiction, too. Education, policy reform, community support—and yes, changing the way the media portrays people with substance use disorder—are all key to helping solve the drug epidemic. Addiction is the single biggest healthcare issue in America. We can't keep ignoring it or justifying our inaction because "addicts did this to themselves." People don't stop being human just because they get sick! We need to improve the way we treat people with substance use disorder, and that starts with one, small, simple change: the names we choose for people who are affected.

I'm not a junkie. I'm a *person*, and I happen to have the disease of addiction. Now I'm a person in long-term recovery from a substance use disorder. I'm a success, and I know that by sharing my experience, I can give many other people hope for themselves and their families, too. I'm proud of my identity as a person in recovery. It's a lot to be proud of.

Recovery is my new "normal." I'm working to make it America's "normal," too.

That was my goal when I started the Voices Project. It was a simple idea: I'd share a picture of a friend or someone from my community who was celebrating a milestone in recovery. I found that, when we tell people who we are, people's hearts and minds open. I wanted to show people what "addicts" really look like, so I collected these photos and added positive, supportive captions, encouraging others to join in. The posts were incredibly popular, sometimes reaching more than 100,000 people.

What was really inspiring were the comments. Instead of the hateful, "go overdose" messages people lobbed at me, I saw thousands and thousands of positive comments, blessings, and prayers. Instead of identifying the people as "addicts," I depicted them as "living in recovery." It was a small, simple change, and it caught on like wildfire. I see strangers using the same term now. The pictures I posted travel all over social media around the world; the trend has caught on. It's nothing fancy, just a smiling person holding a handwritten sign. I've had people reach out to me about Voices and say, "We didn't know this is what recovery looks like." Well, it is. By changing some simple words, I attracted people who were outsiders, who had questions about the transformation. The Voices Project is helping break down many barriers, and tens of millions of impressions later . . . it's a *thing*.

Simple language changes can open the hearts and minds of people who at one time called us the A-word. Imagery is powerful! And the words you use matter. If you're reading this book, changing the way you identify yourself or talk about people in recovery can change how others see us. Use the right language and be recognized as a face and voice of recovery. You'll realize that we can unite around telling our stories. They have real-life impact. Suddenly, our insurance cards work a little faster. Private prisons close. Public policy helps support treatment instead of pushing us into jails. It's all about progress and building a world where recovery is *inclusive* and *included*. It starts with using the right words and not holding ourselves back.

8. BEYOND THE NEEDLE
Harm Reduction Saves Lives. We Have to Get Over Our Prejudice Against People Who Need Help

Harm reduction (noun). The lessening of risks in an intermittent but not total way. With respect to addiction, this means accepting and encouraging improved intervals and markers in a person's active addiction as they journey toward total recovery.

YOU COULD SAY THAT CHAD SABORA was born to advocate for people with substance use disorder. His father had a career in treatment, trying to help people recover. His mom was on the other side of the fence, in the criminal justice system. Her job was prosecuting people for drug-related offenses. Chad was raised on that stuff, starting at the family dinner table, in the Chicago suburbs. Later, he attended law school, hoping to follow in his mother's footsteps. He experimented with a wide range of substances and started drinking in college: nothing out of the ordinary. He managed to maintain his substance use through his education and found a job as a prosecutor in Chicago, for Cook County.

However, when his parents both died unexpectedly, Chad was sent into a spiral of grief and uncontrollable substance use. Chad used opioid painkillers, which quickly led him to heroin. He was arrested in February 2008, lost his job as a result of the charges, and burned through his entire inheritance. The bottom dropped out of his life. Three years later, he'd tried rehab six times, lost his license to practice law, and was homeless. The disease was eating his life. He finally found recovery at the Gateway Foundation.

When Chad left treatment, he wasn't satisfied with staying sober. His individual recovery wasn't enough. He'd seen all sides of the drug epidemic: legal, medical, criminal, pharmaceutical. He connected the dots and concluded that the only way to stop the dozens of daily, fatal opioid overdoses was to launch an all-out campaign on the drug itself. Instead of blaming the drug user, he thought, it was time to deal with the actual substance.

"It's simple," he explained. "When you drive a car, you wear a seat belt, right? We didn't even have those until the 1960s; they weren't mandatory. People died in car accidents all the time. But we weren't blaming the auto industry for that, were we? It was on the drivers. Harm reduction for heroin is the same thing. It's a seat belt. Obviously, the ultimate form of harm reduction is abstinence, but that's not possible for everyone. We have to get them there and they can only get there if we keep them alive. So the next best thing is syringe access. If you give someone the proper gear, they don't die. They maybe get another chance to get sober down the line."

Chad is sharp, fiery. I met him during the summer of 2016, when I was scouting communities to visit for my Addiction Across America tour. His personal story was compelling, because of his unique perspective on the drug epidemic: Like me, he'd lived it, and like me, he'd lost his career, home, and hope for the future. Also like me, he'd dedicated himself to helping people who were still suffering. Chad drove around handing out naloxone and clean syringes to people, set up temporary safe injection sites around his city, and did whatever he could to help stop overdose deaths. He knew that, if he were caught, he'd be arrested—but the people he *didn't* help might end up dead. So he did what he needed to do. I resonated with his passion for recovery and reform and his emphasis on education instead of punishment for people who were sick.

"With a lot of addicts, you have to start on the left and move to the right," he said. "Recovery is a sliding scale for a lot of people. On the left, you've got harm reduction. That's basically keeping people alive until they're ready to try to get sober. Then you've got medication-based treatment, like methadone, where you give someone meds in order to get them away from their substance of choice, and so on." He pointed out that recovery is the result of an intervention of some kind: It could be a doctor's recommendation, or a drug court judge's, or a family's. Since addiction varies in intensity and degree from person to person, a diverse toolbox is needed to address the illness. Recovery is not a one-size-fits-all thing. There are multiple pathways to recovery.

The number one thing I've learned is that people in recovery aren't included when it comes to making decisions that affect our community. *Period.* I've met a few policy makers who have direct experience with addiction, and thankfully, more people in recovery are taking it on themselves to run for office, push for pro-recovery legislation, and get involved in the process. However, when laws are passed, budgets are approved, and protocols are developed, it tends to happen without the recovery community at the table. But the opioid crisis affects more neighborhoods, families, and communities every day, and we are finally seeing the pushback from that. We're not going to remain quiet while our friends and loved ones lose their lives. I'm part of that movement. My passion for recovery has connected me to some amazing advocates, some of whom you've read about in this book. They've helped educate me to see beyond my own experience, so that I can understand the bigger picture. I've learned that there is a lot of work to be done and that it will take many hands and voices to get our nation to where it needs to be. In my recovery group, we have a saying: "Nothing about us without us." That means, don't make decisions about our community's welfare and worth without us in the room.

It may be self-centered, but every time I hear about an intervention, treatment module, or recovery-related policy, I think, "How would this work for me? How would it have worked for me when I was in active addiction? How does this align with what I've already experienced, or what my friends have gone through?" The more people I talk to, the more I learn about what works for us as a community and what doesn't. My network and the hundreds of stories I hear every day from people coping with addiction have helped me learn more about what's out there. This information doesn't come from the news or other media, from government agencies, or any "authority on recovery." It's all grassroots. We are on our own: We always have been. The stigma of addiction is so strong that nobody wants to touch the issues that surround recovery. Nobody wants to fund our organizations, support our outreach programs, or research our harm reduction strategies. As a result, we are left to fend for ourselves, and no one outside the recovery community seems to object. You can see where that's gotten us.

The lack of funding is directly linked to the shame surrounding addiction. Leaders don't want to support any efforts that might be seen as "enabling the addict" or making it easier for people to use illicit drugs. The "Moral Majority boogeyman" scares elected officials into thinking they will be seen as soft on crime or supportive of drug use if they show compassion or take an epidemiologic approach to dealing with addiction. Especially when it comes to harm reduction, the needed help simply isn't there. That's crazy to me, because the people who need those harm reduction strategies, like syringe exchange or safe injection sites, are an extremely vulnerable population. It's like we're saying to them "We'll help you once you help yourself. We'll help you get better once you can show that your disease is already in remission and under control." We want people to get better but expect them to do it without any help. Or we expect them to do it *our way*. We know what works to get someone into recovery, but we don't fund those pathways or provide that support. We want recovery but can't bring ourselves to address the shame of addiction. Our actions as a society and our words don't match. And as a result, people are dying.

I know that long-term, lasting progress doesn't happen just because of experiential evidence. Our nation's reluctant, slow response to the drug epidemic is proof of that. We are building a critical mass of experience, stories, and people raising their voices. We need millions of people to speak up, but we also need more than that. There's been some research about recovery, but almost everything that's out there focuses on the acute stages of addiction or the crisis phase within the first year: very early recovery. There really isn't a focus beyond what is perceived as the emergency phase. Most of the research I've seen is highly specialized, specific data that only talks about a small part of our population, or it's outdated by the time it's released. I'm troubled by how many studies about addiction are funded by pharmaceutical companies or treatment centers—can you say *conflict of interest*?

To solve this conflict, we need people in recovery at the table to help represent our needs and the needs of their individual communities, as well. Otherwise, we're relying on inaccurate, incomplete information. Representing what's *actually* happening in different communities is how we share our message and ask for help.

Devin Reaves, a well-known recovery advocate on the East Coast, says that diversity at the policy table is key to beating the drug epidemic. He told me about a task force meeting in Philadelphia that he attended. He was one of the only people of color there.

"The task force meeting was a big deal," he said. "Everyone who mattered was there: the fire department, the criminal justice people from the prison, a bunch of behavioral health specialists. These were high-falutin' people, and I'm just a baby in those fields, so I wasn't planning to say much. However, when it was time to get up to the podium, I was shocked by how elementary their suggestions were for how we're going to address the crisis. It was the kind of thing that a couple of my friends and I might come up with if we stayed up late drinking Red Bull. Helpful, sure, but not sophisticated in any way. I realized that it was because they were coming at it from a research perspective, and the research, without lived experience, tells you *nothing* about how to solve the problem of addiction."

When it was his turn at the microphone, Devin had planned to just introduce himself as a person in recovery and leave it at that. Instead, he knew he had to speak up. The other people sharing their opinions about addiction knew about it only from limited data or TV shows, like *The Wire*. That wasn't going to cut it. When he got to the mic, he introduced himself and also put forward a couple of ideas for the task force. "I said that first, we have to address the inherent racism of criminalizing drug use, which has a disproportionate effect on people of color, especially in urban centers. That raised a few eyebrows. And then I said that we should strongly consider safe injection sites. It's the best method of intervention there is, it reduces overdoses by 30 percent, and has been used in other countries with good results."

To his surprise, the other people in the room started nodding. Progress was happening.

Devin is used to being the only person of color: Recovery leadership, he says, is overwhelmingly white, educated, middle class, and white collar. In other words, privileged. "Any time I go into one of these meetings, I think, where are the black people? What we need is a real grassroots movement, where there's real diversity at the table. You see recovery community organizations with diversity, but that's just in the community, not higher up the chain. It seems like, as soon as there's grant money involved, that diversity disappears."

He's right. While I'm grateful that I have the platform I do, I know that part of it is because I'm a white guy who wears Warby Parker glasses. People who are in positions of leadership must talk about diversity and make room for others who aren't necessarily from privileged groups.

Inclusiveness is key to saving lives: inclusion of many kinds of people, from diverse backgrounds, and using different approaches to recovery. Especially as the opioid crisis increasingly affects suburban families, Devin says, it's easy for already-marginalized groups, such as African Americans or the LGBTQ community, to fall through the cracks. He knows that raising his voice and sharing his unique experience is critical to making sure the recovery movement doesn't leave others behind. Recovery-related reform that serves the needs of people who are already supported by the system we live in is not enough. The crack epidemic of the 1980s, he said, could easily happen again: But this time, the victims could be white. "The fact is, this opioid epidemic is about kids from the suburbs dying. Their parents are the ones flexing their political power, and that's why this is finally a visible issue. The people who get their names on bills and get meetings with senators are people of influence and people of means. Where does that leave someone who doesn't have that access?"

Speaking up worked at that task force meeting. It was a turning point. Instead of using time-tested but largely ineffective or outdated methods, the group agreed that harm reduction was needed to save lives in Philadelphia. Yet some members also expressed strong prejudice toward the actual methods of harm reduction.

"That kind of thinking kills people," Devin said. "Let's give these people a safe place to go. The safe injection site actually *fixed* the problem, because people won't die if they use in a safe place. You know how many people have died in safe injection sites? Zero. Worldwide, the number is *zero*. We know this method works; we just don't want to do it."

Meeting people where they are is crucial to preventing overdose deaths. However, the shame of addiction is fierce, even within the recovery community. Some people discriminate against others because they use methadone or other medical interventions to stay away from heroin. To many, the only acceptable or "real" path to recovery is total abstinence, which simply doesn't work for everyone. "Just Quit" is about as effective as "Just Say No," especially for someone who's experiencing advanced addiction. Opioids are particularly difficult to stop using overnight: In fact, suddenly stopping certain substances, particularly alcohol and Xanax, can trigger a heart attack, seizures, and other severe physical reactions. Medically supervised detox is necessary and standard. So why wouldn't we accept the use of these medications and interventions earlier in the process, when someone is in active use but might want to stop altogether?

The idea that all addictions are created equal and that all recovery is the same is a deadly myth. Many people enter treatment or a 12-Step program and are explicitly told, "This is the only way to recover." Nothing could be further from the truth. Listening to other people's experiences proves that there are many ways to get to recovery. Some work better than others. Some are more accessible. But at the end of the day, there's no wrong way to get sober, and there's no wrong way to stay sober. There is improvement as determined by the person's needs and goals. Yet it is easy to forget this. Recovery is associated with the idea of total abstinence, but that's not accurate. Also, not everybody reaches total abstinence at the same rate: One person may exit a five-day detox center and be OK, and another one may need a year of Vivitrol shots to control their opioid cravings. Both may find recovery. Does it matter if a cancer patient had chemo or radiation or surgery? No, it only matters that the person is in remission after twelve months.

Preaching abstinence as a superior form of recovery buys

into the idea that addiction is a moral failing. It says that one kind of recovery is better or more pure than another one. That attitude can be extremely harmful because it reinforces the shame of addiction—and makes it less likely that someone will ask for help. It's a diet mentality, an all-or-nothing, black-and-white kind of thinking, and it excludes people who desperately need support. The recovery community is largely to blame for this, as the loudest and proudest tend to be those on the abstinence-only moral high ground.

"We live in a puritanical society," said Brooke Feldman, a recovery advocate in Philadelphia, where she's earning her master's in social work. Although she says she initially shared a lot of the prejudices people have toward harm reduction, through education she's embraced the idea that people find wellness in many different ways.

"The fact is that alcohol kills two times as many people a day as illicit drugs, but we don't talk about that because alcohol isn't an illegal substance. The same is true for tobacco. So much of the stigma around addiction, and the barriers to harm reduction, comes from who decides what's illegal or not," Brooke said.

She falls back on the simple adage that *dead people don't recover*. For many, recovery is a much more complex issue than just putting down the drug or drink.

"First of all, substance use, substance misuse, and substance use disorder are all different things. We don't really talk about that. Each issue can be a response to psychological issues; we're seeing a strong, strong correlation between childhood trauma and substance problems later in adult life. Many people who are addicted have endured intense pain in their lives, from those negative childhood experiences to social, mental, and economic stress," Brooke said. She pointed out that part of harm reduction is treating the *whole person* so that they have a better chance at reaching recovery.

Acknowledging that not everyone experiences the same barriers to recovery is important: That was definitely true for me. I mean, the fact is that not everyone can afford treatment. Not everyone has insurance. Not everyone who needs recovery has a place to call home, a supportive community, or a family they can count on. Some people have other issues, like posttraumatic stress disorder or another mental illness, that needs to be addressed before they can try to deal with their substance use. All types of people have a place in recovery, because recovery is for everyone. We all start in different places, which means that, instead of expecting sick people to conform to our treatment standards, we need to lower the barrier to entry so that *everyone can get help*. Research shows that, big surprise, it's almost impossible to get sober while you're homeless or in a mental health crisis—yet that's the expectation we put on people. The Alcoholics Anonymous book has a line in it that I like: "We are like men who have lost their legs: we never grow new ones." If recovery is a moving train, we can't leave behind the sickest people, who aren't able to run and catch up. We stop the train, so everyone can get on board. It's that simple.

A safe injection site, or comprehensive user engagement site (CUES), is one place where people can access recovery support services. In many ways, this form of harm reduction is common sense: Every advocate I talked to repeated the same message about keeping people alive long enough to recover. Devin said, "Bottom line, the dope we were shooting in 2010 isn't the same as it is in 2017. Fentanyl has been a complete game-changer for people in active addiction. The people selling drugs to you or using drugs next to you aren't worried about your safety."

CUES are a completely safe approach to drug use, which, ironically, is where the controversy is. Many people seem to think that offering clean syringes or HIV tests somehow enables drug use or encourages people to continue using. Where is that idea coming from? It's another boogeyman, calling up images of nineteenth-century opium dens in British-occupied China or gritty scenes from the 1971 movie *The Panic in Needle Park*. We are afraid of realities that simply don't exist anymore, if they ever did.

CUES are a new concept in the United States. Although some activists have handled syringe exchanges from their cars or set up mobile safe injection sites, none of those is legal. In fact, helping someone use heroin or other drugs more safely is illegal. That's right. In certain states, anyone who takes it upon themselves to hand over a clean syringe can be arrested. Yet we don't lock up family doctors who willfully and irresponsibly prescribe addictive pain medication. We don't charge sober living home managers with negligence when one of the people in their care dies. Harm reduction is where the double standard of recovery is painfully apparent. And it kills people. In 2017, one of these people was my friend Tyler.

I'd been sponsoring Tyler, helping him with his recovery program. He was staying in a sober living house in Pasadena, was going to meetings, checking all the boxes. Then, one day, I got a phone call that he had overdosed in his home— he was dead. *Another one.* I'd gotten so many calls just like it that year, but let me tell you, it never gets easier. Tyler was young and held such promise. He was like so many other people whose lives are destroyed by addiction and a system that refuses to understand that *this is an illness, not a moral failing.*

I was angry. Furious! I called the sober living home and demanded to know what had happened. They tried to put me off—but if you know me, you know that was about as effective as trying to put out a forest fire with a wet washcloth. I was mad, and I wanted answers. Finally I got a hold of one of the managers.

"What do you mean, he overdosed?" I said.

"He overdosed," she said.

"That's what I just said! How did he overdose?"

"He came home high and I told him to sleep it off on the couch. When I went to check on him a few hours later, he was turning blue."

"Don't you have naloxone on-site?"

They didn't have naloxone, she told me.

The simplest, most elementary part of harm reduction—a nasal spray or shot that reverses the effect of opioids—wasn't available in a *house full of people coping with their addiction to opioid drugs.* This is a place that charges residents more than $1,500 rent a month, out of pocket. It's like running a home for people with diabetes but refusing to keep insulin on hand. It was the most backward thing ever. And these people were supposed to be *professionals.* They were in recovery themselves!

The argument goes that the mere *presence* of naloxone encourages drug use: that people will use heroin indiscriminately, just because the risk of dying is no longer there. If someone can get high and know that, if they overdose, they'll be magically saved by naloxone, why stop? Unbelievable. It's like saying putting seat belts in cars makes people *want* to drive into walls!

It makes *no sense*. Accidents happen, people get hurt. That doesn't mean they deserve to die, though. Tyler's death was preventable.

Every single public place you go in this country, from airports to libraries, has an automatic defibrillator machine in case someone has a heart attack. Every EMT carries an Epipen for the tiny percentage of people allergic to bee stings. We're always ready for a crisis—as long as it's not an overdose. Can you imagine denying funding for defibrillators because "having them around will just encourage people to eat more junk food"? It's the same logic as not keeping naloxone in a sober living house.

I posted on social media about Tyler's death—how it was preventable, and how the sober living home had put his life at risk by not having an anti-overdose drug on hand. Chad saw my post and called me. I described what had happened, how frustrated I was. He listened and then told me that he was buying a plane ticket and he'd be in Pasadena in a couple of days. We were going to do a naloxone training with every sober living house in my area. Overdose should *not* be a risk someone takes when they choose to go to a sober living house. I agreed and made a few phone calls. By the time Chad arrived, we had appointments with a half dozen homes, a case of naloxone kits, and a mission.

We demonstrated how to use naloxone at every one of the sober living places. Yet we only did these trainings with sober living staff. Only *one* of the homes let Chad and me talk to the residents about naloxone and show them how to administer the medication to save someone's life. *Only one.* When I asked why, their reasoning was the same: having naloxone on hand "encouraged drug use."

I was disgusted. Anyone who works closely with people who are coping with addiction knows that *people who have substance use disorder cannot stop using on their own, even when they know they will die.* We don't get sober just because someone holds a gun to our heads. Having a life-saving medication on hand isn't "enabling." It's like having a lifeboat on a ship or a parachute on a plane. It's like these people are saying to the ship's passengers "If you need a lifeboat, it means you don't trust the captain." Well, look how that worked out with the *Titanic.*

Obviously, even the recovery community isn't immune to our culture's ignorance and fear around addiction. The misinformation seems to be strongest when it comes to harm reduction, especially safe injection sites. When I asked Brooke to describe a CUES, she laughed. No, really, I said: Is it an opium den? Red light bulbs and bean bag chairs? What does a safe injection site really look like?

Brooke laughed. "It's not exactly a dope shooting asylum," she said. I'd seen pictures of some proposed designs for safe injection sites in the United States, and, frankly, they looked clinical. Like some sort of nightmare dentist's office, all stainless steel desks, tiled walls, and a drain in the middle of each concrete floor. Bright, industrial lights that shone into every corner, no soft chairs, and efficient, assembly-line service. Those pictures didn't look welcoming or friendly. They looked like the people who were designing the space were terrified that a heroin user might feel too comfortable. The message they sent was that the only way to stop people from using was to make them as uncomfortable as possible.

Frankly, I'd rather shoot dope next to the Dumpster behind a strip club than go into a place like *that*. Why? Because it's dehumanizing. It's ugly, and it reinforces the idea that addiction is an unclean, immoral behavior—not a disease. For comparison, think about the reception area and treatment rooms in a cancer ward. Ever been to one of those? They're really nice. There's soft music playing. The waiting area has magazines that offer a positive message about life after cancer, pretty watercolor paintings on the walls, cozy chairs to sit on while you're waiting for your doctor, and friendly, smiling medical aides. Some clinics offer private areas, where you can wait without being seen if you feel self-conscious about the way cancer has affected your body. There are special rooms where you can try on different wigs if you've lost your hair. Social workers are permanently assigned to cancer clinics, so you always have someone to talk to about how cancer is affecting your life, job, and family. We expect this type of welcoming environment for patients of one chronic illness; it's a marked contrast to the medieval-looking designs we use for patients of another. I mean, a friendly, warm clinic doesn't automatically cure you; that's what treatment is for. But offering help in a positive, nonshaming environment definitely influences whether people come through the door to ask for support and whether they stay long enough to get better. It works because it acknowledges sick people's humanity and gives them their dignity while they recover.

"Safe injection sites should be places where people want to come," Brooke said. "They should have those inspiring posters on the wall and offer a comfortable place for people who need help. The fact is that people *can* get help while they're using. So a CUES isn't just a place where someone can use safely. It also needs to have access to resources and mental health and substance use treatment. Peer support services show a lot of success, too, where people with lived experience who have been through it go with newer people to support them while they recover. It can be as simple as going to the welfare office with someone, or sitting with them in court. Peer support is a powerful lever in recovery, and a safe injection site is one place where we could provide that connection."

Brooke described the ideal safe injection site as being similar to any community center, with areas for people and their families to relax, spend time together, and get compassionate help to improve their lives. Two of the first safe injection sites in North America are in Vancouver, British Columbia. One opened in 2003 and the other in July 2017. Each facility looks like a low-income clinic, a no-nonsense, sterilized place where people get in, use, and get out. It's a far cry from the welcoming space Brooke described. However, each clinic serves thousands of people every year—the need for help is that significant. I wonder how many more people would gravitate toward a site with a more welcoming atmosphere. The fact is, concerns about aesthetic choices are probably a long way off for many communities. Although many cities have voted in favor of basic harm reduction like syringe exchange programs, limited funding—that is, the willingness to fund recovery services—inhibits what actually is provided.

Daniel Raymond, who's the deputy director of planning and policy for the Harm Reduction Coalition, said that some help is good, but the need is much greater than the services being offered.

"Harm reduction is often pushed aside in favor of other interventions when it comes to funding. Without the community getting involved in policy, it's easy to say 'Let's fund prevention' or 'Let's fund treatment.' There's a lot of focus on improving what we have, and that can really leave people behind who need these other harm reduction strategies. Treatment isn't a magic wand that you wave and make the problem go away. That's a dangerous idea."

Recovery isn't just a single, straight path. It's a puzzle of interlocking pieces. We tend to think of it as one holistic thing, but it's not. If you break down someone's recovery plan, it will probably include aspects of mental health, physical health, housing, peer support, community, employment, and some kind of harm reduction. Some people need to include those things in their plan for the duration of their recovery; some people need them only during certain phases. Recovery is not a zero-sum game, and treating it that way pushes out people with different needs. Instead of ditching a pathway to recovery because it's stigmatized, we should be asking "What do we do to get someone where they need to go?" Put another way, how do we change our standards to be more inclusive and less judgmental, instead of excluding people who don't meet the standards we have?

Making these changes means addressing the NIMBY (not in my backyard) mind-set many people have when it comes to addiction. Once again, we think we want to help people with substance use disorder—we just don't want "them" in our neighborhoods, on our streets, or where we can see them. We want people to recover, but without sober living homes, syringe exchanges, methadone clinics, community programs, shelters, or treatment centers. We want recovery to be integrated—just as we want addiction to be. Anyone who is visibly struggling, sober or not, is ostracized. And frankly, the realities of symptomatic addiction make people extremely uncomfortable. Well, get over it. People are dying!

Daniel said that part of the problem is the idea that, at some point, addiction will go away if we ignore it. He told me a story about a harm reduction outreach effort he'd taken into northern Kentucky. Meeting with the community there and some local partners, he found that the area had been overwhelmed by the opioid crisis. There had been a sharp rise in overdoses, and heroin use was rampant, which made the town a good candidate for a syringe exchange program. In addition to preventing infectious diseases like hepatitis C and HIV, the exchange was also an opportunity to intervene and potentially steer a person toward recovery.

Syringe exchanges are more common in liberal, blue-state, urban areas. San Francisco and New York City have some of the older programs in the United States. This town in northern Kentucky was conservative, suburban, and very new to the drug epidemic. The influx of heroin had wreaked as much havoc on the town's infrastructure as a natural disaster.

"They experienced addiction as though it was a flood," Daniel said. "As I talked with them, I could see that one of the major blocks to getting a good harm reduction program in place was the idea that there might be a light at the end of the tunnel. They thought the flood's waters would eventually recede. They'd never contended with something like this, so they didn't understand harm reduction. The fact is, in a situation like this, you don't go back to 'the good old days.' There's no going back. You have to adapt, but we have such strongly held ideas about addiction that any move forward is seen as capitulation."

American drug policy is astonishingly inflexible on the

issue of harm reduction. Even though the death toll from drug overdoses continues to rise *exponentially*, the needed policy change is very slow to come.

There are two simple things that we can do to greatly increase more people's chances of survival and recovery. First, recovery must be a priority in every single health plan. It might sound crazy, but many of the policies we're working with now say *nothing* about recovery. They focus on the stigma of addiction or the effects of substance use on American communities, but where's the recovery plan? If recovery is not on the table, neither is harm reduction. In spaces where advocates work with policy makers, we've got to start talking about harm reduction as a permanent, viable, and valuable tool for saving lives. We need to advocate for harm reduction as loudly as we're calling for other recovery-related reforms. It doesn't belong under the umbrella of prevention or treatment. Harm reduction must be treated as a cornerstone of our solution. Currently, the federal government's Substance Abuse and Mental Health Services Administration allocates *no funding* for harm reduction; that's got to change.

We also need to fund these programs in a realistic way that reflects the immense amount of need they support. For example, in that same part of Kentucky, thirty other counties have adopted some kind of harm reduction measures. That sounds good, but when you look at it up close, you see that the programs barely scratch the surface of what is needed. It's not lack of compassion; it's lack of money. One syringe exchange program is available only one day per week, from noon to two p.m.: *two hours per week*. Addiction is a twenty-four-hour illness. It doesn't take a day off. Solutions must be available whenever and wherever the problem is. Finally, more conservative states are waking up and enacting programs that allow exchanges and other interventions, but we need to look beyond the needle.

A harm reduction program is a place where people can seek help without judgment, scolding, or stigmatization. For many people, especially those who have already tried treatment a number of times, it's a place where they can go and receive support. I'll be super clear: Syringe exchanges do *not* enable drug use. They're places where people who are motivated to take care of themselves and their health go, just like clinics. What if we treated harm reduction as a necessity, like Planned Parenthood? If every community in America had access to substance use disorder screening and early intervention services in a neutral, compassionate setting, I bet we'd have a lot fewer people in need and a lot more healthy Americans contributing to our nation. Instead of interacting with people affected by addiction in only three places—jail, the ER, and the morgue—we could bridge the gap and offer life-saving outreach.

Harm reduction programs can accelerate someone's escape from addiction. They are opportunities to show people—daily, in some cases—that there's a way out. They provide a connection to recovery that simply doesn't exist when someone is using alone or with people who aren't interested in getting better. Syringe exchange is perceived as a waste, because "people are going to inject no matter what," but that's patently untrue. I'm living proof that it's possible to recover from being an IV heroin user. I got hepatitis C because I didn't have access to clean syringes. Now I'm years into my recovery and past addiction, but I'm still dealing with the effects of hepatitis. So are many of my friends. My story would be completely different if I'd had a way to use safely—if I hadn't had to struggle through this on my own.

Reducing drug use, containing people who are in active addiction, and helping the people who need support are all ways to help someone get away from heroin. But saying "You'll use no matter what" flies in the face of people like me, who have lost friends and loved ones to this illness. We don't use "no matter what." Actually, I'd say that we recover against incredible odds. I'd say that we should make that chance available to more people, through more compassionate, accessible programs.

We have to change our thinking, or die.

9. ACROSS AMERICA
My Road Trip Through America's Drug Epidemic Changed Me Forever

I DON'T REMEMBER WHAT INSPIRED ME to travel across America the month before the 2016 Democratic National Convention. I'd been elected as delegate, and suddenly, it seemed like the sky was my limit. The idea of a cross-country road trip just popped into my head, and the next thing I knew, I was calling Greg Williams.

"Greg, I thought of something," I said.

He always encouraged me, and he listened to me while I told him my plan.

The idea was simple: My best friend Garrett and I would rent a motor home and drive for thirty days across twenty-two states, visiting people in communities hit hardest by the addiction crisis. We'd get their stories, listen to how they were coping, and share it in a series of videos online. We wanted people to experience what the epidemic was *really* like, up close and personal: We wanted to take them to the front lines with us. Most important, we wanted to share how much hope and power we saw in everyday people.

Greg thought it could work, so Garrett and I started collecting donations—just from our friends, community, and supporters. Facing Addiction was immensely helpful in getting us on the road, too. We were lucky to have a small team, a group of guys in recovery who joined us for the month as our film crew. Garrett and I read hundreds of Facebook posts and messaged with people we'd never met before, who offered to speak with us on our tour. I have to be honest: We didn't have a plan. We just had a vision of what we wanted the end product to be—and that was even less defined. We wanted to show the world those stories. So we just took the leap, and the net appeared to catch us. The AddictionX-America project was something that *happened*, as if by magic. That's how things work in our movement. We're inspired, we reach out for support in our community, and amazing things transpire that help others and change lives.

By the time we loaded our stuff into the motor home, we had a plan and plenty of people to meet. However, we had no idea what we were really in for. We had no time to think about what we were getting into or what the trip would mean for us or the hundreds of people we met that month. As usual, we just figured it out as we went along.

Anyone who knows me knows that I love my country. Like, *really* love it. My entire apartment is red, white, and blue. My favorite holiday is the Fourth of July. I love the American flag, the anthem, parades, and fireworks. I love our nation and everything she stands for. I love democracy. I love voting. I watch political races like some people watch the Super Bowl. But my trip gave me a deeper understanding of my country, and the many people who are affected by the political changes I tracked. Once I got into that motor home, I started a journey deep into America's heartland that showed me the incredible strength and grit that makes our nation great. I got to meet people from all walks of life. I met parents who had lost their children to overdoses; people who had been incarcerated for drug-related convictions; leaders who were organizing their communities; people in long-term recovery who were breaking their silence to show what life is like beyond addiction. I met people from all different backgrounds. They all had one thing in common: They were ordinary people doing extraordinary things to fight back against the crisis.

As the trip unfolded, I started to understand how little we actually knew about the drug epidemic. These stories weren't being shared. These people had no voice, beyond their own small reach. When it came to political representation, government support, media attention, or even basics like funding for grassroots efforts—they had nothing.

Garrett and I compiled our interviews into seven videos, which we shared on YouTube, Facebook, and other social media. They reached millions of viewers. It was clear to me that people were desperate for information about this massive issue that was affecting them and their lives daily and that finding a way to lift up their voices would be a game-changer as the recovery movement unfolded. Although my original goal was to show people what addiction really looked like, I learned a lot, too. Some of the most enlightened recovery-related policy I saw was in red states and counties—places I'd been taught were "backward." I learned that *conservative* doesn't always mean *close-minded*. Likewise, I listened to people in so-called progressive states describe some of the crazy stuff they experienced and how addiction was stigmatized, criminalized, and punished. When it comes to recovery, I learned, actions speak a lot louder than the political party on your bumper sticker.

I learned another hard truth: A person's geography often determines their solutions. Not every resource or recovery tool is available to every person, no matter where they live or what their socioeconomic background is. They are just not. It's an uneven patchwork, with some solutions in some areas and random dispersion that makes no sense at all. It's like someone took all the knowledge that we use to explain economic and demographic trends in healthcare and major social issues and threw it out the window. Basic commonsense principles don't apply to addiction treatment and trends. Improving access by actually bringing recovery to people who need it would make a colossal difference for people who are struggling with addiction. Yet access is an elusive moving target for reasons that are so profoundly complex I was truly overwhelmed. How many lives would be saved if we had folks doing naloxone training door to door and offering free anti-overdose kits? How many families would benefit from community groups designed to support people in crisis? How many parents would be able to commit to a program of recovery that included doctor's visits, counseling, and medication if they had low or no-cost, safe child care for their kids? But no unified national approach exists that would make this actually happen.

We need to think about ways to bring recovery *toward* the people who need it instead of locking it away into treatment centers and expensive facilities that aren't accessible to everyone. Sometimes just the message that *we do recover* is enough to get someone started on the right road. We need to ensure that every person who is ready to try making a difference in his or her life also has the necessary tools and support to continue on the journey. We also need to teach community members the roles they need to play in combating the crisis and then hold them accountable for actually doing their part.

The number one issue? Financial support such as block grants and other outside funding. We need what I call the "pink" money: the enormous amount of personal, state, and corporate philanthropy that has been thrown at breast cancer awareness and prevention over the last twenty-five years. That money resulted in real change, real research, and real lives saved. It popularized an important cultural movement to support breast cancer advocacy organizations. Every October is pink, pink, pink! Offices have 5K "Save the Ta-Tas" runs. TV stations hold pledge drives. Brands release pink soda flavors. NFL players wear pink uniforms. This is normal, *and* it is productive. Imagine if we had a "pink revolution" for addiction.

So many of the amazing organizations I was able to meet with are run on a shoestring budget or on donations and get very little support. Yet the solutions they're offering are more effective and innovative than anything that's come from the federal level. It's clear to me that we need to look to Main Street for leadership, not Pennsylvania Avenue. There are real solutions at the community level. There are individuals and groups out on the front lines who have been doing this work for *decades*—since before I was born! They know what they're up against, and they can tell us more about what is needed than someone sitting in an ivory tower on a pile of research and data. Lived experience and firsthand knowledge of addiction is *priceless* in combating the epidemic—so we need to go where the problem is, find out what's working, and share it widely and freely.

Eight thousand miles later—at the average speed of forty-five miles per hour—Garrett and I had circled the country and arrived back home. The trip had completely changed my perception of the crisis, which is saying a lot, because I was definitely living in the middle of it. I realized that my experience was part of a movement. I wasn't alone. I was one of thousands of Americans who were fighting the epidemic in their own living rooms and backyards. Their courage gave me immense hope. At the trip's focal point, the Democratic National Convention, I joined the other delegates. For me, it was a dream come true: I was participating in the democracy I loved, surrounded by people who were passionate about making positive change for our nation. What could be better?

When I got home to California, the light bulb over my head just burned brighter and brighter. I didn't want to let go of the trip. Not yet. I was so inspired that I never wanted to stop. The end of the trip was just the beginning for me. Since then, I continue to travel, meet everyday heroes, and learn more about the incredible work they're doing. When I talk with people about the crisis, one of the first questions they ask me is "What can I do?" God, that gives me so much hope. One person, *just one*, can change the lives of hundreds, thousands of suffering people. One hand. One friend. One phone call. One cup of coffee. One minute. We have so much power and so much potential to help one another. Our community reminds me that, no matter how overwhelming and hopeless the epidemic can seem, good people are out there, working and helping each other, every single day. Here are some of their names.

PREVENTION

Preventing drug use doesn't start with "Just Say No." It begins when we start educating young people about addiction. Anthony Alvarado, who started the youth education group Rise Together, says that having compassionate conversations with students about coping with drugs, alcohol, bullying, mental health issues, and suicide opens the doorway to healing. Instead of telling young people what they should care about, he said, it's more important to ask them what matters in their lives.

Anthony said, "When I was young, I thought I would grow up and change the world. Along the way, I lost that hope in addiction. I know that my life changed in the moment when I was in need but not afraid of judgment and able to ask for support. If I'd had that earlier, my outcome would be different. I might not have suffered as long as I did. So what we're doing is teaching young people to ask for help, and how to be there to support somebody else. That's the number one thing they want to learn, when we go to speak at schools: how to help each other."

The drug epidemic disproportionately affects teenagers and young people, so prevention is incredibly important. People tend to start using illicit drugs before they turn eighteen, and 50 percent of young people continue using substances after their first time.[1] In a culture where illicit drug use is acceptable, normalized, and even encouraged, it can be very hard to just say no. For many young people, one of the hardest things to do is ask for help—Anthony says that's why peer-led support and mentoring relationships are so important in prevention.

"We can change the culture," he said. "We have thousands of testimonies from young people who all say the same thing: They want somewhere to go and they want to learn how to help someone who's struggling. So what we're doing is trying to teach young people how to live. Rise Together offers six direct service programs, where we teach things like coping skills, life skills. The messages and language we use are incredibly important, so we work on that, too. What we want to do is create a situation where they don't take those challenges on by themselves."

Instead of treating young people like they can't learn or are apathetic about addiction, we need to include them. Through reaching out, sharing lived experience, and helping build community, we can create a space where people feel safe and inspired. For many teenagers, isolation and sense of being disconnected from people who care can be lethal. That silence leads to death, in addiction or suicide. Yet we can start saving lives by offering young people positive, supportive messaging and resources at an early age. We can show young people that there is a happy ending for those who struggle with addiction and a productive life in recovery. They can use the tools they learn early on throughout their entire lives.

INTERVENTION

Let's not forget that fifty or sixty years ago, frontal lobotomy was an acceptable method of treating addiction. We're still challenging old, deeply held beliefs about substance use disorder. Some of those ideas actually are promoted by groups that are trying to support families and people affected by the disease. For example, it's a commonly held belief that the sick people have to hit bottom before they get help. For many people, the "bottom" is death. So, what does that really mean? Parents are given the message that they have to watch their son or daughter suffer and struggle, and if they help in any way, they're "hurting" their child. That's just not true. The fact is, it's possible to intervene even when the person *doesn't* want help and hasn't hit bottom yet. Instead of standing by or worrying that we're enabling a loved one's addiction, we can take control of the situation and help break the cycle.

Brad Lamm, an interventionist, says that almost everything we think we know about interventions is wrong. By the time most families are ready to say something, they're worn out, stressed, and scared. They think they'll have to threaten their loved one in order to get him or her to change.

"A lot of families go in with these bullshit bottom lines," Brad said. "But they've used those threats before, and they didn't work. The fact is that the intervention isn't going to make someone better. If talking by itself was going to fix the problem, it would have already. Instead of trapping the person, what I do is *invite* the person to their own intervention."

By identifying which voices are the most important in the person's life—for example, their parents, coworkers, friends, siblings, and partner—Brad helps organize a family meeting. He calls this powerful, influential group the intervention team and draws a family map or *genogram*. There's no letter-reading or consequences, no hard limits. Although letters and "say yes or I'll never talk to you again" are popular methods for intervention, Brad said, hard science suggests that they simply don't work and actually can be damaging because they destroy the life-giving connections between people who love each other.

"Dr. Judith Landau did these wonderful, peer-reviewed studies that show how important the family-centered process is. This intervention method is data-driven; I'm just popularizing it," Brad said. "I'm a big believer in the power of the clan, and I see it work in my interventions. You begin by reaching out to the person who needs help and letting them know you're going to have this family meeting with or without them. They very, very rarely don't show up. That invitation helps open the door, and what I come back to throughout the whole process is just asking them 'Will you say yes?'"

By avoiding emotionalism and emphasizing connection, Brad has been able to help many families intervene. He says that one of the most important aspects of an intervention is having realistic goals: Usually, that means outpatient treatment nearby, or a professional assessment. It's ridiculous to think that one serious conversation will make someone who's in active addiction stop using—yet we've been set up to have those expectations. Asking people to leave their support network, homes, and comfort zones to "demonstrate their willingness to get sober" is, in those cases, cruel, not helpful. There's a temptation to go nuclear on the problem and bombard it, but what does that do to the person who's suffering? In most cases, it just makes things worse, especially with young people.

"The fact is, taking a teenager who is smoking a bit of weed out of their home and sticking them into a facility with a bunch of kids who are shooting heroin is not going to help them. There are other costs associated with treatment, and you want to minimize those," Brad said. "You get better results when you start locally."

At the end of the day, recovery isn't about luck; it's a science. We simply don't apply what we know about human relationships, communication, and families. Brad's work is a great example of how, when you *don't* punish people for being sick, they're more likely to heal.

TREATMENT

Treatment works—when everyone gets it. Carol McDaid, who's the cofounder of the McShin Foundation, a woman in long-term recovery, and a longtime advocate for recovery, says that change at the policy table is key for ensuring more people can access the help they need. Her own experience in getting into recovery, she said, taught her that "treatment was the right of the rich." If people didn't have the money to pay for treatment or family members who could help, they were simply out of luck. To address inequality of access, the McShin Foundation offers a wide range of services to people in immediate need: family intervention services; recovery housing; recovery coaching; drug testing; peer support groups; relapse prevention groups; reentry support services like job assistance, social services assistance, and transportation; help navigating the criminal justice systems, with probation, parole, and pretrial services; and linkage to clinical services, including medical detox, addiction psychiatry, and addiction counseling. The foundation also shares its programs with other groups. John Shinholser, who is Carol's partner, has helped set up peer mentoring and recovery support in communities all over America. Many of the organizations I mention in this book have benefited from McShin's willingness to share and propagate its recovery resources.

Carol said that a lot has changed over the years and that policy is finally catching up with the work being done on the ground. The recovery community, in the 1980s and 1990s, was still very closeted: The stigma surrounding addiction was powerful, and it took a lot of time for advocates to find a place at the policy table. Now that people are speaking up and sharing more about their lived experience, there's a better understanding of what needs to change at the top in order to benefit people in need. "People died to get us here to the table," Carol said. "I wish it weren't so. It's so important to honor those people, and we never forget them. Everyone knows how those deaths affect us, when we lose friends and loved ones. There's no need to raise the stakes emotionally when we're negotiating for these changes. We have the data to back it up. But we never forget where we came from, either. That's why long-term recovery is so valuable in policy. We understand prevention, and we understand why it's key to keep a long-term focus."

Access to good programs, especially for people who are experiencing intense need, is critical. Carol said that having *immediate* help is key. Waiting lists should be a relic of the past. "When people with substance use disorders express a willingness to get help, there is a very short window of opportunity. This window can close very quickly, so it is crucial that services are available the same day the individual expresses a willingness."

That was certainly my experience. I endured a long, painful wait for treatment; many people don't make it through the waiting process. It's common for people with substance use disorders to feel totally rejected if treatment or other recovery support doesn't work the first time—as if they're defective or broken. That's just not the case. The fact is that addiction treatment should be just like any other form of emergency medicine: on demand, accessible to everyone, and available everywhere. It shouldn't take an overdose to get someone into the medical system.

Ideally, McShin Foundation and other recovery aid groups should be covered by Medicaid. Carol thinks that it's possible, even with threatened cuts to federally funded healthcare, in a time when progress is walking backward in Washington, DC. She said, "If Medicaid and federal block grants meaningfully covered recovery support services, places like McShin across the country could immediately provide same-day services and supports like housing that are so desperately needed to reduce the mortality rate."

Longer-term care, better support, and more services all mean a higher quality of care for more people. In the last ten years, significant improvements in healthcare policy for people with addiction show that it's possible for legislation to advance in proportion to grassroots efforts. We've come a long way since the 1970s, and thanks to Carol and other people who create change at the policy level, we're on track to get even more done in the next decade.

SAME-DAY HELP

Karl Soderstrom watched his mother's recovery at AA meetings. By the time he was sixteen, he had a problem with substances, and bounced through the usual maze of jails, hospitals, and rehabs. Sober in his early twenties, he had a passion for behavioral health and substance use treatment. He went back to school to get a counseling degree and was connected to Alaska nonprofit My House for his internship program. Karl said that he noticed a trend at My House: The nonprofit served about 300 kids that year between the ages of fourteen and twenty-four. For 280 of those youngsters, drugs were the primary reason they were at risk. It was clear that this population needed help and support, so Karl started Fiend 2 Clean. He and his friend Kerby Kraus set up a Facebook page and a "hope line" and started sharing information about recovery.

The area where they live, Alaska's Mat-Su Valley, is about the size of Pennsylvania. There's strong recovery in the area, but it's mostly limited to the 12-Step community—and carefully guarded by the tradition of anonymity. Outside of the meetings, there was little support for people who were struggling. When Fiend 2 Clean started, there were only fourteen detox beds in the whole state, and every treatment center had a waiting list. Also, people who lived in rural areas simply didn't have access to recovery services. It was clear that the people who needed help couldn't find it or didn't know where to start. Karl and Kerby shared videos about recovery, what to expect, how to get sober, the difference between enabling someone and supporting them, and more. They also started doing community outreach, talked to young people at local schools, and teamed up with other groups.

"It was like cooking with Crisco," Karl said. "Sometimes there's conflict between recovery efforts on the clinical and nonclinical sides, but that wasn't a problem in Alaska. We were welcomed with open arms. Now we're working to connect people with jobs, meetings, faith-based groups, and housing. We've opened two sober living homes. In 2017, we had 575 hours of recovery support, started the two homes, and created a case management position for peer support. We have forty to fifty active clients and we've helped 200 people since the first of the year."

Giving someone a place to live and access to recovery services and support makes an immense difference. Same-day help is life saving—groups like Fiend 2 Clean offer *immediate* support for people who are reaching out. When Karl's internship ended, he and Kerby continued the work, and they've been able to grow to meet their community's needs.

Karl said, "We became like a referral service. What we do is help people and families navigate recovery. For example, just last week we got a call at eleven at night from someone. I went out and met them at the McDonald's and mapped it all out for them right there—a whole recovery plan—and talked them through what to do next. We've gotten calls to go and do an intervention with families. We came in wanting to help these kids, and it just kind of grew and blossomed. We're just helping people."

FAMILY SUPPORT

"When I found out my daughter was using heroin, I was mystified," said Lori Erion. She herself had been in recovery for seven years and was abstinent from alcohol and other drugs, but she had no idea how to address her daughter's illness. "That was an animal of a different color."

Although her daughter continued using, she taught Lori everything she could about heroin addiction—how it worked, how it affected people, and where it came from. She educated Lori more than anyone did about the culture, how people's minds work in active addiction, and why they do what they do. One major realization? Addiction isn't a choice, and neither are the behaviors that go with it. When the disease is active, Lori said, "They're not able to stop themselves from cutting the locks off the doors."

Lori wanted to share what she learned with other parents

and help families educate each other with their shared, lived experience, so everyone was educated, empowered, and embraced. In 2013, Lori started a Meetup group online for parents and families in Dayton, Ohio, who were affected by addiction. Around the same time, she also saw Greg Williams's groundbreaking documentary *The Anonymous People*. She decided that she wasn't going to stay silent about recovery anymore and that making addiction a front-and-center issue was critical to stopping the disease from stealing more lives.

Her group, Families of Addicts (FOA), is hundreds of families strong. More than 2,200 people attended the group's rally in 2017. They show up, speak out, and raise their voices to call for change. That kind of passion is infectious, and it's common for someone who's used the group as a resource or support to begin stepping up in other ways. Lori said, "Through osmosis, they realize that they're not alone. We need not be ashamed. We're like this little army of people who are out there working for the cause."

The longer she works in the recovery field, the more she can give to people in need. Lori often acts as a guide and a resource to families that are new to addiction, scared, and don't know where to start. Many people contact her from other counties or even out of state, maybe because they're afraid of ending up on a list or not being able to talk to someone anonymously. Lori said, "We get lots of calls from people who don't know where to start. That sounds crazy, with these crisis numbers, but we hear from a lot of people who are at the end of their rope and they're not educated. That's what we're here for. We are looking to add more one-on-one support, so that we can immediately help anyone who calls: a sibling, the person with the problem, family, or teachers calling from schools. A lot of people call to ask for guidance and advice. We're fortunate, because we've created so many relationships with people. The relationship aspect isn't going to change with regard to accessing resources. The most efficient resource guide isn't going to replace relationships."

By building partnerships in her community, both with families and policy makers, Lori is creating positive change. She says, however, that FOA would benefit greatly from funding funneled into Montgomery County's mental health board—which refers clients to FOA but doesn't provide any financial support for services. Lori dreams of being able to expand what she does, and even considered trying to get accredited as a peer-run organization so that she could fulfill FOA's mission, but at the end of the day, it was simply not possible. "I'm a graphic designer, not a policy writer," she said. "It's really disheartening to hear people in leadership roles talk about eliminating the stigma and bringing community together—using all the messaging we've worked so hard to promote—and then not support programs like ours, which have really taken hold, taken off, and had an impact."

Connection and community are invaluable, and Lori's work proves that sharing resources and educating people affected by substance use is critical. In 2017, FOA helped at least 200 people get into treatment and supported thousands of families, friends, and loved ones who were coping with addiction's effects. She said, "I hope we are preventing people from falling through the cracks. We don't have a corner on recovery. We're a recovery *support*."

HARM REDUCTION

To people like me, Florida is Rehab Central. There's a huge population of people with substance use disorder, in part thanks to the pill mills that blossomed in the early 2000s and in part because of the high number of treatment centers that decided to set up shop there. Yet, to many young people in need, recovery isn't even on their radar. The treatment world or recovery world is totally separate from the one they know. Innovations in harm reduction are slow to catch on, because the people who are educated in addiction treatment are opposed to using them. Justin Kunzelman, the founder of Rebel Recovery, said, "It's a weird place because the treatment industry kind of influences what recovery looks like. Treatment has put so many people into the recovery community that their mentality has carried over, too."

For example, Suboxone, a medication used to treat opioid addiction, wasn't made available to patients until 2017—fifteen years after it was approved by the FDA. Abstinence-only thinking means that recovery has a very narrow definition, which limits access for people who don't fit into a one-size-fits-all model. In Florida's treatment industry, Justin said, Suboxone was perceived as "helping people get high." That's completely false: It's an opioid blocker that helps someone abstain from heroin by reducing cravings and can be used as a long-term replacement therapy. Yet, because "recovery" is defined as total abstinence, without medications, the people who need Suboxone weren't able to get help—or they were shamed for needing it in the first place.

Rebel Recovery works primarily with minority populations: people with no insurance, people of color, people who have low incomes, LGBTQ people, and homeless communities. Rebel Recovery focuses on bringing help to marginalized populations that don't find a connection with the mainstream community. Justin said that, based on sheer numbers, there's more of those types of people than abstinence-only 12-Step members. Yet there was no treatment available for this marginalized majority. As he got involved with harm reduction, he realized that it's impossible to disconnect the need for harm reduction and marginalization. Yet some treatment centers try to justify high barriers to access by saying that everyone *should* conform to the same unrealistic standards, based on nothing except their own opinions.

Justin said, "The evidence has been pushed out. Most of my time is spent trying to convince people about this well-established, credible research. I mean, fuck an *opinion*, I have decades of evidence! It's starting to move toward that now, but to get access in 2017 is insane." As a response to the treatment industry's reluctance to adopt medication-assisted programming, Justin said that he insisted they start paying for naloxone. His reasoning? If the rehabs won't accept evidence-based treatment and help people in need, then they'll at least donate medication to help keep people alive.

Rebel Recovery is unique because it's prepared to be on a peer level with any population that it might come across. Justin said that the group works with a mix of rogue, minority groups that together make up the large one of people who don't fit in. Often they've been laughed at because they want to be on medication-assisted treatment, rejected because they were weren't "willing enough," or had shared something in a 12-Step meeting that was really big and led to them being ostracized. Those common experiences actually put their lives at risk—and make Rebel Recovery's services invaluable. Because Justin and the other people in his group look, talk, and act like normal people instead of government employees, they're able to act as a liaison between services and the people who need them. Justin said that Rebel Recovery is the buffer between the community and drug users. Essentially, the state came to the program and said, "'We have all these services but nobody trusts us.' Well, of course not. Addiction is criminalized: a system that's been putting people in jail for 100 years, firing them for having a dirty urine test, and taking their children away hasn't done much to build trust. Not to mention the high barriers to service. Why would anyone reach out, after experiences like that?"

Justin says that he knows he's succeeding when street kids start referring each other to Rebel Recovery: They start telling each other about what's available.

At the end of the day, harm reduction is about respect. Rebel Recovery offers all kinds of resources, for people anywhere on the recovery continuum. It teaches safe use techniques and hands out clean syringes and naloxone. It also can connect people with medical and dental care. The point isn't to provide a benchmark for "how sober you are"; it's about providing a catalyst for someone's recovery. Justin said, "People have a hard time accepting harm reduction stuff. It's just the idea that when you're helping a person, you should be objective. Their story matters to me as a human being, but it doesn't matter to me as a helper. The only reason I listen to someone's story is to make sure they're connected to the right resources, not to judge them. That's what treatment should be."

There's no shortage of kids who need help. Due to the treatment industry's business practices, Rebel Recovery gets everybody else's users as well. There are only forty beds for state-funded treatment and detox for the whole South Florida area. Justin says that it's important to see the big picture: The issue isn't access to syringes or naloxone. It's a civil rights issue. His work is not just to end discrimination against people affected by addiction but also to improve access to resources by changing the way people look at drug users.

CRIMINAL JUSTICE

"We've gotta help people instead of just incarcerating them," said Terria Walters. As a woman in long-term recovery, a faithful Christian, and a mom, she brought her whole heart to starting Fallen Up Ministries. The Alaska group helps provide transitional, supportive housing for people in early recovery and specifically reaches out to people who have been through the criminal justice system.

"Fallen Up Ministries is faith based, but we will work with anybody whether they believe in God or not. We won't turn people away. We just love people. That's it. We strive to be an example of what we believe, which is to be like Jesus, love people regardless, and be an example," Terria said.

Terria has walked a long road with her faith. She'd started using at a young age and eventually was in and out of jail. Finally, she started using meth to get off opioids. She couldn't get help for her addiction and was arrested again within eight months. This time, she ended up going to prison: a twenty-year sentence, with eight suspended. Her son, Christopher, was put in foster care, but they stayed connected. While Terria was serving the five-year mandatory minimum and waiting to become eligible for parole, she went to a fourteen-month recovery program in the prison. She also worked through a faith-based program, for a total of twenty-six months of treatment. She said, "I gave my life to God and wholeheartedly surrendered." When it was time to apply for parole, she got it on the first try. Her spiritual experience had started in that faith-based program, and she used it to help her son get sober, as well. They worked together in a restaurant—she waited tables and mixed drinks, and he was the bar back—to pay the bills. She wanted to start a ministry of some kind but wasn't sure where to begin. Fallen Up Ministries was barely off the ground, just housing people in a motel. The program was aiding people but not doing a lot of speaking out or other support.

Then, in February 2015, Terria's son relapsed. He was murdered, execution-style, a couple of months later. Someone shot him in the head and robbed him—for heroin. When Terria found him, she was devastated. She said that losing her son brought everything into focus. "I could not understand why the opioid problem was not being talked about. I was talking about it, but it wasn't really out there. People weren't listening. I got really loud about it. I said that we needed to start providing services. Our youth are dying, and we're not helping them, even with the most basic services."

She connected with My House, another local recovery group, and Fiend 2 Clean to learn more about sharing the message that people recover when they have access to support. She challenged regional groups and policy makers to step up their resources for people seeking recovery and is calling on Alaska's criminal justice program to make dramatic changes to the way it handles addiction. She says progress has been slow, and there's been a lot of pushback, but they've also had some big wins along the way. "I know in my heart that I'm being called to work on this from a justice and political point of view. We've got to get policies changed within the state, especially within the Department of Corrections. People are released before they get the care they need, and that just sets them up for failure."

She pointed out that the biggest issue is education, especially in criminal justice. Incarceration without recovery programming is ineffective for people who are coping with addiction. It's common sense: Isolating and punishing doesn't work. Love, inclusion, and help *do*.

COMMUNITY

If you ask Fay Zenoff about the mission of Center for Open Recovery in San Francisco, she lights up like a firecracker. "The idea of there being one road to recovery is as ludicrous as the idea that there's one road to identity," she said. "Let's be clear that we're open to share, solve, collaborate, find, and maintain recovery. We asked ourselves, how do we open, like a funnel, to redefine what recovery means and open up to other possibilities? Structurally, there are so many layers of stigma. We've got it in policy, socially, and personally."

COR uses a virtual model to embed its resources directly within the communities where people live, work, and study. That allows it to have greater reach and impact by focusing on population health as a social justice issue. After fifty-eight years offering programs from a specific location, the center realized a few key things. First, affording the rent in San Francisco as a nonprofit was a huge barrier to operating a positive fiscal model. Buying a million-dollar building or paying tens of thousands in rent was simply out of the question. Also, the organization could reach and help only a limited number of people, which was restricted by physical location and by offering direct services to individuals who were court-mandated to attend diversion programs. Most of the funding for recovery went to programs focused on prevention or short-term crisis intervention. There was a gaping absence of resources to support and strengthen those living in recovery.

The solution? Find more ways to reach more people in more places. Inspired by the groundbreaking work of recovery advocate Marty Mann, the center started with the mission of *ending the stigma of addiction*. But it's a lot more complex than it sounds: simple, but not easy. In a broad sense, the goal is to change the understanding of what recovery is and who is "recovered." The Center for Open Recovery aims to create the change by attacking that entrenched stigma. A big part of it is encouraging people to self-identify as being in recovery and invite newcomers to see what recovery is about. Down the road, people who become part of the movement might contribute on a larger scale, by investing money to find a cure for addiction or supporting more paths to recovery. The point is to start a ripple effect, much like ACT UP did for HIV awareness and gay liberation. Fay pointed out that the famous slogan "Silence = Death" is still true today for people with substance use disorder. Silence kills us. Speaking out, and being an ambassador for *all kinds* of recovery, is critical. It saves lives. Most of all, the Center for Open Recovery wants to help those in recovery to become empowered in order to make change to a broken healthcare and criminal justice system and a society in which 90 percent of people who need help are ignored and left to fend for themselves.

Fay said, "Open Recovery is a framework, but it's a way of life, too. It can be a shared community value, where we commit to helping people in recovery. We support someone else's healthy life choice. We think about how we can create recovery conducive environments. If one is able to get to the place where you're in recovery, it's a sense of being open. There's a sense of integration and peace. It's like LGBTQ equality: We should be *free* to experience recovery openly, without backlash and discrimination."

To build a recovery-friendly community that would work for all kinds of people, the center looked at the continuum of where help was needed: housing, research, and medical education. Equally important was the work of raising up people in recovery and sharing the joy, fulfillment, and happiness they find in their lives. Events, festivals, inspirational meetings, and bold media campaigns have all helped empower people and encourage them to feel pride in their recovery. It's a complete 180 from what the center started as: a group that primarily offered information on DUIs, diversion, and urine tests and felt like an extension of the criminal justice system. It's powerful. It spreads inspiration, and *it works*.

Tammy Lofink, who started the group Rising Above Addiction, is also a big supporter of recovery-positive events. A distance runner and mom, Tammy decided to begin her advocacy work on the anniversary of her son Rob's fatal overdose. She said, "I wanted to do something to help myself heal, help other families, and help other young addicts who were struggling. Most of all, we want to avoid this happening to somebody else. We wanted to do something that was out of the box."

Out of the box is an understatement. The inaugural event was a group skydiving trip. Tammy, who used to be afraid of air travel, jumped out of a plane. The next year, thirty people signed up to try it. Visibility, fun events, and inclusiveness have helped Rising Above Addiction share the message and shatter stigma and stereotypes. Tammy has become a community partner with the Maryland state attorney's office. Its members have been on the news and in the media, sharing their experiences with people who might not know about recovery. It hosts a five-mile run every year, as well as various fundraisers and a music festival. Recently, the group was able to open a women's recovery home.

That's an amazing step. Tammy inspires me because she's someone who was just an ordinary person until her life was touched by addiction. She said that after Rob passed away, "a lot of people approached me whose children had also died. They said 'you'll never get over it.' Well, I didn't want pity. I didn't want to be that person who crawled into a corner and gave up. I had to show my daughter that she's important enough for me to keep living. I went running the next day. I feel like every life that is saved through this work shows me that Robert's life wasn't lost in vain."

PEER-SUPPORTED RECOVERY

We can't wait for someone to rescue us, so we've built our own lifeboats. Our community, out of necessity, has created some innovative ways to deal with the drug crisis. Many of us are lucky to live near major cities and find connections there. But recovery, and the tools to get it, should be free and open to *everyone*. Those resources should be available to everybody who needs them, no matter where they live.

One amazing example is the Alano Club in Portland, Oregon. The club is located in a historic mansion downtown, where anyone can just walk in, ask for help, and be connected with a mentor who can guide them through a recovery plan. The club designed a Recovery Toolkit series to focus on holistic, integrated recovery support. It includes weekly yoga and meditation classes, mindfulness workshops, writing sessions for people who want to learn to tell their recovery stories, and even courses on healthy eating, addiction, and relationships. The classes are free and totally open to the community: *Anyone* can get the help they need. The club is also home to hundreds of mutual aid support groups every week, like SMART Recovery, Refuge Recovery, and many 12-Step meetings.

I think the Alano Club is an incredible example of where peer-supported recovery is going. It's not a treatment center; it's a nonprofit. It's a member of the Facing Addiction Action Network, one of 600+ groups dedicated to helping people in recovery. It also looks beyond immediate need to the larger forces at work. The club's advocacy training workshops teach people how to lobby for change and communicate with people who don't know the truth about substance use disorder. Its message is that anyone can get sober and that anyone can be an activist in our community. This is groundbreaking, in the recovery world.

The Alano Club is a one-stop resource for people in Portland, but its mission and materials could easily be adapted to any other recovery club. That's the beauty of recovery: It really *does* go everywhere.

Arnell Evans is also helping people connect with peer recovery resources. She runs alternative peer groups for underserved and underprivileged young people in Houston's inner city. An alternative peer group is "a community-based, family-centered, professionally staffed, positive peer support program that offers prosocial activities, counseling, and case-management for people who struggle with substance use or self-destructive behaviors." Once Arnell and her husband, Bert, got started in Houston, her plate was suddenly very full. She currently oversees two peer groups in a school.

Arnell has an innate understanding of the need for mental health support for people in recovery, especially younger people. She experienced deep depression when her three-year-old daughter was killed in a car accident, and used alcohol and other substances to numb her emotional pain. She said, "We did not have the money or the knowledge that seeing a therapist or psychiatrist could help my depression. I continued to self-medicate with depressants and stimulants for the solution."

Now, with over twenty-six years in recovery, she said that the link between recovery and a healthy, nurturing environment is obvious. "Far too many teens from inner cities are children with adult problems. Many are kids who didn't have dinner the night before or wear dirty clothes. They are so challenged by life that they often can't focus on the curriculum. So, when necessary, we modify the curriculum to fit their cognitive level of understanding. We are constantly morphing the program!"

By helping young people—who may not be aware of the way environmental risks like poverty, emotional and physical trauma, and family stress can influence drug use—Arnell is helping to raise the next generation of sober people. She's educating and supporting the teenagers who will be our leaders in the recovery movement—planting seeds that will flower for generations to come.

CIVIC HEROES

The heroes in our recovery movement don't usually start out wanting to make a difference. They're just normal, good-hearted people whose lives are irrevocably changed by the effects of addiction. Sometimes, like Tammy or Terria, they're moms who lose children to overdoses or drug-related crime. Sometimes, like Fay, they're innovators who think there's a better way to build recovery communities. They see a need and they step up to fill it. Along the way, they change lives—and save many others. They come from all walks of life, but when they step up, raise their voices, and help others, they become leaders. Helpers. Servants. They're amazing examples to me of what is possible. Their work, their dedication, and their love are truly changing America for the better.

When I was in Dayton for a visit in the summer of 2017, I happened to meet Lauren White, who runs a media company called Indigo Life. Lauren is my age, and her brother struggled with substance use disorder. She was tired of seeing the way the media portrayed people like him. They depicted addiction as nothing more than needles, spoons, and dead bodies. This was irresponsible, and it undermined the efforts of recovery organizations that were working hard to fight the epidemic: Who wants to help someone who's a lost cause?

Lauren's reaction was to leverage her expertise with film, marketing, and digital media to start raising up the solutions. She said, "These are people's lives. There is no time to sit back. So many people are affected by addiction, and it is going to take all of us coming together to get through this. The more we can highlight all the positive efforts and strides being made, the more people can gain awareness and get on board with a movement that will literally save lives. The least we can do is contribute our God-given talents to make a difference."

She committed to making twenty-six videos as part of a solution-based media campaign in 2018. She's doing this work pro bono because she believes that we can face addiction and that recovery speaks more loudly than the disease of substance use disorder. She's not alone. She is one of dozens of leaders in Dayton who are giving their time, energy, and talent to finding a way to save lives. She's also, at the end of the day, just a person, too. Just a sister who loves her brother and wants to do the right thing.

These are just a few people doing truly incredible work to fight the drug epidemic. This is in no way a comprehensive list of all the incredible friends, allies, supporters, and advocates I've met—not at all. I could write an entire book about each one of the people I've been fortunate enough to cross paths with on this journey. Literally every one of them has had something to contribute.

One of my biggest inspirations is Jim Hood, whose son Austin died of an accidental drug overdose at age twenty. After Austin's death, Jim left his career to devote his life to ending the American drug crisis. He helped found Facing Addiction and has been a tireless advocate for other families, parents, and communities who have lost loved ones to this disease.

In a letter to Austin on the five-year anniversary of his death, Jim said:

> *In a heartbeat, you were gone. My beautiful boy was dead. No more twice-a-day texts, calls about this crazy world, funny messages, or anything. Nothing more. Forever.*
>
> *At your memorial service, I pledged to do everything I can to help other wonderful, loving people like you from losing their lives, and spare other families that anguish.*
>
> *Since then, many amazing people came together to create Facing Addiction. We are making a difference. And on days, like this, when I can hardly get out of bed, I am inspired by those astonishing people who, like me, want to turn the tide on*

this crisis and bring help and hope to tens of millions. And I am humbled that they all know about you, although none ever met you.

But I still wonder why there is not more outrage. We come together as a nation when there are shootings, earthquakes, and hurricanes—as we should. Yet addiction is the leading cause of death in our country among people under the age of 40. One in 3 households is impacted by this scourge. Somebody, usually a young adult, dies every 4 minutes—the equivalent of a jumbo jet falling from the sky every day, with no survivors. I pray America very soon adds addiction to that list of "disasters" we must care about, and respond to, with our love, concern, help, and money.[2]

To me, Jim and his work with Facing Addiction represents what so many parents in America are facing today. Even in the depths of unimaginable loss, Jim chose to rise up and fight back—so other moms and dads wouldn't have to suffer the way he has. We have to work for change, so that no family sits down to a table where someone is missing. No more empty chairs and bedrooms that are kept just as they were—a shrine to our lost brother, son, loved one, friend.

As a person in recovery, I know how much our families love us and what they'd do to see us get better. They don't want us hurting. They don't want us dying. They just want their kids back. So many of these parents have given more to our movement than I thought was humanly possible. All of them have shown me both the magnitude of this drug epidemic and the wave of human love, compassion, and strength that has risen to meet it.

So, what do we do now? And where's the outrage?

10. RISE UP
Either America Changes,
or We Change America

A man dies when he refuses to stand up for that which
is right. A man dies when he refuses to stand up for
justice. A man dies when he refuses to take a stand for
that which is true.
—MARTIN LUTHER KING JR., March 8, 1965, sermon

HOW WE CHOOSE TO ACT ONCE we know what's right
reveals our character. Integrity is when our actions match our
ideals—when our "insides" match our "outsides." It's a spiritual principle that has guided me through the last few years
of my recovery. Now that I know better, I can do better.
And as I've learned more about the opioid crisis, who's responsible for it, and who's standing up to fight back, I know
what side of history I need to be on.

I was led into activism by the stories of the people I met—
ordinary, everyday people whose lives were indelibly changed
by addiction. Their voices speak loudly about the injustice of
the opioid epidemic. Why are people with substance use disorder treated like second-class citizens? Why are we ignoring the
genocide-level deaths that happen every day in every community across our nation? Why has the federal government

been so slow to acknowledge the crisis, and slower to take any action? Why do we keep pretending that addiction is someone else's problem when it affects *every single person in America*? As I've listened, traveled, talked, and learned, I feel like the answers are clear. We didn't ask for these problems. We didn't create them. But we are empowered to end them.

You too are empowered to do this work. You too can save lives, just by taking a few simple steps. Many other people—whose stories have appeared in this book—started small. What looks to us like an insignificant change, as small as a single mustard seed, can grow into something great. As you make these changes and scatter these seeds, you never know what is going to take hold. For me, it was a Facebook Live video of the Facing Addiction rally in Washington, DC, in 2015. That one-minute clip of people marching on the National Mall, holding signs and openly identifying themselves as being in recovery, changed my life forever. Because of that video, you're holding this book in your hands. My hope is that this book, and what you've read in its pages, will flip the switch for you, too.

If you're waiting for a sign, this is it. Today is your day. It's time to rise up.

How do we create change? We start with ourselves. Simply building awareness of substance use disorder can have a positive effect. For me, that's telling my story. I help raise awareness by putting myself out there, sharing what I've been through, and identifying myself as a person in recovery. I'm loud and proud. Although this was intimidating at first, I quickly connected with other people who had been through similar experiences. I learned the more I told my story, the less shame I felt. I also didn't realize how much shame I was carrying until I started shedding it by being vocal. I decided

I wasn't going to hide anything I had been through. I didn't want to be silent anymore. Telling my story gave me pride in who I am. Instead of weakening me, those experiences are a source of strength. I can express gratitude for what I've endured and be thankful for the many people who have helped me on my journey. Having the courage to say "Yes, addiction affects me" also makes it possible for someone else to say "Me, too."

Telling your story opens the door for the person who is still living in the dark, silenced by stigma, sick and afraid. When we openly admit that our son or daughter is struggling with substance use, we help other people. Talking about substance use disorder the same way we talk about heart disease and breast cancer helps make it feel "normal." We even celebrate it. My dream is that one day, I'll walk into a bookstore and the rack of greeting cards will have a section for recovery anniversaries, right next to birthdays and graduations. Maybe one day the guy in the cubicle next to you will say, "Hey, there are cupcakes in the conference room for Phil's five years of recovery." One day, no one will think that is weird, strange, or needs to be covered up.

We don't need to have the answers; we just need to speak up. We need to share, without fear or shame. Once that barrier is broken, it creates so much freedom! Sharing allows other people to see us, love us, help us. It also gives a new face and a new voice to substance use disorder. Instead of old, harmful stereotypes, we can say, "This is what a person in recovery looks like." We can show people the truth about substance use disorder simply by raising our hands.

I started by telling my story online. Now I share it at recovery rallies, in policy making summits, and in community meetings. It truly does open doors and allows me to educate others. Think about it: When you opt to "come out" as someone affected by addiction within your family, your community, your workplace, and your friend group, you change every one of those groups. When you explain to your sister why the word "junkie" is harmful or ask your boss to offer nonalcoholic options at the holiday party, you're creating small changes that really do have immediate impact on the world. I can't tell you how many times I've said, "I'm in recovery, and that's inaccurate" to someone who was spouting off about substance use. Stepping up and speaking out isn't always easy, but it's always worth it.

Beyond our personal stories, how can we use our voices and our experiences to fight the opioid crisis? Like the civil rights movements before us, it's important to find places to share our message that will reach more people. We can write letters to the editor of our local paper or pen op-eds about how the drug epidemic is affecting our community. We can call for justice by reaching out directly to our elected officials. You can find their contact information online, or message them on social media. Remember: Your mayor, governor, city commissioner, senators, and representatives are supposed to care about what *you* care about. Your issues should be their issues, too. Knock on their doors, make their phones jangle, and fill their mailboxes with your stories. Let them know that if they're not making recovery their top priority, they're not getting your community's support.

Organize a few friends and write letters. Ask other parents and recovery people to add their names to your letter. Most important, do these things more than once. Don't take no for an answer. Make a lot of noise! Senators and other people in public service can and do make time to meet with their constituents. If you want to tell the governor, in person, about your son's issue with prescription painkillers—and if you want to know exactly what your state is planning to do about it—you have the right to do so. We can't let elected officials get away with ignoring us, sweeping us under the rug, or making decisions that harm the people we love. We need to make sure they know *we care about recovery*, and we're not alone. No decisions about us without us!

When I ran for delegate to the Democratic National Convention, I witnessed firsthand how our agenda is pushed aside. I heard how quickly the media reduces our heartbreaking stories and calls to action into newsy sound bites. Addiction is sensationalized and dramatized, and the message of recovery gets lost, every time. We can't let that happen. No change can come unless we are *all* working for it, lifting our voices and choosing leaders who will give us more than pats on the head. Until we demonstrate that we are not satisfied with the status quo, our friends, kids, family members, and neighbors will continue to die from untreated substance use disorder.

Action speaks even louder than words. As I said, the first time I saw a Facing Addiction rally—thousands of families, people in recovery, and advocates, celebrating their recovery and calling for change—it transformed my life. It was an incredibly powerful moment for me. Addiction is so stigmatized. After a lifetime of being told to hide who I am and be ashamed of my illness, I never thought I'd see anyone walking around carrying a sign that said "I'm in Recovery and I Vote." I can't tell you what it means to see parents embracing their children, saying "I'm Proud of My Sober Kid." These milestones were unimaginable only a few years ago. Yet the courage of the few can inspire the many. That's why organizing events, and mobilizing in a *visible* way, is so powerful. When it comes to recovery, we need to have our own Million

Man March. We need our own Pride event. We need to fill public parks and streets, just as the Occupy movement did. We need elected representatives who are willing to work with local groups and grassroots activists to create change. We need people from our community in office, crafting policy that benefits people with substance use disorder. We need recovery to be center stage, not treated like a sideshow. We must *let it be known* that we're here and we deserve the same equal, fair treatment as everyone else.

Addiction dehumanized us. But we are people, too. Our leaders, and even our neighbors, seem to have forgotten that *we are human beings*. We are still Americans. We live here, too. We work, raise kids, and vote here. We deserve to be supported, just like anyone else affected by a chronic illness. We deserve that visibility, that respect, and that love. But we're not going to get it unless we reach out and demand it. We must rise up.

Building a more just and equal America begins with us. I mean *all* of us. A 2016 study by the Pew Research Center showed that Americans were discouraged and pessimistic about pretty much everything.[1] Gun control, immigration, security from terrorism, women's rights—every issue that mattered was looking bad, from both Democrats and Republicans. The one thing that both sides could agree on was prioritizing recovery. "Majorities of Trump supporters (62%) and Clinton backers (56%) said drug addiction was a very big problem." This is absolutely true, because addiction affects everyone, regardless of their race, religion, political party, gender, or class. It affects all of us, which means we must all work toward the solution together. In fact, if we all come together around this issue, we will be able to fix it much faster. I would say that the drug epidemic is the single unifying issue in America right now. Candidates whose campaigns focus on recovery win. A huge constituency of unreached, single-issue voters care about recovery. They're waiting for leaders who represent those values, have a plan, and follow through on their campaign promises. The candidates who can do that will win, and win big. That's not an overstatement. Addiction was a leading topic in the 2016 presidential election, as the number one topic for many voters. Yet both parties made huge promises that they have yet to follow through on. Once again, recovery is being swept under the rug instead of being put in the center, where it belongs.

We must have dramatic, sweeping, government-wide change *at every level* if we are going to stop this crisis. There is not a moment to waste. Policy is key, yet nobody is stepping up to lead the charge. Meanwhile, local and grassroots groups are caring for people in desperate need of help. They can't support this crisis indefinitely. We have to do something. We need more people to get involved, we need them in decision-making positions, and we need policy change to reverse the epidemic's course.

One of those people needs to be you.

I know we've got it in us. People are willing to fight for *hours* about healthcare, or a woman's right to choose, or travel bans. They'll go back and forth forever, hashing out the fine points of a new bill or the merits of one candidate or another. However, we don't fight when it comes to addiction. We know it's killing us, our families, and our nation. We know that. It's not up for debate. The issue is following through and not letting our message die once it reaches the federal level. We are more than a sob story or a perfectly packaged sound bite. We are people, we vote, and we have the numbers to create real change in America.

That's why I think that the drug epidemic may be the key to unity. I think we can reach across the aisle and listen to one another in order to create lasting solutions to drug-related deaths. In fact, I know we can. In this book, you read how Sheriff Karl Leonard implemented an extremely progressive peer recovery model in the Chesterfield Jail in Virginia. That's Republican country—one of the reddest counties in a very purple state. Yet some of those red counties are leading the charge in our fight against addiction. It's time to look at what is working, not at which party is doing the work. This is not about party affiliation; it can't be. It's about saving people's lives. There are no teams on a sinking ship, and this one is filled with desperate, drowning people. The only choice we have is to work together, as hard as we can, to end this crisis before we are completely underwater. We must transcend our resentments, old grudges, and fears about "what will happen when the other party is in power." We have to. Our children's lives are at stake. An entire generation's future rests on whether we can cooperate long enough to make recovery the number one issue in America.

As my sister Lorraine would say, "If you're not at the table, you're on the menu."

We deserve a seat at the table. To get it, we need to get loud. Addiction affects more than one-third of Americans— yet where are our recovery voters? Policy is made without anyone from our community at the table, by people who don't know anything about addiction and have no lived experience in recovery. We can't keep letting that happen. We need to lift up our voices and demand that the recovery community is represented in the process.

My own experience running for delegate in California showed me that it *is* possible to win an election on a recovery platform. But we need to go much further if we are going to save lives. Our actions must match our words; we don't need more of the same. The status quo is killing us. I learned how complacent our political system is when it comes to recovery. Every time a candidate makes hollow promises about reform, access to treatment, and more compassionate policies for people with substance use disorder, millions of sick people are condemned to a tragic, avoidable, unnecessary death. When we continue to enable the systems that thrive on keeping us sick, we are signing up for more of the same. However, I learned that by getting on the front lines and working with other grassroots efforts, we can change the narrative around addiction and change hopelessness to hope.

I hope many others feel empowered by my example and consider throwing their hats into the ring, as well. If you have solutions to the drug epidemic—if you're tired of sitting by and watching politicians do nothing to stop the deaths—you can get in the middle, get into office, and be the change. If you refuse to hand your child's life over to a committee of uninformed, uncaring, uneducated "professionals," you can get involved with decision-making groups. You can form a task force. You can reach out to local leadership and ask them what they're doing to bring recovery to your community. You can petition your local medical board to require new certification that is specific to addiction and recovery.

You can rise up!

You won't be alone in this work. This year I have committed to registering *1 million recovery voters* by the 2020 election. Yep. One million people who think that recovery and solving the opioid crisis should be our nation's number one issue. A recovery voter is someone who has substance use disorder or someone whose life is affected: a parent, friend, sibling, or neighbor. A recovery voter believes that we need to solve the addiction problem to get America back on its feet—and we can do it humanely, in a way that will save billions of taxpayer dollars.

I know that, if we work together on this problem, we can solve it for *everyone*. Not just in cities, and not just in small towns. We can make recovery happen everywhere.

I want our elected officials and representatives to *know* that recovery is important to us. I want substance use disorder to be a term they are all familiar with. I want them to educate themselves about recovery and get to know the ways that both recovery and addiction have impacted their community. But words and a few handshakes aren't enough. Words aren't going to save lives. We saw how useful those empty promises were on the 2016 campaign trail. As recovery voters, how do we know who is a pro-recovery candidate and who is just trying to look good for the media? To help define a "pro-recovery" candidate, I've created an easy seven-point rating system.

1. Is the person in recovery? Is the candidate or someone close to him or her in recovery or affected by substance use disorder? First-person, lived experience is the best measurement of whether someone is on our side. Also, recovery is a human issue, not a partisan issue. *Putting recovery first* means that we can find real solutions to our problems.

2. What does the candidate know about recovery? How did they learn it? Are they endorsed by any pharmaceutical companies? Big Pharma spends tens of millions every year on political candidates, influencing FDA scientists, and protecting its own interests. If we want reform, we don't need Big Pharma in politics.

3. How does the candidate make their living? By the same token, we don't want millionaire treatment center owners pretending to be recovery experts, either. Just because they run a rehab doesn't mean they've cracked the code on recovery. It's important to look closely at the candidate's role in the recovery community. Did they profit off sick people and potentially abuse desperate families? If they ran a treatment center, was it private payer only, or did they accept Medicaid and patients who were unable to pay? Are they truly invested in the recovery community, or are they investing in themselves?

4. How do they feel about the Eighth Amendment? This is the amendment that protects us from "cruel and unusual punishment," and it's key to cleaning up the criminal justice system. The Eighth Amendment means that jails and prisons should not withhold life-saving medical care from people with substance use disorder and requires facilities to provide humane, accessible, realistic recovery supports. No more overdoses in prison, and no more deaths behind bars due to inadequate care during detox. No more cages, solitary confinement, and zero recovery. Sick people shouldn't be incarcerated. Does the candidate have a plan to solve this problem?

5. What is the candidate proposing? Harm reduction sites, on-demand care, universal naloxone, and funding for nonprofit recovery services are all signs of a pro-recovery candidate. Helping people on every part of the recovery spectrum, from overdoses and active addiction to long-term recovery support groups, is critical. Does the candidate's plan take *all* of us into account or cater to only one type or group? If other groups, such as people who need harm reduction, are excluded, why is that? Also, rather than funding do-nothing groups, like more drug enforcement officers or more jail cells, the candidate needs to focus on community efforts that are already having a positive impact.

6. How will the candidate pay for the programming? The golden rule is that every dollar we spend funding recovery services frees up an additional seven dollars from America's economic burden. How will this candidate balance the budget while keeping recovery first? There is a huge financial incentive to fund services for people with substance use disorder. All candidates should put this programming first, since relieving drug-related pressure on the system affects the police, courts, low-income housing and food stamps, and almost every other conceivable social service. Does the candidate's plan benefit *people* or *politicians*?

7. Who are the helpers? Any plan's success rests on people, infrastructure, and grassroots support. What recovery groups and organizations are endorsing this candidate, and why? We need a pro-recovery candidate who has good relationships with existing community organizations and can work with them to follow through. These grassroots organizations include activists, parent groups, nonprofits, volunteer organizations, and task force leaders. Grassroots groups often work for years without support or recognition but get great results. Instead of trying to reinvent the wheel, a smart candidate will leverage existing relationships and learn from people who are already active and on the front lines.

We need activism to keep leaders working for real change. There is a lack of accountability for elected officials, except when large, influential advocacy groups and lobbies hold them to their word. For example, the National Rifle Association (NRA) has an enormous influence because it appears as a single voting bloc. It focuses only on gun-related laws. Every candidate gets graded on his or her gun control stance. NOW, the National Organization for Women, has historically been a powerful advocacy organization concerned with equal rights issues, especially abortion and a woman's right to choose. Both groups have influenced the outcome of important policy decisions that affect every person in our nation.

There is no such unified, vocal, respected group for addiction or recovery rights—*yet*. If an elected official makes a horrible policy decision that further isolates those who are addicted, or cuts resources for treatment, there is no NRA or NOW to speak up. Nobody mounts a publicity campaign on a seismic scale, calls the media, or organizes a protest march. More dangerously, if an elected official wants to push forward *good* policy that will truly save lives, there is no organized group that drums up support, grabs the media's attention, and makes sure we get that bill passed.

A good example of this was the Comprehensive Addiction and Recovery Act (CARA), which President Obama signed into law in July 2016. The original bill was authored and sponsored by a Republican and a Democrat. The votes in both houses in Congress were all in favor, with the exception of four congressmen. That's almost unanimous support. (You don't need a career in politics to understand how rare that is.) Yet, despite its incredible momentum and support, CARA sits as a nascent law with no allocation of funding. Congress has never actually followed through to fund the act's many helpful initiatives. The act is in limbo. No one has challenged Congress's indecisiveness and dismissal of everything CARA was supposed to accomplish, and in the year since it was passed and put on the shelf, 64,000 people have died. This is infuriating! Congress's inaction persists because 23 million people in recovery do not have an NRA, NOW, or American Civil Liberties Union to hold elected officials accountable. Nobody is pushing for laws to be enacted once they pass.

One of my great inspirations is Patrick Kennedy, who wrote and fought for the Mental Health Parity Act when he was a congressman in 2008. The bill said that insurance companies must pay for mental health and substance use treatment, the same way they cover cancer and diabetes. It leveled the playing field and made it impossible for insurance companies to opt out of the problem. Eight years later, at the Democratic National Convention in Philadelphia, Patrick led a panel of experts to solve the issue of actually enforcing the law that he wrote and passed. In 2016, the life-saving act was still on the shelf. In almost a decade, nobody was using it or enforcing it. No attorney general had brought any action against a major insurer for dodging reimbursement. Not one! Why? *Because no one was holding elected officials accountable.*

Our government has quite literally gotten away with murder by avoiding its responsibilities to the recovery community. Our elected officials make horrific addiction-related policies with impunity. The result is systemic genocide: laws that target, punish, and kill people with substance use disorder. That ends now. Those of us who have survived the struggle cannot allow politicians to make laws that hurt us, cut funding that will help us, and compare our deadly disease to a moral failing. We will no longer be abused. We will no longer be ignored. We will no longer be denied. There are 23 million of us, and we are rising up. *We demand justice.*

In the years of my recovery, I have seen the strength of our community and their families. We can harness our collective pain and frustration and turn it into accountability. Here is how:

Show Up. If we get active, we can gain influence. We need to show up on the news and at events surrounding elections, just as labor unions, gun rights advocates, civil rights leaders, African American and Hispanic community leaders, and evangelical clergy do. We will join in, as people in recovery, families of loss, and families supporting loved ones through active addiction.

Get Your Scorecard. We are going to grade each elected official. We will review everyone, starting at the federal level and state chapters and at the municipal level. This includes cabinet appointments, like the secretary for Health and Human Services, directors of the Substance Abuse and Mental Health Services Administration, the National Institutes of Health, the Centers for Disease Control, the Food and Drug Administration, and the Surgeon General. People in these positions are the decision makers who can truly bring progressive reform and save lives. For example, former US Surgeon General Vivek Murthy, M.D., had the courage to write the first-ever *Surgeon General's Report on Alcohol,*

Drugs, and Health. His work ended the medical debate about many aspects of our disease, while shining a light on evidence-based practices that work.

The people in these positions affect system-wide change. President Obama's director of National Drug Control Policy, Michael Botticelli, changed the vernacular name of his office from "drug czar" to "recovery czar." He held town halls with President Obama to address the opioid crisis. These offices *must* be occupied by people who understand, care, and are not afraid to make bold, unpopular decisions. We need leaders who will commit to standing up to people who want us dead.

We need to know who is qualified for these vital posts and who isn't. How does a family in Amarillo or Pawtucket know how their local congressional candidate will vote on significant addiction issues? We need to empower our community to make decisions that support recovery with their votes.

We will do the auditing. We will research, vet, and grade everyone running. We will review the statements they have given on addiction and listen to their interviews. We'll look at their voting record. We'll call each of their offices or campaigns and ask them about their stance on various addiction-related issues. We'll alert newspapers and television stations if a candidate is particularly bad or good. We'll make sure journalists are armed with an accurate assessment of every candidate, so they can ask the questions that matter in interviews. We will make our ratings public and accessible online.

I want every candidate running to earn an A+ from us. I want our rating to make or break a campaign: Does the recovery community approve? Does the candidate's plan serve the needs of families who are coping with addiction? Our grading system will force a national conversation around recovery.

I know that many people who hold elected office genuinely care about this issue. For example, former Florida governor Jeb Bush has been an ally to our community. So has Boston mayor Marty Walsh, who's in long-term recovery. I have prepared a pledge for people like them; they are our allies.

For anyone who cares about addiction issues, this pledge is a no-brainer. For those on the fence, it should be a conversation starter. For those who aren't supportive, it should help turn them around. Our nonpartisan pledge will give people running for office or already in office an opportunity to tell the electorate where they stand. They can show their commitment to ending the greatest public health crisis of our time. There are ways that both parties can help end this crisis, but I am optimistically looking at *a bipartisan goal.* I want everyone running for president and Congress to take the following pledge:

As an elected official, I pledge to commit my support on matters related to combating addiction based on the following five guiding principles:

1. Humanizing Addiction for Both the Afflicted and the Affected

This means simply telling our stories. We need to show the world when they talk about "those people," they mean us. We are smart, caring, compassionate, bright, creative, everyday Americans. We are your neighbors. Our kids go to school with your kids and sleep over at our houses. We live with a chronic disease, and we nurture its remission.

We need to be out, loud, and proud so the world sees who we are. We need leaders to sit with us and walk among us;

speak with us in town halls; visit recovery night celebrations at treatment centers; and march in our parades.

2. Suffering from Addiction Is Not a Crime—Reforming Public Safety Responses

This means not locking up people who are addicted to illegal drugs. It does not mean legalizing dangerous drugs; rather, it means not turning people with substance use disorder into criminals. We're going to stop locking people up without treatment, rendering them unemployable, and letting their addiction progress in prison. People who commit nonviolent crimes because of their addiction should have their charges and sentences commuted, once they have achieved successful recovery.

Criminal justice reform is an opportunity for every elected official to make a profound difference in ending the crisis by voting for measures that support recovery.

3. Dramatically Expanding Prevention, Screening, and Early Intervention Programs

So many lives could be saved and repaired if our government funded the evidence-based measures in the Surgeon General's report. In proportion to the actual need, we need more funding. The total need may never be funded, but elected officials must allocate, earmark, designate, and pass deliberate budgetary support to combat addiction. We've got to make treatment universally available. We can't let Congress unanimously pass a law and then let it disappear.

4. Promoting Multiple Pathways of Recovery for Individuals and Their Families

Leaders will support the obvious clinical solutions and expand treatment. More important, they will support medication-assisted treatment just as much as abstinence-based programs. Faith-based groups like Catholic Charities and Jewish Family Services that provide addiction care to everyone should receive government grants for their work. We're going to recognize faith as a pathway to recovery. We're going to show that there isn't *one* definition of recovery and that there are no absolutes in treatment. Nobody is "less worthy" because of the way he or she reached remission.

5. Mainstreaming Addiction Health Services

We will treat addiction health services just like every other medical service: with parity and accountability. This means increasing the amount of credit hours about addiction a student is required to take in medical school. We need standardized screenings for substance use disorder and other recovery support tactics right in your primary care physician's office. We should require sick leave and other employer support for a worker battling addiction. We need to ensure that communities build and nurture adequate treatment availability relative to their population, the same way we expect hospitals to.

The more politicians sign the pledge, the more influence we can exert on ending this crisis. And we must exert it, or we will continue to lose our loved ones. We must have justice. We need recovery reform and we need it now. *We will find consensus.* Don't forget, recovery voters alone outnumber voters of both major parties, in terms of people affected by the crisis. We will find a way to make these changes, we will seek office, and we will put pro-recovery candidates into every elected office in this nation. We will fight for justice in every arena. *And we will win.*

Together, we can create meaningful policy that helps get funding to groups that are already having an impact on the crisis. We can expand services to people in need, including harm reduction, housing, healthcare, and treatment. We can improve access to recovery services so that anytime people need help, no matter who they are or where they live, they can get care immediately. Without impacting chronic pain patients, who legitimately need these medications, we can limit the distribution and production of lethal opioids that turn normal people into sick ones—and find alternatives to "medicines" like OxyContin, which have a high risk for overdose and dependence. We can educate doctors so that they learn about addiction in medical school, not from a pharmaceutical company's marketing materials. We can make sure naloxone is available *everywhere*, from libraries, to ambulances, to bus stops, to bathrooms. We can improve drug education and prevention by telling kids the truth about drugs and addiction and empowering them to support one another instead of just saying no. We can shatter the stigma of addiction by telling the truth about substance use disorder and refusing to stay silent while our friends and loved ones die. We can decriminalize drug use and offer treatment instead of jail time, freeing billions of dollars in funding and making our neighborhoods safe places to live, work, and thrive. We can stop unfairly targeting minorities for drug-related crimes and stop incarcerating people whose only crime is their addiction.

Working together, we can go a lot further, too. Beyond basic, humane treatment of people with substance disorder, I think there is a lot more to achieve.

The treatment industry needs dramatic reform, and its methods must be dictated by data, not outdated ideas about addiction. Insurance companies shouldn't limit inpatient treatment to a mere twenty-eight days: We need a ninety-day minimum for inpatient services. Parity, which was established as the law of the land years ago, *must* be enforced. Furthermore, every treatment center in America must provide publicly funded beds as well as scholarships for people who need help but can't afford treatment. Treatment shouldn't be something that is available only to affluent people. Medical bills related to substance use treatment shouldn't create hardship for families in need.

Addiction needs to be treated like any other life-threatening condition. Anyone should be able to walk into an emergency room or urgent care clinic and receive care—just like a person who's experiencing cardiac arrest or is in labor. It is unconscionable that someone who is struggling with the symptoms of acute substance use disorder or is overdosing might be turned away. We need enforcement of malpractice laws that are specific to addiction and recovery treatment. Irresponsible medical care and prescriptions *kill people*, and the doctors who persist in those practices are criminal and should be held accountable. I don't mean making an example of a few bad apples: I mean a rigorous, thorough reform of the entire medical industry, from the first semester of medical school to a requirement for continuing education in addiction treatment.

Pharmaceutical companies must also be held accountable for their role in creating, promoting, and profiting from the American drug epidemic. We deserve reparations from Big Pharma: Every death should cost the companies, and cost them big. Companies should pay billions of dollars into a disaster relief fund—an independent, national disaster relief fund run by a blind trust, administered state by state, to stem the drug epidemic. The companies that created this deadly crisis *do not deserve our praise*. They don't get to pretend to be our saviors. They do need to pay for the irreparable damage they did to the communities they profited from destroying.

Also, some of the products these companies manufacture should be severely restricted and taken out of emergency rooms and dental clinics. They're dangerous, not for acute care, and practically guarantee that patients will either develop an addiction or a dependence. Limiting prescriptions won't stop the problem. I find it hard to believe that our nation can put a man on the moon but can't figure out a more compassionate, ethical, responsible way to treat pain than just tossing a prescription bottle at someone.

To that end, I think we need to reform the FDA appointment process and take politics *out* of the FDA. It should be a truly independent, agnostic organization. Currently, those officials are appointed by the president, and, last time I checked, the president is not a doctor. Those appointments shouldn't come from the executive branch but from a qualified entity, like the United States Department of Health and Human Services. My experience, and that of many others, has demonstrated that addiction *can't be solved* through political enmity but only through collaboration, cooperation, and hard work from both parties. We need leaders who are in our corner, fighting for us no matter who is sitting in the White House.

Most of all, we need to change our ideas about substance use disorder. Instead of a twenty-eight-day treatment cycle, we need to think *long term* about recovery. What about a five-year timeline that includes ninety days of inpatient treatment, long-term outpatient support, quality mental health care, and vocational training? How about, instead of dumping people on the street after they've completed treatment, we ensure that they'll have a safe, stable place to live while they rebuild their lives? Guaranteed sober living housing for two or three years would make an immense impact on positive outcomes for people starting out in their recovery, especially those who have contended with homelessness, bankruptcy, and domestic abuse, among other obstacles.

I can imagine a world where people are allowed to *live*, despite past drug use. Where people with substance use disorder are not shunned as criminals or treated like lepers. I imagine us as valued citizens who are part of society. What could we do, if we were free of this epidemic and the stigma of addiction? I imagine a vitalized, healthy, and powerful America, where everyone is included.

These might sound like huge changes, but they all started with one voice. One story. One person. Today, that person can be you.

I'm ready for change. I'm ready for action. I'm ready to rise up.

Are you?

Connect with me:
RyanHampton.org
Facebook: facebook.com/AddictionXAmerica
Twitter: @RyanForRecovery
Instagram: @ryanjhampton

Facing Addiction helped me find my voice.

They are leading the charge to unify the voices of over 45 million Americans and their families who are directly impacted by addiction.

Find them at facingaddiction.org.

ACKNOWLEDGMENTS

I could not have written *American Fix* without the love, patience, and help of the following people.

Claire Foster, you've been more than a co-writer. You've become like a sister to me. Thanks for always picking up the phone, making me laugh, and channeling my passion, grief, outrage, and hope onto paper.

My best friend Garrett Hade, thanks for putting up with me, day in and day out. I'm grateful every day that we met in that public detox in 2012. We haven't left each other's side since.

Tim Sullivan, thanks for lightening the mood and teaching me not to take myself too seriously as we brought this book to life.

My editor Adam Bellow, thanks for giving me a chance and allowing me to write a story that needed to be told.

My agent Jennifer Cohen, whose enthusiasm is contagious. Your support is invaluable.

The entire team at Facing Addiction: Jim Hood, Greg Williams, Michael King, Ivana Grahovac, Laszlo Jaress, Aisha

271

Waheed, Christian Quilici, Dave Noble, Beth Wilson, and Aaron Kucharski. Through your guidance, I've found my purpose.

Tom Coderre, thank you for taking my phone call in November 2015. You opened my eyes to what advocacy can do and be. If I made it this far, it's because you showed me the path.

Carol McDaid, thanks for sharing your passion and knowledge with me. Your friendship is invaluable, and I'm forever grateful for your help.

The guys who helped save my life and have stood by my side since Day One: Abram B., Mikey B., Alex B., Dan G., Jimmy H., Justin D., and Chris H.

I could name so many more friends who have mentored me, educated me, guided me, and opened my eyes on this journey. I am truly blessed to be part of the recovery community. Thank you, to everyone who has put their faith in me.

Because you believed in me, I believed in *us*.

NOTES

INTRODUCTION

1. Laura Northrup, "President's Commission on Opioid Crisis Says Death Toll Is Like 9/11 Happening Every Three Weeks," *Consumerist*, August 1, 2017, https://consumerist.com/2017/08/01/presidents-commission-on-opioid-crisis-says-death-toll-is-like-911-happening-every-three-weeks/.

2. Nicholas Kristof, "Opioids, a Mass Killer We're Meeting with a Shrug," *New York Times*, June 22, 2017, https://www.nytimes.com/2017/06/22/opinion/opioid-epidemic-health-care-bill.html.

3. Max Blau, "STAT Forecast: Opioids Could Kill Nearly 500,000 Americans in the Next Decade," *STAT*, June 27, 2017, https://www.statnews.com/2017/06/27/opioid-deaths-forecast/.

1. IT STARTED WITH A PILL

1. Julie Donohue, "A History of Drug Advertising: The Evolving Roles of Consumers and Consumer Protection," *Milbank Quarterly* 84, no. 4 (December 2006): 659–699, doi: 10.1111/j.1468-0009.2006.00464.x.

2. "CNN: 1986: Nancy Reagan's 'Just Say No' Campaign," YouTube, published by CNN on February 28, 2011, https://www.youtube.com/watch?v=lQXgVM30mIY&feature=youtu.be.

3. "Fact Sheets—Alcohol Use and Your Health," Alcohol and Public Health, Centers for Disease Control and Prevention, January 3, 2018, https://www.cdc.gov/alcohol/fact-sheets/alcohol-use.htm.

4. Grace Medley et al., "Sexual Orientation and Estimates of Adult Substance Use and Mental Health: Results from the 2015 National Survey on Drug Use and Health," SAMHSA: Substance Abuse and Mental Health Services Administration, National Survey on Drug Use and Health Data Review, October 2016, https://www.samhsa.gov/data/sites/default/files/NSDUH -SexualOrientation-2015/NSDUH-SexualOrientation-2015/NSDUH -SexualOrientation-2015.htm.

5. "CDC Fact Sheet: Trend in US HIV Diagnoses, 2005–2014," National Center for HIV/AIDS, Viral Hepatitis, STD, and TB Prevention, Centers for Disease Control and Prevention, February 2016, https://www.cdc.gov/nchhstp /newsroom/docs/factsheets/hiv-data-trends-fact-sheet-508.pdf.

3. NOT ANONYMOUS

1. "Historical Data: The Birth of A.A. and Its Growth in the U.S./Canada," Alcoholics Anonymous, https://www.aa.org/pages/en_US/historical-data-the -birth-of-aa-and-its-growth-in-the-uscanada.

2. "Barack Obama's Final State of the Union Address," YouTube, published by ITV News on January 13, 2016, https://www.youtube.com/watch?v=suDEynUvw FM&feature=youtu.be.

3. U.S. Department of Health and Human Services (HHS), Office of the Surgeon General, "Early Intervention, Treatment, and Management of Substance Use Disorders," *Facing Addiction in America: The Surgeon General's Report on Alcohol, Drugs, and Health* (Washington, DC: HHS, November 2016), chapter 4, https://addiction.surgeongeneral.gov/chapter-4-treatment.pdf.

4. AMA Opioid Task Force, "Help Save Lives: Co-Prescribe Naloxone to Patients at Risk of Overdose," American Academy of Family Physicians, August 2017, https://www.aafp.org/dam/AAFP/documents/patient_care/pain_management /co-branded-naloxone.pdf.

5. U.S. Department of Health and Human Services (HHS), "Introduction and Overview of the Report," *Facing Addiction in America*, chapter 1, https:// addiction.surgeongeneral.gov/chapter-1-introduction.pdf.

6. "About Facing Addiction," Facing Addiction with NCADD, https://www .facingaddiction.org/about.

4. "WE SAVE LIVES"

1. http://www.hazeldenbettyford.org/education/bcr/dan-anderson-research -award.

2. U.S. Department of Health and Human Services (HHS), Office of the Surgeon General, "Early Intervention, Treatment, and Management of Substance Use Disorders," *Facing Addiction in America: The Surgeon General's Report on Al-*

cohol, Drugs, and Health (Washington, DC: HHS, November 2016), chapter 4, https://addiction.surgeongeneral.gov/chapter-4-treatment.pdf.

3. http://passagesmalibu.com/.

4. Cat Ferguson, "Searching for Help," *The Verge*, September 7, 2017, https://www.theverge.com/2017/9/7/16257412/rehabs-near-me-google-search-scam-florida-treatment-centers.

5. Pat Beall and Christine Stapleton, "Addiction Treatment Bonanza: How Urine Tests Rake in Millions," *My Palm Beach Post*, August 1, 2015. http://www.mypalmbeachpost.com/news/addiction-treatment-bonanza-how-urine-tests-rake-millions/rvmrD8VMBwykDtd6TCSALJ/.

6. Kelly Puente, "$40 Million Medical-Insurance Fraud Went Down in Orange County, Elsewhere, Law and State Officials Say," April 20, 2017, *Orange County Register*, http://www.ocregister.com/2017/04/20/40-million-medical-insurance-fraud-went-down-in-orange-county-elsewhere-law-and-state-officials-say/.

7. Michael Corkery, "Google Sets Limits on Addiction Treatment Ads, Citing Safety," *New York Times*, September 14, 2017, https://www.nytimes.com/2017/09/14/business/google-addiction-treatment-ads.html.

8. Evan Allen and David Armstrong, "Behind the Luxury: Turmoil and Shoddy Care Inside Five-Star Addiction Treatment Centers," *Boston Globe*, August 25, 2017, https://www.bostonglobe.com/news/nation/2017/08/25/behind-luxury-turmoil-and-shoddy-care-inside-five-star-addiction-treatment-centers/HzNBLYyMCIjSkaKyUZgfSN/story.html.

9. Brendan Pierson, "Deerfield Management Agrees to Settle Charges Related to Insider Trading," Reuters, August 21, 2017, https://www.reuters.com/article/usa-crime-healthcare-leaks/deerfield-management-agrees-to-settle-charges-related-to-insider-trading-idUSL2N1L7193.

5. ONE NATION, OVERDOSED

1. "Monologue: Trump in the Wind | Real Time with Bill Maher (HBO)," YouTube, published by *Real Time with Bill Maher* on September 8, 2017, https://www.youtube.com/watch?v=_Z_mkjzRcAs&feature=youtu.be.

2. Jarrett Murphy, "Rush Limbaugh Arrested on Drug Charges," *CBS News*, April 28, 2016, https://www.cbsnews.com/news/rush-limbaugh-arrested-on-drug-charges/.

3. Barry Meier, "In Guilty Plea, OxyContin Maker to Pay $600 Million," *New York Times*, May 10, 2007, http://www.nytimes.com/2007/05/10/business/11drug-web.html.

4. Center for Behavioral Health Statistics and Quality, *2014 National Survey on*

Drug Use and Health: Detailed Tables (Rockville, Maryland: Substance Abuse and Mental Health Services Administration, 2015), http://www.samhsa.gov/data /sites/default/files/NSDUH-DetTabs2014/NSDUH-DetTabs2014.pdf.

5. Josh Katz, "The First Count of Fentanyl Deaths in 2016: Up 540% in Three Years," The Upshot (blog), *New York Times*, September 2, 2017, https://www .nytimes.com/interactive/2017/09/02/upshot/fentanyl-drug-overdose-deaths .html.

6. "Overdose Death Rates," National Institute on Drug Abuse, September 2017, https://www.drugabuse.gov/related-topics/trends-statistics/overdose-death -rates.

7. Katz, "The First Count of Fentanyl Deaths in 2016."

8. Dina Gusovsky, "Americans Consume Vast Majority of the World's Opioids," CNBC, April 27, 2016, https://www.cnbc.com/2016/04/27/americans -consume-almost-all-of-the-global-opioid-supply.html.

9. Alex Berenson, "Merck Agrees to Settle Vioxx Suits for $4.85 Billion," *New York Times*, November 9, 2007, http://www.nytimes.com/2007/11/09/business /09merck.html.

10. Catherine Saint Louis, "FDA Approval of OxyContin Use for Children Continues to Draw Scrutiny," *New York Times*, October 8, 2015, https://www .nytimes.com/2015/10/09/health/fda-approval-of-oxycontin-for-children -continues-to-draw-scrutiny.html?mtrref=www.nytimes.com.

11. David Armstrong, "'Who Treats You Matters': Some ER Doctors Three Times More Likely Than Others to Prescribe Opioids," *STAT*, February 15, 2017, https://www.statnews.com/2017/02/15/opioid-prescribing-er-doctors/.

12. Casey Ross, "Doctors Who Attend Lower-Tier Medical Schools Prescribe Far More Opioids, Study Finds," *STAT*, August 7, 2017, https://www.statnews .com/2017/08/07/doctors-opioid-prescriptions/.

13. "Almost All U.S. Doctors Are Overprescribing Narcotic Painkillers, Research Suggests," *Health*, March 8, 2016, http://www.health.com/pain /nearly-all-u-s-doctors-overprescribe-addictive-narcotic-painkillers-survey.

14. Michael Nedelman, "Doctors Increasingly Face Charges for Patient Overdoses," CNN, July 31, 2017, http://www.cnn.com/2017/07/31/health/opioid -doctors-responsible-overdose/index.html.

15. Marc R. Larochelle, MD, MPH, et al., "Opioid Prescribing After Nonfatal Overdose and Association with Repeated Overdose: A Cohort Study," *Annals of Internal Medicine*, January 5, 2016, http://annals.org/aim/article -abstract/2479117/opioid-prescribing-after-nonfatal-overdose-association -repeated-overdose-cohort-study.

16. https://www.statnews.com/2017/02/15/opioid-prescribing-er-doctors/ STAT. (Ibid.)

17. Ashley Welch, "Drug Overdoses Killed More Americans Last Year Than the Vietnam War," *CBS News*, October 17, 2017, https://www.cbsnews.com/news /opioids-drug-overdose-killed-more-americans-last-year-than-the-vietnam -war/.

18. Dean Reynolds, "Overdoses Now Leading Cause of Death of Americans Under 50," *CBS Evening News*, June 6, 2017, https://www.cbsnews.com/news /overdoses-are-leading-cause-of-death-americans-under-50.

6. END THE WAR ON DRUG USERS

1. "Pres. Reagan's Nov. 11, 1983 statement on National Drug Abuse Education Week Proclamation," YouTube, published by Jason Saltoun-Ebin on August 12, 2009, https://www.youtube.com/watch?v=xxfwGdMUNsc&feature=youtu .be.

2. "Overdose Death Rates," National Institute on Drug Abuse, September 2017, https://www.drugabuse.gov/related-topics/trends-statistics/overdose-death -rates; "Stand Up for Recovery, Face Addiction," Substance Abuse and Mental Health Services Administration, August 13, 2015, https://blog.samhsa.gov /2015/08/13/stand-up-for-recovery-face-addiction/#.Wqf5AqLwJqu.

3. "Drug and Alcohol Use in College-Age Adults in 2016 Infographic," College-Age & Young Adults, National Institute on Drug Abuse, https://www .drugabuse.gov/related-topics/college-age-young-adults.

4. Laura Jarrett, "Sessions Nixes Obama-Era Rules Leaving States Alone That Legalize Pot," CNN, January 4, 2018, http://www.cnn.com/2018/01/04 /politics/jeff-sessions-cole-memo/index.html.

5. Noelle Crombie, "Oregon Pays Out $85 Million in Pot Taxes to School Fund, Cops, Other Services," *The Oregonian*, http://www.oregonlive.com/marijuana /index.ssf/2017/10/oregon_pays_out_85_million_in_1.html.

6. Nancy Gertner and Chiraag Bains, "Mandatory Minimum Sentences Are Cruel and Ineffective. Sessions Wants Them Back," http://www.washingtonpost .com/amphtml/posteverything/wp/2017/05/15/mandatory-minimum -sentences-are-cruel-and-ineffective-sessions-wants-them-back/.

7. Lauren Carroll, "How the War on Drugs Affected Incarceration Rates," *Politifact*, July 10, 2016, http://www.politifact.com/truth-o-meter/statements/2016 /jul/10/cory-booker/how-war-drugs-affected-incarceration-rates/.

8. "Criminal Justice Facts," The Sentencing Project, http://www.sentencingproject .org/criminal-justice-facts/.

9. "Attorney General Jeff Sessions Delivers Remarks on Efforts to Combat Violent Crime and Restore Public Safety Before Federal, State and Local Law Enforcement," press release, United States Department of Justice, March 15, 2017, https://www.justice.gov/opa/speech/attorney-general-jeff-sessions-delivers -remarks-efforts-combat-violent-crime-and-restore.

10. "Evaluation Research: Adler and Clark," http://www.d.umn.edu/~bmork/ 2155/2155Readings/evaluationadlerclark.htm.

11. D. R. Lynam et al., "Project DARE: No Effects at 10-Year Follow-Up," *Journal of Consulting and Clinical Psychology* 67, no. 4 (199): 590–593, http://dx .doi.org/10.1037/0022-006X.67.4.590.

12. "The Facts on Drugs and Crime in America," National Association of Drug Court Professionals, http://www.nadcp.org/sites/default/files/nadcp/Facts%20 on%20Drug%20Courts%20.pdf; Jennifer Bronson, PhD, et al., "Drug Use, Dependence, and Abuse Among State Prisoners and Jail Inmates, 2007–2009," Bureau of Justice Statistics of the U.S. Department of Justice, June 2017, https:// www.bjs.gov/content/pub/pdf/dudaspji0709.pdf.

13. Sheldon X. Zhang, Robert E. L. Roberts, and Valerie J. Callanan, "Preventing Parolees from Returning to Prison Through Community-Based Reintegration," *Crime & Delinquency* 52, no. 4 (October 2006): 551–571, doi: 10.1177/0011128705282594; "Drug Rehab Instead of Prison Could Save Billions, Says Report," Rehab International, https://rehab-international.org/blog /drug-rehab-instead-of-prison-could-save-billions-says-report.

14. "The Facts on Drugs and Crime in America."

15. Jonah Engel Bromwich, "Guards Paraded Alaska Inmates Naked on a 'Dog Leash,' Report Finds," *New York Times*, October 4, 2017, https://www.nytimes .com/2017/10/04/us/alaska-inmates-stripped-naked.html.

16. Amy Julia Harris and Shoshana Walter, "They Thought They Were Going to Rehab. They Ended Up in Chicken Plants," *Reveal News*, October 4, 2017, https://www.revealnews.org/article/they-thought-they-were-going-to -rehab-they-ended-up-in-chicken-plants/.

17. Heroin and Prescription Opiate Addiction Task Force, About page, KingCounty.gov, https://www.kingcounty.gov/depts/community-human-services /mental-health-substance-abuse/task-forces/heroin-opiates-task-force.aspx.

7. DIRTY WORDS

1. Andrew Blake, "Overdose Victims Charged with 'Inducing Panic' Under New Law in Ohio," *Washington Times*, March 9, 2017, https://www .washingtontimes.com/news/2017/mar/9/overdose-victims-charged -inducing-panic-under-new-/.

2. Cleve R. Wootson Jr., "One Politician's Solution to the Overdose Problem:

Let Addicts Die," *Washington Post*, June 30, 2017, https://www.washingtonpost
.com/news/to-your-health/wp/2017/06/28/a-council-members-solution
-to-his-ohio-towns-overdose-problem-let-addicts-die/?utm_term=
.5c37a8e90504.

3. "Languages and Stigma," Faces & Voices of Recovery, https://facesandvoiceso
frecovery.org/resources/language_stigma.html.

4. "'I Was Drunk When I Met President Bush' TV Anchor Laurie Dhue Ad-
mits as She Opens Up About Struggle with Alcoholism," *Daily Mail* (UK),
July 16, 2013, http://www.dailymail.co.uk/news/article-2366250/I-drunk-I
-met-President-Bush-TV-anchor-Laurie-Dhue-admits-opens-struggle
-alcoholism.html.

5. Zac Auter, "Beer Reigns as Americans' Preferred Alcoholic Beverage," Gallup News, August 3, 2016, http://news.gallup.com/poll/194144/beer-reigns
-americans-preferred-alcoholic-beverage.aspx.

9. ACROSS AMERICA

1. "Youth Survey," We All Rise Together, https://www.weallrisetogether.org
/prevention/.

2. "5 Years After Son's Drug Death, Jim Hood Asks: 'Where Is The Outrage?'"
06880: Where Westport Meets the World (blog), October 27, 2017, https://
06880danwoog.com/2017/10/27/5-years-after-sons-drug-death-jim-hood
-asks-where-is-the-outrage/.

10. RISE UP

1. "A Divided and Pessimistic Electorate," Pew Research Center, U.S. Politics and Policy, November 10, 2016, http://www.people-press.org/2016/11/10
/a-divided-and-pessimistic-electorate/.

INDEX

celebrities, 72–3, 7, 94, 113, 136–7,
182–5. *See also* Rush Limbaugh;
Tom Petty
Center for Drug Safety and
Effectiveness (Johns Hopkins
Bloomberg School of Public
Health) (Baltimore), 132–3
Center for Open Recovery (COR)
(San Francisco), 235–6 Centers
for Disease Control and
Prevention (CDC), 12, 135,
210, 259
Chesterfield Jail recovery program
(Virginia), 154–62, 167–8, 252
choice, and addiction, 20–1, 28, 93,
125–8, 147, 150–1, 157–8,
177–8, 188, 227
Christian Alcoholics & Addicts in
Recovery (CAAIR),166–7
Christianity, 19–20, 113, 154–5,
166–7, 182, 233
civil rights, 74–82
classism, 1–4, 19–24, 38–43, 73, 94–5,
100–2, 110–13, 144–6, 177
Clinton, Bill, 70, 111
Clinton, Hillary, 67, 110, 250
cocaine, 102, 114, 144, 148, 178
codeine, 135–6
compassion, 21, 47, 106–7, 162, 195,
207, 210–12
Comprehensive Addiction and
Recovery Act (CARA), 257–8
comprehensive user engagement site
(CUES),168, 193–8, 201–2
conservative politics, 112–13, 154,
158, 209, 211, 215
Conway, Jack, 139
COPS, 175
COR, *see* Center for Open Recovery
Cox, Spencer, 74
craving, 18, 30–1, 36, 92–3, 150,
178, 199, 230
and anxiety and depression, 18

Crime & Delinquency, 161
criminal justice system reform,
143–66, 233–5
criminalization of addiction, 143–69,
174–8, 232, 262. *See also* racism
CUES, *see* comprehensive user
engagement site
culture and addiction, 179–88

D.A.R.E. program, 11, 15–18, 150–2
statistics on, 152
Darwin, Charles, 55
"dealer" doctors, 7–33, 117–36,
153–4
and discrimination, 32–3
and Dr. Leah, 12–15
and Dr. Sullivan, 32–3, 153–4
and general practitioners, 128–9
grooming of, 133–4
and heroin, 153–4
and lack of training, 23, 117,
128–9, 133–6
and "pain management," 10–16
responsibility of, 127–9, 134
and withdrawal, 7–9, 25–33
See also Big Pharma; OxyContin;
"pill mills"; Purdue Pharma
decriminalizing addiction, 165–9.
See also prison system
dehumanization, 160–4, 169, 176–7,
188, 206, 250, 261–2
Democratic National Convention
(2016), 63–71, 213, 218, 249,
252–3, 258
Democratic party, 16
dentists, 135–6
depression, 14–15, 18, 41–2, 92, 98,
150, 240
detox, medical, 37–9, 48, 80, 85–6,
89–92, 119, 160, 164–5, 178,
199, 223, 226, 232, 255, 271
as medical specialty, 89
Dhue, Laurie, 185–7